Learn JavaScript

In a Weekend®

2nd Edition

Jerry Lee Ford, Jr.

Premier
Press

JavaScript is a trademark of Sun Microsystems, Inc. in the United States and other countries. Microsoft, Windows, Internet Explorer, Notepad, JScript, and VBScript are either registered trademarks or trademarks of Microsoft Corporation in the United States and/or other countries. Netscape is a registered trademark of Netscape Communications Corporation in the U.S. and other countries.

All other trademarks are the property of their respective owners.

Important: Premier Press cannot provide software support. Please contact the appropriate software manufacturer's technical support line or Web site for assistance.

Premier Press and the author have attempted throughout this book to distinguish proprietary trademarks from descriptive terms by following the capitalization style used by the manufacturer.

Information contained in this book has been obtained by Premier Press from sources believed to be reliable. However, because of the possibility of human or mechanical error by our sources, Premier Press, or others, the Publisher does not guarantee the accuracy, adequacy, or completeness of any information and is not responsible for any errors or omissions or the results obtained from use of such information. Readers should be particularly aware of the fact that the Internet is an ever-changing entity. Some facts may have changed since this book went to press.

ISBN: 1-59200-086-X

Library of Congress Catalog Card Number: 2003108348

Printed in the United States of America

04 05 06 07 08 BH 10 9 8 7 6 5 4 3 2 1

Premier Press, a division of Course Technology
25 Thomson Place
Boston, MA 02210

SVP, Professional, Trade, Reference Group:
Andy Shafran

Publisher:
Stacy L. Hiquet

Senior Marketing Manager:
Sarah O'Donnell

Marketing Manager:
Heather Hurley

Manager of Editorial Services:
Heather Talbot

Acquisitions Editor:
Arlie Hartman

Associate Marketing Manager:
Kristin Eisenzopf

Project Editor:
Kim V. Benbow

Technical Reviewer:
Burt LaFontaine

Retail Market Coordinator:
Sarah Dubois

Copy Editor:
Gene Redding

Interior Layout:
Shawn Morningstar

Cover Designer:
Mike Tanamachi

Indexer:
Katherine Stimson

Proofreader:
Deana Casamento

To Alexander, William, Molly, and Mary.

ACKNOWLEDGMENTS

There are a number of individuals who deserve a lot of credit for the effort that they put into this book. I especially want to thank Arlie Hartman who served as the book's acquisitions editor. I also want to thank the book's project editor, Kim Benbow, for her guidance and suggestions. Finally, I want to acknowledge the book's copy editor, Gene Redding, and its technical editor, Burt LaFontaine, as well as everyone else at Premier Press for all their hard work.

ABOUT THE AUTHOR

Jerry Lee Ford, Jr. is an author, educator, and an IT professional with over 15 years' experience in information technology, including roles as an automation analyst, technical manager, technical support analyst, automation engineer, and security analyst. In addition, he has a master's degree in business administration from Virginia Commonwealth University in Richmond, Virginia. Jerry is also the author of 13 other books including *Learn VBScript In a Weekend, Microsoft Windows Shell Scripting and WSH Administrator's Guide, VBScript Professional Projects* and *Microsoft Windows XP Professional Administrator's Guide.* He has over five years' experience as an adjunct instructor teaching networking courses in information technology. Jerry lives in Richmond, Virginia, with his wife, Mary, and their children William, Alexander, and Molly.

CONTENTS

Introduction

Congratulations on your decision to learn JavaScript and JScript. JavaScript is a powerful scripting language that, when combined with HTML, allows you to create exciting and powerful Web pages. You can use these Web pages to run a small business or to share information with family and friends over the Internet. JScript is a Microsoft implementation of JavaScript that can be used as a scripting language for automating repetitive or complex desktop and system tasks.

What you are probably asking yourself is, "Can I really learn to program using JavaScript and JScript in a single weekend?" The answer is "Yes!" I am not promising that you will become a programming guru in just a few days, but if you will dedicate a full weekend to this book and follow along with its examples, you will be able to write your own JavaScripts and JScripts. In no time you will be able to make dramatic improvements to your Web pages as well as develop scripts that automate any number of Windows desktop tasks.

Syntactically, JavaScript and JScript are virtually identical. So by learning how to write JavaScripts, you are also learning how to work with JScript as well. Where the two languages differ is in the environments in which they execute. JavaScripts are embedded inside HTML pages and run by Web browsers. JScripts, on the other hand, are written as plain text files that are executed directly from the Windows desktop by the Windows Script Host or WSH.

As long as you have basic Windows skills and a good HTML background, you'll find that this book will provide you with all the information and examples you need to get up and running with both of these exciting scripting languages in a single weekend.

What This Book Is About

This book is about learning how to write JavaScripts in order to create exciting Web sites. It is also designed to teach you how to leverage the skills and knowledge that you'll develop working with JavaScript in order to create JScripts that automate desktop tasks. Basic experience with Windows and HTML is assumed. The book provides the rest for you. By the time the weekend is over, you will have learned how to do the following:

- Integrate JavaScripts into your Web pages
- Use JavaScript to take control of the browser status line
- Use JavaScript to display pop-up alert, prompt, and confirmation dialog boxes so that you can interact with your visitors
- Use JavaScript to add graphic effects to Web pages
- Use JavaScript to create Web page banners, clocks, and other animation effects
- Use JavaScript to validate forms and e-mail the contents of those forms to yourself
- Write JavaScripts that collect and save visitor information

- Write JScripts that automate Windows tasks, such as the creation of new user accounts and disk and printer management
- Write JScripts that can read text files and create log and report files
- Write JScripts that can create shortcuts and configure the Windows Start menu and Quick Launch bar

Who Should Read This Book?

This book is for anyone who is ready to begin spicing up their Web pages using JavaScript, or anyone who wants to become more efficient by learning how to automate the execution of repetitive or complex Windows tasks. Before working with JavaScript, you'll need to be comfortable working with Netscape Navigator or Microsoft Internet Explorer. Of course, you'll need to know a little HTML as well. Likewise, you'll need to know the basics of working with Windows in order to be able to leverage the power of JScript. This means that you should already know how to perform such tasks as well as know how to create a shortcut, how to create, delete, and modify text files and folders in addition to knowing how to configure the Windows Start menu.

NOTE If you feel that your HTML skills are a little weak, you might want to brush up on them by reading Premier Press's *Learn HTML In a Weekend*. However, if you are only a little rusty, you'll probably be able to pick things back up by reviewing the HTML code used in this book.

It is also helpful (but not required) that you know another programming language such as Basic, Perl, or C. This book provides an ideal quick start guide for more seasoned programmers. Although knowledge of another computer programming language is not a prerequisite for success, having this type of background will make your learning experience this weekend a little easier and less stressful. Do not worry if you lack this experience; everybody has to start somewhere. JavaScript and JScript are perfect languages to start with.

What You Need to Begin

The great thing about JavaScripts and JScripts is that they are easy to create. You do not have to spend a lot of money on programming tools before you can begin developing scripts. To begin developing JavaScripts, all that you'll need is

- **A computer.** Just about any computer will work because you don't need a lot of horsepower to develop and test JavaScripts.
- **Internet access.** Whether it is from work or home, you must be able to access the Internet so that you can upload your Web pages to your Web site.
- **An Internet Web browser.** Several Internet browsers support JavaScript, including Microsoft Internet Explorer, Netscape Navigator, and Opera. You need at least one of these browsers to test your JavaScripts. However, it's a good idea to have copies of all of them to make sure that your JavaScripts work correctly with each browser.
- **A Web site.** If you do not already have your own Web site, the odds are that your local Internet service provider can set you up with one.
- **A text editor.** You can use any basic text editor to write and save your JavaScripts. You can even use the Windows Notepad application.
- **A graphics editor.** This tool is optional, though it is required if you plan to add any graphic images to your Web pages. For example, you might want to design your own banner pages or Web site logo.

Unlike many programming languages, JScript doesn't require you to learn how to work with a complicated *integrated development environment* or IDE before you can develop scripts that run directly from the Windows desktop. To begin developing JScripts, all that you'll need is

- **Windows 95, 98, Me, NT, XP, 2000, or 2003.** Only Windows computers support JScript.
- **The Windows Script Host or WSH, version 5.6.** Available for free at http://msdn.microsoft.com/scripting.
- **JScript 5.6.** Available for free at http://msdn.microsoft.com/scripting.
- **A text editor.** Like JavaScript, any text editor, including Notepad, will do.

How This Book Is Organized

This book is written so that you can complete it in seven sessions over the course of a single weekend. Of course, you can read it anytime you want. The first five chapters focus on providing you with a strong JavaScript programming foundation. The last two chapters leverage this material by teaching you how to apply what you have learned to the development of JScripts. The basic outline of the book is shown here:

- **Friday Evening: "Introducing JavaScript and JScript."** This chapter provides prerequisite background information for working with JavaScript and JScript. It overviews the kinds of enhancements you can make to Web pages using JavaScript. Background information includes a brief history of JavaScript and a discussion of browser compatibility. You'll then learn how to write your first JavaScript. This chapter also includes an overview of JScript and the WSH. This will include an overview of both technologies and a brief examination of the WSH architecture, which provides the environment in which JScripts execute.

- **Saturday Morning: "Learning the Basics of JavaScript Coding."** This chapter provides you with a programming foundation. It discusses scripting and script syntax before starting a series of lessons that outline the basic programming statements that comprise the JavaScript and JScript languages. You will learn how to work with variables, literals, functions, expressions, operators, statements, and arrays. The chapter concludes by covering object-oriented programming and outlining the JavaScript object model.

- **Saturday Afternoon: "Using JavaScript to Build Better Web Pages."** This chapter reviews objects made available to JavaScript by browsers and demonstrates how to access these objects. The chapter also provides a discussion on JavaScript events and how to handle them with event handlers. The chapter concludes with a discussion on how to use JavaScript to control HTML frames and forms.

- **Saturday Evening: "Doing Really Cool Things with Your Web Pages."** In this chapter, things start getting really exciting. You'll learn how to write JavaScripts that manipulate the browser status line, create scrolling messages, and open pop-up dialog boxes. The chapter includes a discussion on the differences between Netscape Navigator and Internet Explorer and how to work with both browsers using JavaScript. The chapter concludes by covering the use of plug-ins and the application of graphics and animation.

✪ **Sunday Morning: "Advanced JavaScript Coding."** This chapter concludes the book's JavaScript coverage by exploring how to use cookies to store and retrieve information about visitors to your Web site. The chapter also provides a solid review of the techniques involved in debugging JavaScripts. Finally, the chapter ends by demonstrating how to put your new JavaScript programming skills to use by developing the On-line Bookmall Web site.

✪ **Sunday Afternoon: "Learning How to Use JScript and the WSH."** This chapter covers the objects that make up the WSH object model, including their properties and methods. It also goes over JScript's runtime objects. It teaches you how to write JScripts that can access the Windows file system and shows you different ways of performing file and folder administration. You'll learn how to create text documents and log files as well as how to open and read text files.

✪ **Sunday Evening: "Using JScript to Automate Windows Tasks."** This chapter focuses on showing you how to use JScript and the WSH to perform a number of different automation tasks. These tasks will include the creation of Windows shortcuts, the customization of the Windows Start menu and Quick Launch Toolbar, how to write messages to the Windows Event Log, and how to read and write to the Windows registry. In addition, you will learn how to work with Windows commands, access network resources, and schedule script execution.

✪ **"What's on the Web Site?"** This tells you where you can find examples of all the scripts that are presented in this book. Copies of each are available for download from http://www.courseptr.com.

✪ **Glossary:** This presents a list of terms used throughout this book.

Please go to http://www.courseptr.com to find Appendixes A, B, and C.

✪ **Appendix A: "A Brief JavaScript and JScript Object Reference."** This appendix provides a brief outline of JavaScript objects and identifies the properties and methods associated with them.

✪ **Appendix B: "A Summary of JavaScript Events and Event Handlers."** This appendix provides a brief outline of JavaScript events and the event handlers associated with them.

✪ **Appendix C: "JavaScript and JScript Reserved Words."** This appendix identifies JavaScript and JScript reserved words.

Special Features of This Book

This book applies a number of conventions to help make it easier for you to use, including

 ✪ **Notes** provide additional information that is good to know but which may not be essential to the topic being discussed.

 ✪ **Tips** suggest alternative techniques and shortcuts that can help you to work faster and more efficiently.

 ✪ **Cautions** warn you of situations where errors or unforeseen problems could arise.

✪ *Italics* are used to highlight new terms and emphasize key pieces of information.

Introducing JavaScript and JScript

- ➤ What are JavaScript and JScript?
- ➤ Integrating JavaScript into HTML pages
- ➤ Writing your first JavaScript
- ➤ Understanding JScript and the Windows Script Host
- ➤ Configuring the JScript execution environment

Welcome to Learn JavaScript in a Weekend. This book will teach you everything that you need to know to get started using this exciting and fun Web scripting language. By the time the weekend is over, you'll be ready to update your Web site to make it a lot more interactive and entertaining for your visitors. This book also will teach you how to create scripts using JScript (which is Microsoft's version of JavaScript) to automate all sorts of tasks on Windows operating systems.

In this chapter you will learn the background information that you need to know about JavaScript. This will include learning where it came from, what browsers support it, and the steps involved in creating and testing your JavaScripts.

To develop JScripts that run directly from the Windows desktop, you'll also need to learn about the Windows Script Host (WSH). This chapter will explain the WSH's basic architecture and show you how to configure it and use it to run your first JScript. By the time you go to bed tonight, you'll have the foundation you need to finish the rest of this book and begin your journey as a JavaScript and JScript programmer.

Introducing JavaScript and JScript

JavaScript is a computer language specially designed to work with Internet browsers. It lets you create small programs called *scripts* and embed them inside Hypertext Markup Language (HTML) pages in order to provide interactive content on your Web pages. *JScript* is Microsoft's implementation of JavaScript. In addition to running within Internet Explorer, Microsoft also provides a version of JScript that can be used as a desktop scripting language with the Windows Script Host.

The WSH is an optional scripting environment that supplies Windows operating systems with the capability to run scripts directly on the Windows desktop. Both languages support the same collection of programming statements.

JavaScript and JScript are *interpreted* languages. This means that scripts written in these languages are not compiled before they are executed (as is typical of most programming languages such as C++). Every script statement must first be converted into *binary code* (a computer language made up of 0s and 1s that the computer can understand) in order to execute. Unlike complied programs, which are converted to binary code in advance, JavaScript and JScript statements are processed at execution time. This means that they run a little slower than compiled programs. The upside is that this makes writing and testing JavaScripts and JScripts very intuitive and easy. You simply write a few lines of code, save your script, and test it without having to stop and compile it into executable code.

JavaScript and JScript are *object-based* scripting languages. This means that they view everything as *objects*. For JavaScripts, the browser is an object, a window is an object, and a button in a window is an object. JScript has access to a different set of objects. For example, JScript has the capability to access objects such as files, drives, and printers.

Every object has *properties*, and you can use JavaScript and JScript to manipulate these properties. For example, with JavaScript you can change the background color of a browser window or the size of a graphic image. In addition to properties, objects have methods. *Methods* are the actions that objects can perform. For example, JavaScript can be used to open and close browser windows. By manipulating their properties and executing methods, you can control objects and make things happen.

JavaScripts support *event-driven* programming. An *event* is an action that occurs when the user does something such as click on a button or move the pointer over a graphic image. JavaScript enables you to write scripts that are triggered by events. Did you ever wonder how buttons dynamically change colors on some Web sites when you move the mouse over them? It's simply a JavaScript technique known as a *rollover*. The event is the mouse moving over the button (object). This triggers the execution of an *event handler*, which is a collection of JavaScript statements that replaces the button with another one that uses a different color.

JavaScripts and JScripts that run within Web browsers have access to objects located on Web pages. On the other hand, JScripts that run within the WSH have access to desktop resources such as toolbars, files, printers, and the Windows registry.

Because JavaScript and JScript run in different environments, they work with different objects, and they have different capabilities. For example, using JScript you can create scripts that can copy and move files, access data stored on network drives, administer local and network printers, and configure the Windows desktop and Start menu.

Because JavaScript and JScript are so closely related, you can learn one language by learning the other. The difference between the two resides in the location in which they execute and the objects to which they have access. Tomorrow morning you will get a thorough language review of all the statements that make up JavaScript and JScript. Because the first part of this book focuses on JavaScript, all the examples will be presented using that language. However, from a programming standpoint, most of the scripting statements that you will see can be applied directly to JScript programming.

What Kinds of Things Can You Do with JavaScript and JScript?

The relatively simple and straightforward HTML that helped to make the Internet explode upon the scene in the mid-1990s enables you to create Web pages that display static information. Over the years, HTML has lost much of its luster. Markup languages are great for formatting the display of text, but they lack the capability to interact with visitors. People surfing the Internet have come to expect and demand more than a static presentation of data from Web sites. If you want people to visit your Web site, to enjoy themselves, and to return again, then you have to find ways to make it more interesting. One of the best ways to do this is with JavaScript.

JavaScript provides your Web pages with the capability to do many exciting things. The following list provides a preview of what you will learn how to do with JavaScript in this book.

- Display pop-up messages that display and collect information from visitors
- Create rotating banners
- Open new windows
- Redirect people using older browsers to non-JavaScript HTML pages
- Detect the browsers and plug-ins being used by people visiting your Web site
- Validate forms and package their contents in an e-mail message
- Perform simple animations such as rollovers
- Exercise greater control over HTML frames and forms
- Take control of the status bar and create scrolling messages

JavaScript can do a lot of different and exciting things. However, there is one thing that it cannot do. JavaScripts cannot run outside of the browser. This "limitation" helps make JavaScript more secure because users do not have to worry about somebody writing a JavaScript that might erase their hard drive or read their address book and extract private information.

NOTE JavaScript, as covered in this book, focuses on client-side scripting. By *client-side* script-ing I means scripts that execute within the browsers of people that visit your Web pages. A *server-side* version of JavaScript also exists. This version of JavaScript is designed to run on Web servers and is used by professional Web site developers to create scripts that provide dynamic content based on information received from visitors, as well as from information stored in a server-side database. A discussion of server-side JavaScript is beyond the scope of this book. From this point on, when I refer to JavaScript, I will be talking about client-side scripting.

Like JavaScript, JScript is limited by the constraints of its execution environment. When run by the WSH, JScripts don't have access to Web content. They don't work with HTML frames or forms. Instead, the WSH opens up a whole new execution environment that provides JScripts with the capability to access both local and network computer resources. In this context, JScript's primary reason for existing is to facilitate the development of scripts that automate tasks.

JScript provides an especially powerful tool for developing scripts that can automate repetitive and mundane tasks or tasks that are complicated and prone to error when performed manually. The following list provides a preview of what you will learn how to do with JScript in this book.

- Create and configure desktop shortcuts
- Generate text reports and log files
- Manage the Windows file system by copying, moving, and deleting files and folders
- Manage operating system resources such as Windows services, the registry, and event logs
- Create and administer user accounts
- Manage local and network resources such as network printers and disk drives
- Interact with and control other applications

A Little History Lesson

Years ago, the programmers at Netscape Communications Corporation recognized that HTML alone was not robust enough to support interactive Web programming. In 1995 they developed a scripting language called LiveScript, which gave Web page developers greater control over the browser.

Later, Sun Microsystems came along and developed a new programming language named Java. Java quickly became a hot item and received an enormous amount of media and industry attention. Netscape added support for Java in Netscape Navigator 2. At the same time, Netscape decided to change the name of LiveScript to JavaScript, which earned the scripting language a little more attention thanks to its name. That's about all the two languages have in common. Neither is related to the other, although both are supported by modern Internet browsers as a way of delivering interactive Web content.

Netscape has continued to enhance and improve JavaScript over the years and has released a number of new versions of Netscape Navigator along the way, as shown in Table 1.1.

TABLE 1.1 HISTORICAL VIEW OF INTERNET BROWSER SUPPORT FOR JAVASCRIPT		
JavaScript	**Netscape Version**	**Internet Explorer Version**
1.0	Navigator 2	Internet Explorer 3
1.1	Navigator 3	Internet Explorer 4
1.2	Navigator 4	Internet Explorer 4
1.3	Navigator 4.5	Internet Explorer 5
1.5	Navigator 6 and 7	Internet Explorer 5.5 and 6

One problem that has plagued Internet development over the years is a lack of standardization. The European Computer Manufacturing Association (ECMA) has taken a lead role in working toward standardizing JavaScript, which it refers to as ECMAScript. The ECMA-262 specification outlines standards with which JavaScript 1.3 is compliant. JavaScript 1.5 is compliant with ECMA-262 revision 3.

Like the JavaScript 1.5, JScript 5.6 is a based on ECMA-262 revision 3.

 NOTE Netscape is now working on JavaScript 2.0, which it promises will be compatible with the fourth revision of ECMAScript. At the same time, JScript .NET, Microsoft's next version of JScript, is also being developed based on ECMAScript revision 4.

Microsoft first released JScript in 1996 as a scripting language for Internet Explorer 3.0, which was basically just Microsoft's own implementation of JavaScript 1.0. Later, JScript 2 was released as a component of IIS 3.0, turning JScript into a server-side scripting language that, when embedded inside ASP pages, could access server-side databases and create HTML pages with dynamic content.

 NOTE *Internet Information Server* (IIS) is a Microsoft Web server application that supports the creation of Web sites and is used by companies all over the world to host their Web sites. *Active Server Pages* (ASPs) are executable files that run on IIS and deliver dynamic HTML content.

JScript 3 was released in a number of different environments, which include the following:

- Internet Explorer 4
- IIS 4
- Windows Scripting Host

As one of the two default scripting languages provided as part of Microsoft's new Windows Scripting Host, JScript 3 became a desktop scripting language capable of interacting directly with computer resources. Next, JScript 4 was delivered as part of Microsoft's Visual Studio development suite. The major feature added to this version of JScript was the capability to interact directly with the Windows file system.

NOTE   Microsoft's Visual Studio development suite is a collection of different software languages and software development tools that assist software developers in creating robust professional applications.

JScript version 5 was released along with the joint introduction of Internet Explorer 5 and Windows 2000. The current version of JScript, version 5.6, was introduced in 2001 along with Windows XP and Internet Explorer 6.

JavaScript and Browser Compatibility

When JScripts are processed by the WSH, browser compatibility issues do not affect JScript programmers.

However, browser compatibility has always been a major issue for JavaScript programmers. The two most popular Internet browsers since the mid-1990s have been Microsoft's Internet Explorer and Netscape's Communicator. Microsoft and Netscape traditionally have had different opinions as to how browsers should work. As a result, Netscape Communicator versions 2, 3, and 4 performed differently in many situations than Internet Explorer versions 3, 4, and 5. HTML pages and JavaScripts often behaved differently when asked to do the same thing on either browser.

One key difference between these earlier versions of Internet Explorer and Netscape Communicator was their object models. Browsers abstract their content and functionality in the form of objects. JavaScript interacts with browsers by interacting with these objects. The problem was that Netscape and Internet Explorer had different object models, so some objects that existed in one browser did not exist in the other. However, with the advent of the ECMAScript standards, things have become a lot more consistent in recent years. As a result, in most circumstances, HTML or JavaScript processed by Netscape Communicator version 6 or 7 should be processed pretty much the same as if it were processed by Internet Explorer 5.5 or 6. However, even with the latest versions of both browsers, small differences in implementation still exist. The only way to be sure that your JavaScripts will behave as expected on both browsers is to test them using both browsers.

Another browser issue that JavaScript programmers still have to be concerned with is what version of JavaScript the various browsers support. JavaScript support began with the Netscape 2 browser, but that browser supports only the initial version of JavaScript. Microsoft began to provide JavaScript support only in Internet Explorer 3. The problem is that there are still a lot of people out there running older versions of both browsers, and trying to accommodate them all is very difficult.

Not all browsers are created equal. In fact, things are made more difficult because Microsoft and Netscape are not the only companies that make browsers. Other browsers provide varying degrees of JavaScript support. For example, the Lynx browser, shown in Figure 1.1, is a simple text-based browser that does not support graphics or JavaScript.

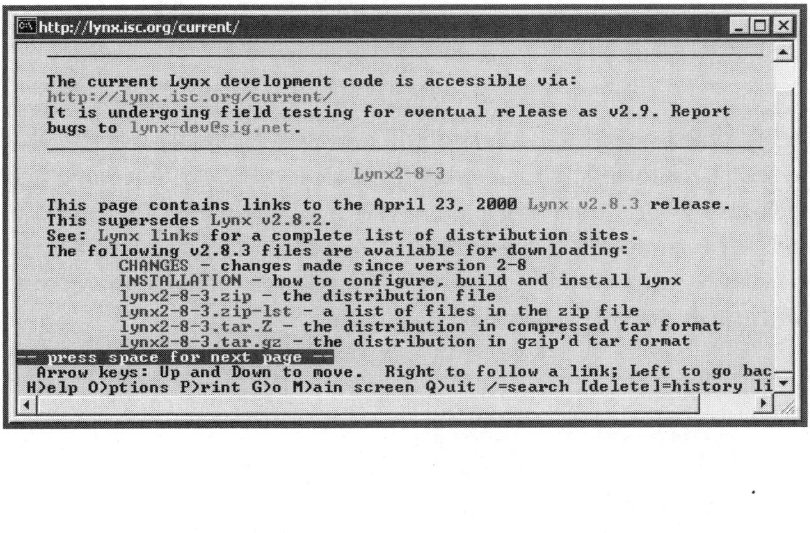

Figure 1.1

The Lynx browser is lightning fast when interacting with Web sites that support text-only content.

One option is to ignore all non-JavaScript browsers and stay with Netscape Navigator and Internet Explorer. You might also write scripts that support only the latest versions of both browsers. This will probably satisfy 98 percent of your potential visitors. However, if you want to attract as many people as possible to your Web site, you may want to consider finding ways to accommodate older browsers. We'll look at different options for dealing with that problem tomorrow.

One other Internet browser that you might want to be on the lookout for it called Opera, pictured in Figure 1.2. It is currently available for trial download at www.opera.com. It is less than half the size of its Netscape and Internet Explorer competitors. Still, it provides support for all the features that you'd expect, including support for JavaScript. Best of all, it loads Web pages fast. There is just one catch: It is not free. More and more people are starting to pay attention to it, and you may want to get a copy of it for testing.

Integrating JavaScript with HTML

JavaScripts are collections of programming statements that you embed in HTML documents by placing them within the <SCRIPT> and </SCRIPT> tags. These tags can be placed within either the head or body section of an HTML page. Figure 1.3 outlines the syntax that you must follow when using these tags in an HTML page.

Testing your JavaScripts with multiple browsers is simply a matter of downloading and installing them and then using them all to see how they handle your scripts. If you also want to test how older versions of those browsers work, you may need another computer. As of the writing of this book, I was able to download versions as old as Netscape 3 and Internet Explorer 3 from popular shareware sites such as www.tucows.com and www.download.com.

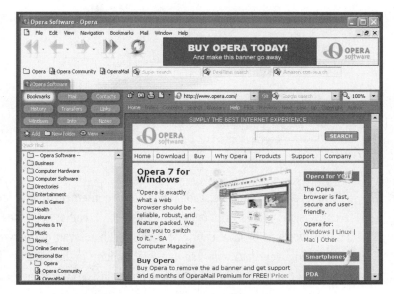

Figure 1.2

The Opera
Internet browser

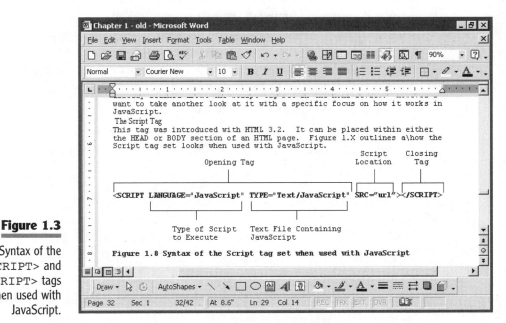

Figure 1.3

Syntax of the
<SCRIPT> and
</SCRIPT> tags
when used with
JavaScript.

Several arguments can be included within the first <SCRIPT> tag. The
LANGUAGE attribute specifies the version of JavaScript you want to use.

Here are your available options:

```
LANGUAGE="JavaScript"

LANGUAGE="JavaScript1.1"

LANGUAGE="JavaScript1.2"

LANGUAGE="JavaScript1.3"

LANGUAGE="JavaScript1.5"
```

NOTE Different versions of the Netscape Navigator and Internet Explorer browsers support different versions of JavaScript (as shown in Table 1.1, earlier in this session). With so many different versions of JavaScript and browsers, things can get very confusing. You may want to write your JavaScripts so that they conform to the lowest common denominator (that is, so that your scripts don't use features in versions of JavaScript newer than the oldest version that visitors to your Web site are likely to have). Another option is to write your JavaScripts to accommodate different browser versions.

The LANGUAGE attribute is the old way of specifying the type of script embedded within an HTML page. According to the HTML 4.0 specification, the TYPE attribute is now the proper way to go. However, you can continue to use both attributes if you want, in order to ensure that older browsers don't get confused. When working with JavaScripts, the TYPE attribute will always be Text/JavaScript.

Another way to work with JavaScripts is to store them in external files that have a .js file extension and then to reference those files from within your HTML pages. To accomplish this, you use the SRC attribute to specify the location of an external JavaScript file. Referencing an external script makes it a little more difficult for users to view your JavaScript source code. It also makes it possible to share the same JavaScripts among multiple HTML pages. Once you have defined the opening and closing tags, you can begin placing JavaScript statements between them.

Your First JavaScript—"Hello World"

So far, we've introduced JavaScript and JScript, discussed their capabilities and differences, and gone over their history. We then discussed JavaScript browser compatibility issues and learned the syntax required to use the `<SCRIPT>` and `</SCRIPT>` tags to embed JavaScripts within HTML pages. Now it's time to create your first JavaScript. It's going to be a very basic example, so don't get your hopes up too high. By tomorrow night, you'll be writing much more sophisticated scripts.

In this example, you will create the classic "Hello World" script that every programming book since the beginning of time has used as its introductory example. After all, who am I to defy such an honored tradition?

Before you get started, I want to say a quick word about HTML and JavaScript editors. There are plenty of them available, and their features and capabilities vary as much as their prices. It really does not matter which editor you ultimately decide to use. In fact, for the code you see in this book, I used the Notepad program that comes with Windows XP Home Edition.

TIP

Most JScript programmers have a script editor that they always work with. Modern script editors provide a number of features that facilitate and expedite script development, making them a lot more useful than Notepad. For example, most script editors will provide statement color coding. In addition, they can be configured to indent script statements automatically. Script editors may also provide wizards or templates that assist in the creation of new scripts. Some editors will even let you test your scripts from directly within the editor, saving you the trouble of having to load your HTML pages into your Web browser each time you want to test them. For example, HomeSite is a very popular editor among Web developers and can also be used when developing JScripts. To learn more about HomeSite, check out its home page at http://www.macromedia.com/software/homesite.

The first thing I did before approaching any of the coding examples in this book was to create an HTML template that I could use over and over again. Every time I worked on a new script, I used Notepad to open my template and type in my JavaScript statements. Then I chose File and selected Save As from the Notepad menu to save my script with a new file name. If you are using a full-featured HTML editor, it may automatically provide you with a starting template whenever you create a new HTML page. If not, you may want to build and use a template like I did. My template is shown here:

```
<HTML>

  <HEAD>

    <TITLE>Script 1.1 - Insert Descriptive Title Here</TITLE>

  </HEAD>

  <BODY>

  </BODY>

</HTML>
```

As you can see, my template contains the `<HEAD>` `</HEAD>`, `<TITLE>` `</TITLE>`, and `<BODY>` `</BODY>` tag sets all wrapped inside the starting and ending `<HTML>` `</HTML>` tag set. If you want to do so, create your own template now. When you are done, add the following lines inside the body section:

```
<SCRIPT LANGUAGE="JavaScript" TYPE="Text/JavaScript">

  document.write("Hello World");

</SCRIPT>
```

These three statements will make up your first JavaScript. You should recognize the first and last lines as script tags that tell your browser to execute the enclosed JavaScript statements. This script has just one statement. This statement tells the browser to write the message "Hello World" on the current document, which is the window in which the HTML page opened.

Once you have added the three lines of JavaScript to your template, it should look like this:

```
<HTML>

  <HEAD>

    <TITLE>Script 1.2 - Sample HTML Page</TITLE>

  </HEAD>

  <BODY>

    <SCRIPT LANGUAGE="JavaScript" TYPE="Text/JavaScript">

      document.write("Hello World");

    </SCRIPT>

  </BODY>

</HTML>
```

Testing Your First Script

Now that you have typed in your first script, you need to save it. I called my script `HelloWorld.html`. The HTML extension identifies the page as an HTML page. Your computer uses the information in the file's extension to associate the file with a particular application. An `.html` extension tells the operating system to open its default browser and pass the HTML file to it. Alternatively, you can use the `.htm` extension, which is also recognized as an extension for HTML pages.

If you are using a full-featured HTML editor, the editor may enable you to test your script with the click of a button. Because Notepad has no such automatic HTML testing feature, I simply started up a browser and used it to open the `HelloWorld.html` file. The browser opened my page and ran the script.

Depending on the browser installed on your computer, the process of testing your script is slightly different as outlined in the following procedures.

Testing with Netscape Communicator:

1. Start Netscape Navigator.
2. In the menu bar, click on File and then click on Open Web Location.
3. Type the location of your HTML page and click on Open. Alternatively, click on the Choose File button to browse and find the HTML page and then select it and then click on Open. Netscape Navigator opens the page as shown in Figure 1.4.

Testing with Internet Explorer:

1. Start Internet Explorer.
2. In the Internet Explorer menu bar, click on File and then click on Open. The Open dialog box appears.
3. Type the location of your HTML page and click on OK. Alternatively, click on the Browse button, locate and select your HTML file and then click on OK. Internet Explorer opens the page as shown in Figure 1.5.

Figure 1.4

Testing your first JavaScript using Netscape Communicator

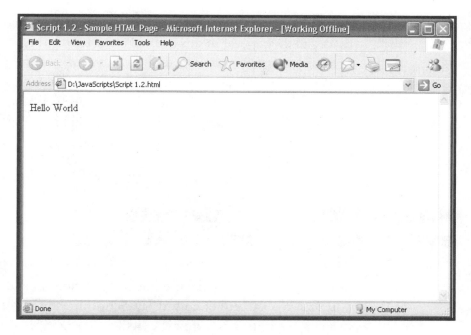

Figure 1.5

Testing your first
JavaScript using
Internet Explorer

After loading your new script and making sure that it works the way that you intended in both Netscape Navigator and Internet Explorer, you know that you probably have a good script. However, both Internet Explorer and Netscape Communicator do a really good job of hiding errors when they occur. I will show you how to look for and fix these errors on Sunday morning. If you did not see the Hello World message displayed, then you probably mistyped something, so go back and reopen your HTML page and double-check your work. For now, I'll assume that you saw what you expected when you loaded your Web page and everything is okay.

JavaScript and Case Sensitivity

You have to be extremely careful when keying in the text of your JavaScripts. JavaScript is a case sensitive programming language (unlike HTML, which enables you to use different capitalization when defining

HTML tags). *Case sensitivity* means that you must type JavaScript elements exactly as they appear in this book in order for them to work. For example, as far as JavaScript is concerned, the words *document* and *Document* refer to two different things, so pay special attention when typing your scripts. If I had accidentally typed a capital *D* in the `document.write()` statement used in the preceding example, my script would have experienced an error. As a result, the `Hello World` message would not have been displayed as I intended.

Different Ways to Integrate JavaScript into Your HTML Pages

As you know, there are two places you can put your JavaScripts in an HTML page: in either the head or body section. In addition, I have told you that you can either embed JavaScript directly into the HTML page or reference it in as an external `.js` file. One more way you can integrate JavaScript into an HTML page is as a component in an HTML tag.

Placing JavaScripts in the Body Section of the HTML page

JavaScripts embedded with the `<SCRIPT>` and `</SCRIPT>` tags can be placed anywhere in the body section of an HTML page. Scripts embedded in the body section are executed as part of the HTML document when the page loads. This enables the script to begin executing automatically as the page loads. For example, the statements shown below demonstrate how to embed a JavaScript within the body section of an HTML page.

```
<BODY>

  <SCRIPT LANGUAGE="JavaScript" TYPE="Text/JavaScript">

    document.write("This JavaScript is located in the body
section");

  </SCRIPT>

</BODY>
```

Similarly, you can embed multiple JavaScripts in HTML pages:

```
<BODY>

  <SCRIPT LANGUAGE="JavaScript" TYPE="Text/JavaScript">

    document.write("This first JavaScript is located in the
body section");

  </SCRIPT>

  <BR>

  <SCRIPT LANGUAGE="JavaScript" TYPE="Text/JavaScript">

    document.write("This second JavaScript is also located in
the body section");

  </SCRIPT>

</BODY>
```

Placing JavaScripts in the Head Section of the HTML page

JavaScripts also can be placed anywhere within the head section of your HTML pages. Unlike scripts embedded within the body section of HTML pages, scripts embedded in the head section are not necessarily automatically executed when the page loads. In some cases, they are executed only when called for execution by other statements within the HTML page. Most JavaScript programmers move all functions and most variables to the head section because this ensures that they will be defined before being referenced by scripts located in the body section of the page.

 NOTE *Variables* are containers for storing information in computer memory. *Functions* are groups of JavaScript statements that you can call to perform a specific task. I'll talk more about the benefits of using functions and variables tomorrow.

The following statements show an HTML page with a JavaScript embedded in the head section. This script will automatically execute when the HTML page is loaded.

```
<HTML>

  <HEAD>

    <TITLE>Script 1.3 - Sample HTML Page</TITLE>

    <SCRIPT LANGUAGE="JavaScript" TYPE="Text/JavaScript">

      window.alert("This JavaScript is located in the head
section");

    </SCRIPT>

  </HEAD>

  <BODY>

  </BODY>

<HTML>
```

As Figure 1.6 shows, this script displays a message in a pop-up dialog. I'll explain how the script did this tomorrow.

This next HTML page contains an embedded JavaScript that will not automatically execute when the HTML is loaded by the browser.

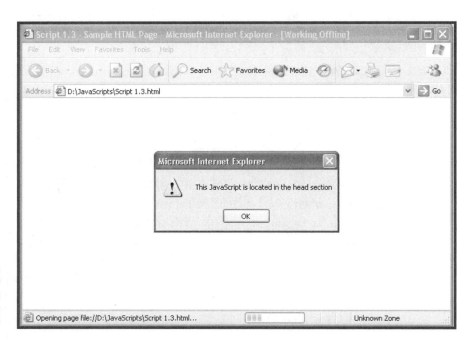

Figure 1.6

Testing your first JavaScript using Internet Explorer

```
<HTML>

  <HEAD>

    <TITLE>Script 1.4 - Sample HTML Page</TITLE>

    <SCRIPT LANGUAGE="JavaScript" TYPE="Text/JavaScript">

      function DisplayMsg() {

         window.alert("This JavaScript is located in the head
section");

      }

    </SCRIPT>

  </HEAD>

  <BODY>

  </BODY>

</HTML>
```

This pop-up dialog is not displayed this time because the JavaScript statement that displays it has been embedded within a function called `DisplayMsg()`. As a result, the JavaScript is executed only when called upon to execute from someplace else in the HTML page. For now, don't concern yourself with worrying about what a function is. Just understand that they can be used to create JavaScripts in the HTML page's head section that do not execute automatically.

Referencing JavaScript in an External .js File

To store your JavaScripts in external files, you need to save them as plain text files with a `.js` file extension. You then need to add the SCR attribute to the opening `<SCRIPT>` tag in your HTML page as demonstrated here.

```
<SCRIPT SRC="Test.js" LANGUAGE="JavaScript"
TYPE="Text/JavaScript"> </SCRIPT>
```

In this example, an external JavaScript named `Test.js` has been specified. This external JavaScript can contain any number of JavaScript statements.

However, it cannot contain any HTML whatsoever. Otherwise you'll end up with an error. For example, the contents of the `Test.js` script might be as simple as this:

```
document.write("This is an external JavaScript.");
```

There are many advantages to putting JavaScripts in externally referenced files. For starters, by moving JavaScripts out of your HTML pages you make your HTML pages smaller and easier to work with. In addition, you can reuse the JavaScripts stored as external files over and over again by referencing them from any number of HTML pages. This way if you create a script that you want to reference from multiple HTML pages, you can do so without having to embed the same script in different HTML pages over and over again. As a bonus, should you ever want to modify the functionality of an externally stored script, you may do so without having to visit every HTML page where you would otherwise have embedded it.

NOTE References to external JavaScripts can be placed in either the head or the body section of the HTML page. There is no limit to the number of external references that you can make, and there is no limit to the number of statements you can place in an external JavaScript.

Placing JavaScript in an HTML Tag

JavaScript can also be placed within HTML tags, as shown in the following example.

```
<BODY onLoad=document.write("Hello World!")> </BODY>
```

In this example, the JavaScript `onLoad=document.write("Hello World!")` statement has been added to the HTML `<BODY>` tag. This particular JavaScript statement tells the browser to write the enclosed text when the browser first loads the HTML page.

Placing small JavaScript statements inside HTML tags provides an easy way to execute small pieces of JavaScript code. Of course, this option really is beneficial only when executing small JavaScript statements and is impractical for larger JavaScript statements or situations that required multiple lines of code. However, as you will learn tomorrow, you can also trigger the execution of JavaScripts embedded in an HTML page's head section by embedding calling statements inside HTML tags.

NOTE You may have noticed the unusual spelling of the word onLoad in the previous example. The L in the middle of the word is capitalized, and rest of the word is in low-ercase letters. This type of notation is known as *camelback notation*. This is a perfect example of JavaScript's case sensitivity. If you change the capitalization of this word in any way, you'll get an error when you run your JavaScript.

Taking a Break

Okay, now is probably a good time to take a few minutes and stretch your legs before we continue. When you return I will start your overview of JScript and the WSH. This will include an examination of the WSH architecture and a look at how JScript fits into it. In addition, you will learn a little bit about how to work with the Windows command prompt. Finally, the chapter will conclude by showing you how to configure the WSH so that it works the way you want it to, both from the Windows command prompt and from the Windows desktop.

Introducing JScript

JScript is one of two default scripting languages supplied by Microsoft to use with the WSH. The other scripting language supplied with the WSH is VBScript. Functionally, JScript and VBScript are pretty much equivalent. Both are great scripting languages for automating small tasks.

NOTE

VBScript is a scripting language based on a subset of the Visual Basic programming language. Like JavaScript, VBScript can also be used for Web page development. However, while Internet Explorer supports VBScript, it does not work with Netscape Communicator. This makes VBScript a less universally accepted scripting language. In addition, VBScript is proprietary. This means that Microsoft owns it, whereas the current version of JavaScript and JScript are based on the ECMAScript standards, so no one company controls its future. As a result, many people prefer JavaScript and JScript to VBScript.

JScript and JavaScript provide a better collection of built-in mathematical functions that assist in performing complex calculation. VBScript, on the other hand, provides better support for working with arrays. I'll talk more about functions and arrays on Saturday morning. The decision as to whether to use JScript or VBScript to automate Windows tasks is really just a matter of personal preference. People with a JavaScript background will be able to make the move to JScript with very little effort. Likewise, people with a strong Visual Basic programming background may prefer learning VBScript.

NOTE

Several other third-party scripting languages are available that also can be used with the WSH. These languages include PERL, Python and REXX. A discussion of these scripting languages is beyond the scope of this book. To learn more about compatible versions of PERL and Python visit www.activestate.com. To learn more about REXX visit www-4.ibm.com/software/ad/obj-rexx.

The main reason for using JScript and the WSH is to save you time by automating system tasks. At the heart of every one of Microsoft's Windows operating systems is an intuitive *graphical user interface* (GUI). This GUI is designed to make the computer easy to use. All that you have to do is grab on to the mouse and point and click your way around.

Unfortunately, the GUI is not well suited to many tasks, particularly those that are highly repetitious or that involve many steps. For example, suppose that you are responsible for defining new user accounts on a shared computer in your department at work, and one day your boss comes in with a floppy disk containing a file with a list of 100 newly hired employees.

Using the GUI, you'd probably spend hours in front of the computer defining new user accounts, during which time no one else could use the computer to get any work done. On the other hand, you could write JScript and use the WSH to run it in less than an hour. This script could even be designed to read the file provided by your boss and to create a new user account for each name stored in the list. Once executed, the script would create the new user accounts within seconds. Best of all, once it is written, you could return and run the script again in the future with no additional work on your part to create new user accounts.

NOTE On Windows NT, XP, 2000, and 2003 operating system, Microsoft also supplies a built-in scripting language known as *Windows shell scripting*. Unlike the WSH, which supports script execution on all Windows operating systems (starting with Windows 95), Windows shell scripting is not supported by Windows 95, 98, and Me. While not as robust as the WSH, Windows shell scripting does provide a viable scripting option. If you want to learn more about Windows shell scripting, I recommend that you check out *Windows Shell Script Programming for the Absolute Beginner*, written by Jerry Lee Ford, Jr. You might also want to check out the *Microsoft Windows Shell Scripting and the WSH Administrator's Guide* (Premier Press), also by Jerry Lee Ford, Jr.

Introducing the Windows Script Host

The WSH is an optional software component that supports the execution of scripts on Windows operating systems. It is tightly coupled with the operating system, meaning that it provides direct access to a number of Windows resources, including these:

- The Windows desktop and Start menu
- The Windows Quick Launch Bar

- The Windows file system
- Local and network printers and drives
- Windows applications
- Windows services
- User accounts
- The Windows registry

The WSH provides the most complete scripting environment available today for all Windows operating systems. When combined with a scripting language such as JScript, it provides a perfect platform for developing scripts that can automate virtually any Windows task.

What Operating Systems Are Compatible with the WSH?

So far Microsoft has released three versions of the WSH. WSH 1.0 was released initially as an add-on for Windows NT and 95. It was also supplied with Windows 98 when that operating was released. WSH 2.0 was introduced with Windows Me and 2000. The current version of the WSH is version 5.6, which was shipped with Windows XP and 2003.

Table 1.2 summarizes the versions of the WSH that were shipped with various Windows operating systems. As you can see, WSH does not support execution on Windows 3.X operating systems.

Regardless of which of the Microsoft operating systems you own or support, you will want to make sure that you have upgraded the version of the WSH that is installed to the most current version. Microsoft provides access to the most current version of the WSH through its official scripting Web site, msdn.microsoft.com/scripting, where you can download WSH for free.

TABLE 1.2 WSH OPERATING SYSTEM SUPPORT		
Operating System	**Support for WSH**	**Version No.**
Windows 3.X	No	-
Windows 95	Yes	-
Windows 98	Yes	1.0
Windows Me	Yes	2.0
Windows NT	Yes	-
Windows 2000	Yes	2.0
Windows XP	Yes	5.6
Windows 2003	Yes	5.6

A Brief Overview of the WSH Architecture

The WSH provides built-in support for both JScript and VBScript. In addition, it can support any third-party, WSH-compatible scripting language, including PERL, Python, and REXX. In the future, third-party software developers may provide other WSH-compatible scripting languages. Microsoft designed the WSH to be very extensible, as evidenced by the number of third-party scripting languages that have already been set up to work with it. However, because JScript and VBScript are supplied with the WSH, they are the most commonly used scripting languages.

To work effectively with the WSH, you need to understand its architecture. Figure 1.7 provides a depiction of the different components that make up the WSH. As you can see, the WSH consists of scripting engines, execution hosts, and a core object model. In addition, it can work directly with object models supplied by other software applications.

NOTE

If you are comfortable developing scripts using more than one WSH-supported scripting language, the WSH enables you to create a special kind of script known as a Windows script file. These script files enable you to combine two or more scripts into a single script. This enables you to create scripts that take advantage of the strengths of different languages when automating tasks. For example, you might want to create a Windows script file that takes advantage of JavaScript's collection of mathematical functions and VBScript's strong support for creating and manipulating arrays. Since teaching you scripting languages other than JavaScript and JScript is outside the scope of this book, I won't be going into Windows script files any further. However, if you already know another scripting language, after you have completed reading this book you might want to visit msdn.microsoft.com/scripting to learn more about this WSH feature.

The WSH is a 32-bit application. Its architecture consists of three separate layers. First there are the various WSH-supported scripting engines. These scripting engines interpret script statements and pass them on to an execution host for processing.

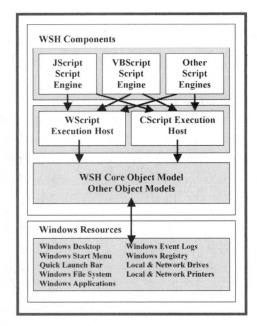

Figure 1.7

The WSH is composed of a number of integrated components.

The WSH provides two different execution hosts. The WScript execution host is designed to support the execution of scripts directly from the Windows desktop. The CScript execution host, on the other hand, is designed to support the execution of scripts from the Windows command prompt. Each of these execution hosts exists as a separate executable file named `Wscript.exe` and `Cscript.exe`, respectively.

With one exception, the WScript and CScript execution hosts provide the same level of functionality. This exception is the WScript execution host's capability to enable scripts to display text messages and collection input from users using graphical pop-up dialogs. This makes the WScript execution host the proper choice for scripts that need to interact directly with users. The CScript execution host, on the other hand, generally is used to run scripts that do not interact with users or to run scripts for users who are comfortable working from the Windows command prompt. However, the WScript execution host can be used to run scripts from the command line as well. Unless your script is designed to generate graphical pop-up dialogs, the choice of which script execution host to use is completely arbitrary.

The purpose of the WSH core object model is to provide access to Windows resources. It accomplishes this by defining objects that represent actual resources. These objects can then be accessed and manipulated by scripts, thus allowing the scripts to access and manipulate the resources that the objects represent. Examples of the types of objects that the WSH makes available include objects that represent Windows shortcuts, files, folders, and disk drives. The WSH also provides objects that represent network resources such as network drives and printers. On top of all this, the WSH object model also provides access to system resources such as Windows events logs and the Windows registry.

Every object that is presented by the WSH is associated with a collection of properties and methods. For example, a file is an example of an object. File objects have file names and file extensions. By accessing these file object properties, your JScripts can locate files that they want to work with. In addition, by modifying file object properties, your JScripts can rename files and change their file types.

The file object also provides JScripts with access to a number of different methods that enable you to create, delete, rename, copy, and move Windows files. Figure 1.7 provides a partial listing of the kinds of system resources exposed by the WSH core object model. On Sunday afternoon I'll cover the objects exposed by the WSH core object model and provide you with examples of how to access and manipulate them.

Writing Your First JScript

In order to create a JScript, you only need to open your text editor, create a plain text file, add a few JScript statements to it, and then save it with a .js file extension. For example, create a new JScript called Script 1.5.js and add the following statements to it.

```
//Script 1.5 - Your first JScript
WScript.Echo("Hello World!");
```

The first statement is a comment that was embedded within the file to document the script's name and purpose. The second statement displays a text message. The composition of the second statement is as follows. First the WScript object is referenced. This object is different from the WScript execution host. Then a method called Echo, which belongs to the WScript object, is executed and passed the text string "Hello World!". Don't worry if this all sounds a little confusing or overwhelming now. By the time that you get through Sunday evening, you'll understand how this stuff works. For now, just follow along and focus on the steps involved in creating and executing your first JScript.

When executed by either the WScript or CScript execution host, this JScript displays its message. However, depending on which execution host you choose to use when running the script, the results will vary significantly. For example, if you were to run this script from the Windows command prompt using the CScript execution host, you'll see the output shown in Figure 1.8.

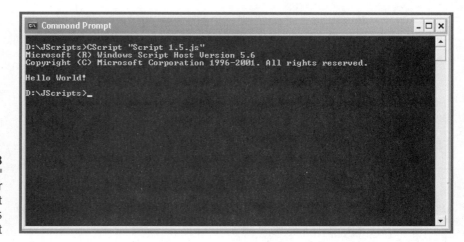

Figure 1.8

Running your
first WSH JScript
at the Windows
command prompt

You may have noticed in Figure 1.8 that the name of the JScript file to be run was enclosed within a matching pair of double quotation marks. I had to do this because the script's file name contained a blank space. Otherwise the use of the double quotation marks would not have been required.

If you were to run the scripts directly from the Windows desktop by double-clicking on it, Windows would, by default, run it using the WScript execution host. As a result, the script's output would be displayed in the form of a graphical pop-up dialog, as shown in Figure 1.9.

You can also use the WScript execution host to run scripts from the Windows command prompt, in which case the script will run exactly as if you had started it from the Windows desktop.

Getting Comfortable with the Windows Command Prompt

Even some of the most experienced computer users have limited experience working with the Windows command prompt and little if any

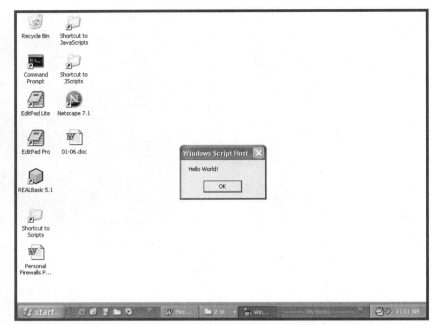

Figure 1.9

Running your
JScript from the
Windows desktop

understanding of the Windows commands that are available. However, if you plan on becoming a serious JScript programmer, you need to get comfortable working with the Windows shell.

The Windows shell provides a text-based interface between the user and the operating system. Instead of using the computer's mouse to point and click your way through the Windows graphical user interface, you work with the Windows shell by typing in text commands. The Windows shell translates these commands into a format the operating system can understand. Likewise, the Windows shell translates any output returned by the operating system into a format that people can understand.

You enter commands for the Windows shell to process by typing them in at the Windows command prompt. For example, on a computer running Windows XP, you would start up a new Windows shell session by clicking on Start, All Programs, Accessories, and then Command Prompt. The Command Prompt window appears and displays the Windows command prompt, as shown in Figure 1.10.

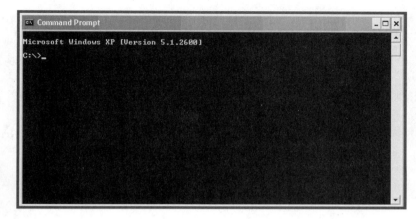

Figure 1.10

The Windows
command prompt

TIP

As a shortcut, you can start up a new Windows shell session and access the Windows command prompt by clicking on Start, Run, typing CMD, and then clicking on OK.

As you can see in Figure 1.11, by default the Windows command prompt is represented in the form of a drive letter followed by a colon, a backslash, and the greater than character (>). Just to the right of the command prompt you will see a blinking cursor, which indicates that the Windows shell is ready to accept new command input. As an example, type VER and then hit the Enter key. The VER command instructs the Windows shell to display information about the version of Windows currently running on the computer, as demonstrated here.

```
C:\>ver


Microsoft Windows XP [Version 5.1.2600]


C:\>
```

The Windows shell passes the command to the operating system, collects the results of the command, and displays them in the back in the Windows console, after which the Windows command prompt is redisplayed.

Now, let's look at how to use the command prompt to run your new JScript using the CScript execution host. All that you have to do is type CScript, a space, and the name of your script and then press the Enter key as demonstrated below.

```
CScript "Script 1.5.js"
```

Likewise, to run your script from the command prompt using the WScript execution host, you would type the following.

```
WScript "Script 1.5.js"
```

NOTE If your script resides in a folder other than the folder upon which the Windows shell is currently focused, you must supply the complete path to the folder where the script is stored. For example, if your script were stored in C:\Jscripts, then you would need to use the following command to run it using the WScript execution host.

```
WScript C:\Jscripts\"Script 1.5.vbs"
```

When you are done running your script and want to close the Command Prompt Window, you can do so by clicking on Close in the upper right corner of the Windows. You can also close the Command Prompt window by right-clicking on the Command Prompt icon in the upper-left corner of the Window and selecting Close.

TIP If you are faster at the keyboard than you are with your mouse then you can also close the Command Prompt windows by typing EXIT and pressing the Enter key.

NOTE A detailed discussion of the Windows shell is beyond the scope of this book. If you would like to learn more, check out the *Microsoft Windows Shell Scripting and the WSH Administrator's Guide* (Premier Press), written by Jerry Lee Ford, Jr.

Setting up WSH Execution Hosts

You can use the WScript and CScript execution hosts to run any JScript. The manner in which these execution hosts run scripts depends on how the execution hosts have been configured. Both the WScript and CScript execution hosts have their individual configuration settings. In addition, you can configure the WScript execution host to run differently when executed from the Windows command line and the Windows desktop.

In addition to enabling you to configure default execution host settings, the WSH also provides you with the capability to override these default settings when running individual scripts. This way you can temporarily change the execution settings that are in effect for a given script's execution without affecting the way the execution host runs other scripts.

Finally, if you have a few JScripts that require their own unique sets of configuration settings, you can store a customized set of configuration settings for each script in its own `.wsh` file. Each of these different execution host configuration options is further explored in the sections that follow.

Configuring Command-Line Execution

Both the WScript and CScript execution hosts support command-line execution. The syntax required to configure the execution setting for the CScript and WScript execution hosts is outlined below.

```
CScript ScriptName [//Options] [Arguments]
WScript ScriptName [//Options] [Arguments]
```

`ScriptName` specifies the name of a script that is to be executed. `//Options` represents a collection of one or more optional parameters that configure a particular aspect of the execution host's operation. The `Arguments` attribute represents a list of arguments that can be passed to the script for processing.

The execution settings available for both execution hosts are identical. Table 1.3 briefly outlines these settings.

TABLE 1.3 WSCRIPT AND CSCRIPT COMMAND-LINE OPTIONS

Option	Description
//?	Displays the syntax requirements to use both the WScript and CScript commands.
//b	Instructs the execution host to run the script in batch mode in order to suppress the display of errors and any other text output.
//d	Turns on active debugging.
//e:jscript | e:vbscript	Specifies the type of WSH script engine that should be used to interpret script statements and convert them to binary code.
//h:wscript | h:cscript	Specifies which WSH execution host is to be used when executing the script.
//i	Instructs the execution host to interactively execute the script in order to enable error and text output to be displayed.
//job:id	Identifies a specific job within a Windows script file that is to be executed.
//logo	Tells the CScript or WScript execution host to display its logo before executing the script.
//nologo	Tells the CScript or WScript execution host not to display its logo before executing the script.
//s	Saves the specified execution settings, making them the default settings for future script executions.
//t:nn	Specifies the timeout value used to limit the script's maximum execution time. By default, no time limit is imposed on script execution.
//x	Executes the script in debug mode.

Let's look at a few examples of different ways that the CScript and WScript execution hosts can be configured. For example, the following command can be used to tell the CScript execution host to run a script named `Script 1.5.js` without permanently modifying any of the execution host's configuration settings.

```
CScript "Script 1.5.js"
```

Likewise, you can run the same script using the WScript execution host using the following command.

```
WScript "Script 1.5.js"
```

Instead of running JScript using the execution host's default settings, you can temporarily override the execution host's configuration settings as demonstrated below.

```
WScript "Script 1.5.js" //T:10
```

In this example, the JScript is run using a 10-second execution time limit. By default, Windows operating systems set up the WScript execution host as the default WSH execution host. In other words, if you type the name of the script without specifying which WSH execution host to use, the WScript execution host will be used. To set the CScript execution host up as the default execution host, you could enter the following command.

```
CScript //H:CScript
```

Similarly, you can change the execution host back to WScript as shown below.

```
WScript //H:WScript
```

You can override more than one execution setting at a time by adding more options, each of which must be preceded by `//` characters as demonstrated below.

```
WScript "Script 1.5.js" //T:10 //nologo
```

In this example, the WScript execution host is used to run a script named `Script 1.5.js` with a 10-second time limit without first displaying the WScript execution host.

Each of the commands that we have looked at to this point affects only the execution for the specified script. To make the changes permanent, you'll need to add the `//s` option as demonstrated below.

```
WScript //nologo //s
```

This statement configures the WScript host so that it will not display its logo each time it runs a script from the Windows command prompt. Because you can configure the command-line execution of the WScript and CScript execution hosts separately, you can assign a completely different set of configurations to the CScript execution host.

NOTE

Configuration changes made to the WSH's execution hosts are specific to the person who makes them. Therefore, any changes you make will not be in effect for other people who share the same computer you use.

Configuring WScript Desktop Execution

The WScript execution host's execution from the Windows desktop is configured separately from its command-line execution. When it is configured for Windows desktop execution, you can limit the amount of time that the script will be permitted to execute, as well as specify whether or not the WScript execution host's logo should be displayed. The following procedure outlines the steps involved in modifying the WScript execution host's desktop execution settings.

1. Click on Start and then Run. The Run dialog box appears.
2. Type `wscript` and then click on OK. The Windows Script Host Settings dialog box appears, as shown in Figure 1.11.

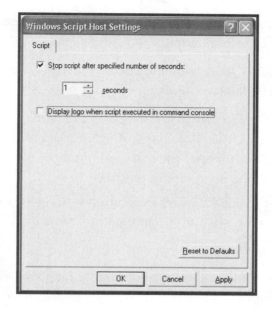

Figure 1.11

Configuring the way the WScript execution host runs scripts that are started from the Windows desktop

3. By default no execution time limit is applied to script execution. To specify one, select Stop Script after Specified Number of Seconds and enter a number specifying the number of seconds within which scripts must finish executing.

4. By default, the WScript logo is displayed when you run your JScripts. To prevent its display, clear the Display Logo when Script Executed in Command Console option.

5. Click on OK.

Configuring Individual Script Execution

If you write a JScript to which you will never want to apply default execution host settings when you run it, you can create an individual Windows script host or .wsh file that specifies custom execution host settings for the script. The .wsh file must be assigned the same file name as the script with which it is associated but with a .wsh file extension. A script named Script 1.5.js would be named Windows script host file Script 1.5.wsh.

The following procedure outlines the steps involved in creating a Windows script host file for a given script.

1. Right-click on your script and select Properties. The script's Properties dialog box appears.

2. Select the Script property sheet, as shown in Figure 1.12.

3. If desired, select the Stop Script after Specified Number of Seconds option and then specify the maximum number of seconds that the script should be permitted to execute.

4. To prevent the display of the execution host's logo, clear the Display Logo when Script Executed in Command Console option.

5. Click on OK.

Once you have completed the previous procedure, you should see a new file with the same file name and a .wsh file extension stored in the folder where your JScript is stored. Its contents will resemble this:

```
[ScriptFile]
Path=D:\Script 5.1.wsf
[Options]
Timeout=5
DisplayLogo=0
```

[ScriptFile] is a header that identifies the file as a Windows script file. Path identifies the path and name of your JScript. [Options] is a header that identifies the start of a list of execution host configuration settings. Timeout sets the script's timeout settings. DisplayLogo specifies whether or not the execution host's logo should be displayed when the script is executed from the Windows command prompt. Set DisplayLogo equal to 0 to prevent the display of the execution host's logo and set it equal to 1 to enable its display.

NOTE If you prefer, you can create a script's Windows script host file manually. However, be careful when doing so to make sure that you don't make any typos when editing the file.

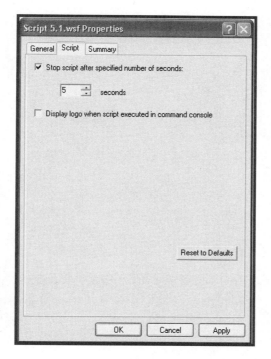

Figure 1.12

Configuring
execution settings
for individual
scripts

Once you have created a `.wsh` file for your JScript, the WSH will automatically refer to it the next time you run your script. However, if you
delete the `.wsh` file or move your script to a different folder and forget to
move its associated `.wsh` file also, the execution host will run the script
using its default execution host configuration settings.

What's Next?

Well, I think that is about enough for tonight. Get a good night's sleep
because there is a lot to do tomorrow. Tomorrow morning you'll get a
basic overview of JavaScript and JScript programming. Then in the afternoon and evening you'll begin focusing on JavaScript as you learn how to
use it to spice up your Web pages by making them more interactive and
graphical. You'll even learn how to take control of the browser itself.

Learning the Basics of JavaScript Coding

- ➤ A few words about scripting
- ➤ Working with values
- ➤ Working with JavaScript statements
- ➤ Streamlining your JavaScripts with functions
- ➤ Using arrays
- ➤ Using built-in JavaScript objects

Good morning! I hope you had a good night's sleep and that you are rested and ready to go. There is a lot for you to do today.

Yesterday, I focused on providing you with the background that you need to get started working with both JavaScript and JScript. Today you will begin to learn about the programming statements that make up these two languages. To keep things as simple as possible and because the focus of the first half of this book is on JavaScript, I will present everything in this chapter using JavaScript examples. However, as you will see on Sunday, just about everything that you learn in this chapter can be applied to JScript.

If you have not already done so, now is a good time to pull together all the tools you plan to work with. While you can certainly use Window's Notepad application to write all your scripts, you also might want to download a more advanced script editor from the Internet. Its also a good idea to download copies of Internet browsers such as Netscape, Internet Explorer, and Opera. In addition, you might also want to check out the various shareware sites such as www.shareware.com, www.download.com, and www.tucows.com for other alternatives.

Assuming that you have everything you need, let's review what I have planned for this morning and then jump right in. You will start out by learning the basic programming statements available to you in JavaScript and JScript. These statements enable you to do such things as storing information for later use, comparing values, and developing logical routines to handle different circumstances. You'll also learn to streamline your script using loops, functions, and arrays. Finally, I'll go over built-in JavaScript and JScript objects, explaining what they are and how to use them.

A Few Words about Scripting

Perhaps you are wondering what the difference is between *scripting* and *programming*. The answer is nothing. They are the same thing. Many people like to think of scripts as small units of program code that perform a specific function and of programs as larger, more robust code. As you will soon learn, scripts can be written that fulfill both of these definitions.

One possible way to differentiate a script from a program is to define scripts as interpreted programs that are processed one line at a time and to define programs as collections of code that must be compiled before they can execute. *Compiling* is the process of converting a program's instructions into machine language so that the computer can process them. Because JavaScript and JScript are *interpreted languages*, they need something to interpret the code as they execute. This is the job of the Internet browser and the WSH, which also provide scripts with a programming environment complete with environment-specific *object models* that provide JavaScripts with access to resources such as windows and browser history information and provide JScript with access to files, folders, drives, and so on.

I know that I keep mentioning objects and object models; I will continue to do so throughout the morning before I finally provide detailed coverage later this morning and in the first part of the afternoon. Learning a new programming language is not always easy and is made only more difficult by the fact that just about every new concept depends on your knowing another one. Unfortunately, I can only teach you one concept at a time. So hang in there!

Getting Comfortable with Statement Syntax

JavaScript and JScript are case sensitive. This means that you must be careful to use correct spelling and capitalization when typing script statements. For example, in a few minutes you are going to learn how to work with variables. If you create a variable in the beginning of your script with the name `total-Value`, you must use this exact spelling throughout your script. Change a single element of spelling and you will get an error because JavaScript and JScript will think that you are referencing a different variable.

■ ■

TIP If you are like me, you will never be able to remember the correct spelling of every JavaScript language element. That means you'll be checking Appendix A, "A Brief JavaScript and JScript Reference," a lot. This appendix provides a list of JavaScript objects, properties, and methods. If you are ever in doubt about how to spell any of these elements, check the appendix first. It will save you a lot of time and frustration.

■ ■

With the exception of its case-sensitivity requirement, JavaScript and JScript are very easygoing languages in that they do not impose a strict set of rules about how you should format your scripts. Statements can begin on one line and end on the next, or you can place multiple statements on a single line by typing a semicolon (;) at the end of each statement. The semicolon tells JavaScript and JScript explicitly where a statement ends. However, packing more than one statement on a single line of code can get ugly if you do it too much.

■ ■

TIP Although the ; is not required for any JavaScript statement, it's a good idea to get into the habit of ending all your statements with one. It makes your script easier for the next person to read and work with.

■ ■

Hiding JavaScript Statements

HTML comments begin with the characters <!-- and end with -->. The browser knows not to display anything between these sets of characters. You also know that the HTML <SCRIPT> tag is used to embed JavaScript into HTML pages. Both JavaScript and non-JavaScript browsers know not to display the <SCRIPT> tags.

However, non-JavaScript browsers do not know what to make of the statements within the <SCRIPT> tags, so they will display the actual lines of the script right in the middle of the HTML page. I am sure that this is not what you want your visitors to see. To get around this unsightly mess, you can enclose all the JavaScript statements starting after the beginning <SCRIPT> tag and before the ending </SCRIPT> tag within HTML comments, as demonstrated in the following example:

```
<HTML>

  <HEAD>

    <TITLE>Script 2.1 -Example of Comment Statements</TITLE>

  </HEAD>

  <BODY>

    <SCRIPT LANGUAGE="JavaScript" TYPE="Text/JavaScript">

    <!-- Start hiding JavaScript statements

      document.write("Non-JavaScript browsers will not see
this message.");

    // End hiding JavaScript statements -->

    </SCRIPT>

  </BODY>

</HTML>
```

Since browsers are smart enough not to process any HTML that they do not understand, the starting and ending <SCRIPT> tags are ignored by non-JavaScript browsers. At the same time, non-JavaScript browsers will view everything between the HTML comments tags as one big comment and ignore it, thus hiding all JavaScript statements and preventing their display.

JavaScript-enabled browsers, on the other hand, will recognize the starting and ending <SCRIPT> tags and process them accordingly. These browsers also will recognize the opening HTML comment tag and ignore it, while simultaneously seeing the line beginning with the // characters as a JavaScript comment and ignoring it as well.

TIP

You also can use comments to make your JavaScripts and JScripts self-documenting by using them to add descriptive comments to your scripts.

As long as you model your scripts after this example, you'll trick old browsers into thinking that your JavaScript statements are just HTML comments, without affecting what JavaScript-aware browsers see.

Working with Values

JavaScripts and JScripts store information as *values*. For example, if you were to create a form for your users to fill out, each entry in the form would contain a separate value. Your scripts can store these values in variables and then use the variables throughout your script.

Table 2.1 shows the list of the types of values supported by JavaScript and JScript.

TABLE 2.1 JAVASCRIPT AND JSCRIPT VALUES	
Value	**Description**
Boolean	A value that indicates a condition of either `true` or `false`
Null	An empty value
Numbers	A numeric value such as 99 or 3.142
Strings	A string of text such as "Welcome" or "Click here to visit ptpmagazine.com"

Declaring Variables

To use a variable in your script, that variable must first be declared. You have two ways of doing this. The first option is to use the `var` keyword as demonstrated in the following example:

```
var firstName = "Alexander";
```

This example creates a variable named `firstName` and assigns it the value of `Alexander`. Your scripts would probably contain other variables that also contain information such as last names, phone numbers, and so on.

Optionally, you can also declare a variable by simply referencing it for the first time as shown in the following example:

```
firstName = "Alexander";
```

USE THE <NOSCRIPT> TAG TO TALK TO NON-JAVASCRIPT BROWSERS

Although more than 95 percent of the browsers being used today support JavaScript, there are still many that do not. In addition, both the Netscape and Internet Explorer browsers enable users to turn off JavaScript support. What can you do to make your JavaScript-enhanced pages available to those visitors who want to view them while still making basic information available to visitors who do not have JavaScript-enabled browsers?

One option you can explore is to create both JavaScript and non-JavaScript versions of your HTML pages and display the appropriate set of pages based on an inspection of the user's browser. I will talk more about this option later today.

A simpler solution is to display an HTML page that provides two links with an instruction to your visitors to click on one link if their browser supports JavaScript and to click on the other if it does not. However, you may be taking a big risk by assuming that all your visitors even know what JavaScript is and that their browsers support it.

A really simple alternative is to use the <NOSCRIPT> tags. Every browser, even those with JavaScript support disabled, will recognize these HTML tags. Their purpose is to display a message for browsers that do not process your JavaScript. JavaScript-enabled browsers will ignore everything within the <NOSCRIPT> tags.

The following example demonstrates how to set up a page that can provide information to browsers, regardless of their level of JavaScript support.

```
<HTML>
  <HEAD>
    <TITLE>Script 2.2 - The NOSCRIPT tag</TITLE>
  </HEAD>
  <BODY>
    <SCRIPT LANGUAGE="JavaScript" TYPE="Text/JavaScript">
    <!--Start hiding JavaScript statements
      document.write("Non-JavaScript browsers will not see this
message " +
```

```
            "but JavaScript-enabled browsers will.");
        // End hiding JavaScript statements -->
        </SCRIPT>
        <NOSCRIPT>
          JavaScript-enabled browsers will not see this message but
          JavaScript handicapped browsers will see it.
        </NOSCRIPT>
      </BODY>
    </HTML>
```

In this example, a value of `Alexander` is assigned to a variable named `firstName` (if the variable exists), thereby changing its value. If the referenced variable does not yet exist, it is created and assigned a value.

Whether you choose to use the `var` keyword or not when creating variables is really just a matter of personal preference. The main benefit of using `var` is that it makes your scripts easier to read and also lets you declare variables for later use in your scripts without assigning them an initial starting value.

Working with Variables

I have to go over a few more things relating to variables before we move on. These important aspects of variables include the rules that govern the naming of variables and how to define variable scope.

Rules for Variable Names

Keep the following rules in mind when creating variables:

- ✿ Variable names can consist only of uppercase and lowercase letters, the underscore character, and the numbers 0 through 9.
- ✿ Variable names cannot begin with a number.

○   JavaScript and JScript are case sensitive. If you declare a variable with the name `totalCount`, you must refer to it using the exact same case throughout your script.

○   Variable names cannot contain spaces.

○   You cannot use any *reserved words* as variable names. Refer to Appendix C, "JavaScript and JScript Reserved Words," for a list of JavaScript and JScript reserved words.

The following list is not a set of rules but is a set of guidelines you may want to follow when working with variables:

○   JavaScript and JScript are considered to be a *loosely typed* languages because they do not force you to define variables before using them. However, using the `var` keyword makes your code easier to understand.

○   You should create variable names that describe their contents. For example, `lastName` is a much better variable name than `ln`. Variable names of only a few characters may be easier to type and may seem quite obvious when you are writing your scripts, but they may not be so obvious to you a year later or to someone else who is trying to read your script.

Defining Variable Scope

You can create variables that can be accessed by JavaScripts located throughout an HTML page or from any location within a JScript. Alternatively, you can create variables that can only be accessed within the constraints of a small section of code known as a *function*. Defining the space in which the variable is effective is known as defining the variable's *scope*. A variable can be either *local* or *global* in scope.

Local Variables

A *local variable* is one that is declared explicitly using the `var` statement inside a function. A *function* is a collection of script statements that can be called by another script statement to perform a specific action.

For example, the following code shows a function called `ShowNotice()` that displays a message every time it is called. This function uses the alert method belonging to the `window` object to display a text message specified by a local variable named `textMessage`, which has been set to "`Are you sure you want to quit?`". Because this variable is local in scope, any statements located outside the function where it is defined cannot reference it.

```
function ShowNotice()
{
  var textMessage = "Are you sure you want to quit?";
  window.alert(textMessage);
}
```

You'll learn more about functions in just a few minutes.

NOTE The `window.alert(textMessage)` statement in the preceding example is one of many types of pop-up dialogs that JavaScript and JScript can display. This particular example works only for JavaScripts because it relies on the browser's `window` object. I will go over how to display text messages using other options in greater detail later today.

Global Variables

A *global variable* is any variable defined outside of a function. Such a variable is global because any script statement located in the Web page or script file can refer to it. You can create a global variable in several ways, including:

- Creating the variable by referencing it inside a function without first declaring it using the `var` keyword.

- Creating the variable anywhere else in a JavaScript with or without the `var` keyword.

The following example demonstrates the differences between local and global variable scope. Three variables are created with a global scope. The first is `glVarMsg1` in the head section of the page. The second and third variables are `glVarMsg2` and `glVarMsg3` in the body section of the page. The glVarMsg2 variable is global in scope even though it is located within a function because it was not created using the var keyword. The lcVarMsg1 variable is local in scope because it is in a function and was created with the var keyword.

```
<HTML>
  <HEAD>
    <TITLE>Script 2.3 - A demonstration of variable
scope</TITLE>
    <SCRIPT LANGUAGE="JavaScript" TYPE="Text/JavaScript">
    <!-- Start hiding JavaScript statements
      glVarMsg1 = "Global variables created in the HEAD
section can be " +
        "referenced anywhere in this page.";
      function CreateVariables()
      {
      var lcVarMsg1 = "Local variables created inside a
function cannot " +
        "be referenced anywhere else.";
      glVarMsg2 = "Global variables created inside functions
in the HEAD " +
        "section can be referenced anywhere in this page.";
      }
    // End hiding JavaScript statements -->
    </SCRIPT>
  </HEAD>
  <BODY>
    <SCRIPT LANGUAGE="JavaScript" TYPE="Text/JavaScript">
    <!-- Start hiding JavaScript statements
      CreateVariables();
      glVarMsg3 = "Global variables created in the BODY
section can be " +
        "referenced anywhere in this page.";
```

```
        document.write(glVarMsg1 + "<BR>");

        document.write(glVarMsg2 + "<BR>");

        document.write(glVarMsg3 + "<BR>");

        document.write(lcVarMsg1 + "<BR>");

      // End hiding JavaScript statements -->

      </SCRIPT>

    </BODY>

  </HTML>
```

TIP   Note the use of the + character in the previous example. It provides the ability to break up lengthy strings and spread them out over multiple lines.

TIP   You may have noticed that I embedded the `<BR>` tag inside the `document.write()` statement. Doing so provides me with one way of controlling line breaks with JavaScripts. To make this work, I placed the `<BR>` tag in parentheses and concatenated it with the rest of the text in the `document.write()` statement using the + operator.

TIP   You may also have noticed that the JavaScript in the head section contains a function named `CreateVariables()`. This line and the statements following it are part of a function. This function does not execute until it is called by the `CreateVariables()` statement in the body section of the page. Don't worry if this seems a bit confusing; I'll explain functions in greater detail later this morning. You might want to bookmark this example to come back and look at again after reading the material on functions.

Figure 2.1 shows what happens when the preceding script executes. The four `document.write()` statements attempt to display the value of each variable. However, because `lcVarMsg1` is not global in scope, it is not displayed. Instead, only three of the `document.write()` statements execute correctly.

The fourth statement, which attempts to display the value assigned to `lcVarMsg1`, generates an error.

The script ran but experienced an error

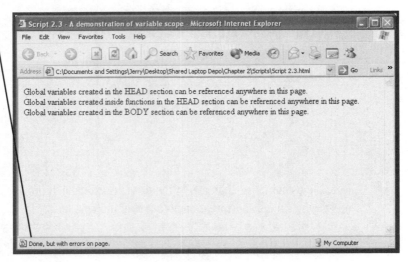

Figure 2.1

Only global variables or those local in scope to the `document.write()` statements will appear when the page is displayed.

 NOTE   Depending on how you have configured your browser, the error message may or may not be displayed. For example, if you are using Internet Explorer to load the HTML page that contains the script and you have not configured it to display all error messages, the only indication of an error will be a small yellow icon and an error message displayed on the browser's status bar.

Manipulating Variables

You can alter the value of a variable by simply assigning it a new value as follows:

```
variableName = 100;
```

JavaScript also provides a number of other operators you can use to modify the value of variables. These are outlined in Table 2.2.

I'll bet you are wondering what's going on with the last four operators in Table 2.2. I will take a moment to explain them a little further.

TABLE 2.2 JAVASCRIPT AND JSCRIPT OPERATORS

Operator	Description	Example
x + y	Adds the value of x to the value of y	`total = 2 + 1`
x - y	Subtracts the value of y from x	`total = 2 - 1`
x * y	Multiplies the value of x and y	`total = x * 2`
x / y	Divides the value of x by the value of y	`total = x / 2`
-x	Reverses the sign of x	`count = -count`
x++	Post-increment (returns x, then increments x by one)	`x = y++`
++x	Pre-increment (increments x by one, then returns x)	`x = ++y`
x—	Post-decrement (returns x, then decrements x by one)	`x = y—`
—x	Pre-decrement (decrements x by one, then returns x)	`x = —y`

Both x++ and ++x operators increment the value of x by 1. The difference between them is when the update occurs. I can best demonstrate this difference with an example. Suppose that I have a script with two variables, totalCount and noUnitsSold. Suppose that noUnitsSold is equal to 10 and that I added the following line of code somewhere further down in my script:

```
totalCount = ++noUnitsSold;
```

What happens here is that first noUnitsSold would be incremented by 1 to a value of 11. Then totalCount would be set to 11. Now suppose that I rewrote the assignment statement to be the following:

```
totalCount = noUnitsSold++;
```

What happens here is totally different than in the preceding example. This time, `totalCount` is first set to the value of `noUnitsSold`, which is `10`. Then the value of `noUnitsSold` is incremented by 1 to `11`.

The –x and x– operators work the same way, only they decrease the value of the variables by 1.

Assigning Values

As I have already alluded to, you assign values to variables using an *assignment operator*. For example, the following statement assigns a value of `44` to a variable named `totalCount`:

```
totalCount = 44
```

In this example, the assignment operator is the old-fashioned equals sign. JavaScript and JScript provide many ways to assign values to variables, as outlined in Table 2.3.

TABLE 2.3 ASSIGNMENT OPERATORS (ASSUME THAT Y = 5)

Operator	Description	Examples	Result
=	Sets a variable value equal to some value	x = y + 1	6
+=	Shorthand for writing x = x + y	x += y	11
-=	Shorthand for writing x = x - y	x -= y	6
*=	Shorthand for writing x = x * y	x *= y	30
/=	Shorthand for writing x = x / y	x /= y	6
%=	Shorthand for writing x = x % y	x %= y	1

The following example demonstrates the use of each of these operators. In this example, the script establishes two variables, x and y, and assigns a value of 10 to x and 5 to y. The next statements then test the five assignment operators listed in Table 2.3 to make sure they work as advertised. The first two of these statements set x = y + 1 and then use the `document.write()` statement to display the results. The remaining statements duplicate this methodology, changing only the mathematical formula each time. Figure 2.2 shows the result of running this script.

```
<HTML>
  <HEAD>
    <TITLE>Script 2.4 - A demonstration of JavaScript opera-
tors</TITLE>
  </HEAD>
  <BODY>
    <SCRIPT LANGUAGE="JavaScript" TYPE="Text/JavaScript">
    <!-- Start hiding JavaScript statements
      var y = 5;
      var x= y + 1;
      document.write("x = y + 1 ...Result = " + x);
      x += y;
      document.write("<BR>x += y ...Result = " + x);
      x -= y;
      document.write("<BR>x -= y ...Result = " + x);
      x *= y;
      document.write("<BR>x *= y ...Result = " + x);
      x /= y;
      document.write("<BR>x /= y ...Result = " + x);
    // End hiding JavaScript statements -->
    </SCRIPT>
  </BODY>
</HTML>
```

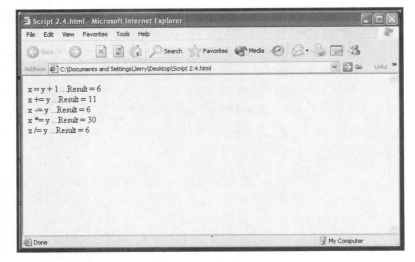

Figure 2.2

A demonstration of
JavaScript and
JScript operators

Comparing Values

One of the things you will find yourself doing in your scripts is comparing
the values of variables. For example, you might take one action if a variable
has a value less than 10 and a different action when the variable is greater
than 10. Table 2.4 provides a list of JavaScript and JScript comparison operators you can use in your scripts.

The following JavaScript demonstrates the use of the greater-than operator.
In this example, the two variables x and y are initialized with values of 12
and 5, respectively. Next, the script tests to see whether x is greater than 10.
This condition is true, so the script writes a message to the browser window.
Then the script tests the value of y to see whether it is greater than 10. This
test is false, so no action is taken.

```
<HTML>

  <HEAD>

    <TITLE>Script 2.5 - Example of a Value Comparison</TITLE>

  </HEAD>

  <BODY>

    <SCRIPT LANGUAGE="JavaScript" TYPE="Text/JavaScript">
```

TABLE 2.4 JAVASCRIPT AND JSCRIPT COMPARISON OPERATORS

Operator	Description	Example	Result
==	Equal to	x == y	true if both x and y are the same
!==	Not equal to	x !== y	true if x and y are not the same
>	Greater than	x > y	true if x is greater than y
<	Less than	x < y	true if x is less than y
>=	Greater than or equal to	x >= y	true if x is greater than or equal to y
<=	Less than or equal to	x <= y	true if x is less than or equal to y
!x	Not	!x	true if x is false
&&	Both true	x && y	true if x and y are both true
||	Either true	x || y	true if either x or y is true

```
<!-- Start hiding JavaScript statements
   var x = 12;
   var y = 5;
   if (x > 10);
   {
      document.write("x is greater than 10!");
   }
```

```
    if (y > 10)
    {
       document.write("y is greater than 10!");
    }
  // End hiding JavaScript statements -->
  </SCRIPT>
 </BODY>
</HTML>
```

Writing Text with Strings

We have spent a lot of time already this morning learning about how to work with values. One object in particular, the String object, you will find yourself using over and over again in your scripts. I thought I'd spend a little time going over the String object now, even though the lesson on JavaScript and JScript objects isn't until this later this morning. Consider this a sneak preview.

The String object is made up of a collection of text characters. You create an instance of a String object using the new keyword, as shown in the following example:

```
MyString = new String("This is an example of a text string.");
```

This statement creates a String object called MyString and assigns text to it. The new keyword is used to create objects. However, you are not required to use it. You can also create a String object by simply referring to it as in the following example:

```
MyString = "This is an example of a text string.";
```

You can change the value assigned to a String object by assigning it a new value. The following example changes the value of the MyString string:

```
MyString = "This is a second example of a text string.";
```

String Properties

Because a `string` object is a built-in JavaScript and JScript object, it has properties. In the case of the `string` object, there is just one property, its length. You can refer to an object's property by typing the name of the object, followed by a period and the name of the property. In the case of the `MyString` object's `length` property, you'd use `MyString.length`. The `length` property contains the number of characters in the string. The following example demonstrates how to display the value of this property, which is 40.

```
document.write("The length of MyString is " +
MyString.length);
```

String Methods

Although the `string` object has only one property, it has many methods. A *method* is an action that can be taken against the object. For example, you can use the `string` object's `bold()` method to display the string in bold, as shown in this example:

```
document.write(MyString.bold());
```

When referencing an object's methods, the correct syntax to use is the name of the object, a period, the name of the method, and the left and right parentheses. In this example, the parentheses did not contain anything. Some methods enable you to pass *arguments* to the method by placing them inside the parentheses.

For example, you can display strings in all uppercase characters using the `toUpperCase()` method:

```
document.write(MyString.toUpperCase());
```

Similarly, there is a `toLowerCase()` method. Other methods enable you to set the string's font color and font size or to display it in italic, blinking, or strikethrough text. A particularly useful method is `substring()`. This method enables you to extract a portion of a string's text.

For example, you might create a string that contains people's names and addresses. You could reserve the first 15 character positions of the string for the person's name, the next 20 characters for his street address, and the last 17 characters for the city, state, and ZIP code information. Below you will find three examples of this type of string.

```
cust1Info = "Bobby B Jones   9995 Park Place Ct   Richmond VA
23232   ";

cust2Info = "Sue K Miller    1112 Rockford Lane   Richmond VA
23232   ";

cust3Info = "Bobby B Jones   9995 Richland Drive Richmond VA
23223   ";
```

Now, using the String object's substring() method, you can extract just the name portion of any string, as shown in the following example:

```
<HTML>
  <HEAD>
    <TITLE>Script 2.6 - Substring Method Example</TITLE>
  </HEAD>
  <BODY>
    <SCRIPT LANGUAGE="JavaScript" TYPE="Text/JavaScript">
    <!-- Start hiding JavaScript statements
    var cust1Info = "Bobby B Jones   9995 Park Place Ct
Richmond VA 23232";
      var cust2Info = "Sue K Miller    1112 Rockford Lane
Richmond VA 23232";
      var cust3Info = "Bobby B Jones   9995 Richland Drive
Richmond VA 23223";
    document.write(cust1Info.substring(0,14),"<BR>");
    document.write(cust2Info.substring(0,14),"<BR>");
    document.write(cust3Info.substring(0,14),"<BR>");
    // End hiding JavaScript statements -->
    </SCRIPT>
  </BODY>
</HTML>
```

As you can see, the `document.write(cust1Info.substring(0,14),` `"<BR>");` statement copies the contents of the first 15 characters in the string, starting with character 0 and ending with character 14, and writes those characters to the browser window. The script then repeats this logic for the remaining `String` objects. Figure 2.3 shows the result of loading this page.

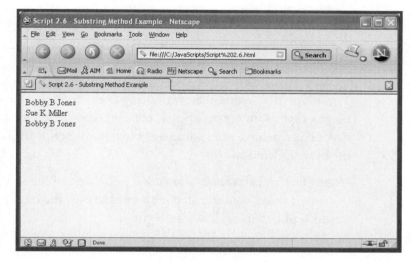

Figure 2.3

A demonstration of how to extract portions of a string using the `String` object's `substring()` method

String Concatenation

You can do many cool things with strings. For example, you can concatenate two or more of them together using the + operator, as shown in the following example:

```
<HTML>

  <HEAD>

    <TITLE>Script 2.7 - Example of String
Concatenation</TITLE>

  </HEAD>

  <BODY>

    <SCRIPT LANGUAGE="JavaScript" TYPE="Text/JavaScript">
```

```
<!-- Start hiding JavaScript statements
  var stringOne = "Once upon a time, ";
  var stringTwo = "there was a little house on a hill.";
  var stringThree = stringOne + stringTwo;
  document.write(stringThree);
// End hiding JavaScript statements -->
</SCRIPT>
</BODY>
</HTML>
```

The script first establishes two strings, stringOne and stringTwo, and assigns them some text. Then it concatenates these two strings to create a new object named stringThree. Finally, the script displays the results in the browser window.

Notice that an extra space was added to the end of the stringOne object so that when it was concatenated with stringTwo, the resulting stringThree would read better, as shown in Figure 2.4.

 NOTE In many computer languages, the programmer must specify the type of data that a variable will contain. This is known as the variable's data type. JavaScript and JScript support a range of data types, including numeric, Boolean, and string values. One nice thing about these languages is that they do not require you to specify a data type. In fact, they don't even allow it. Based on the context within which a value is created, JavaScript and JScript know what type of value it is. If you use the + sign with two numeric variables, they will be added together. If you use the + sign with two strings, they will automatically be concatenated. Finally, if you use the + sign with a numeric value and a string, the numeric value is converted automatically to a string and then is concatenated to the other string.

The Math Object

Having introduced you to the String object, it seems only proper at this point in the discussion that I talk a little about the Math object as well. This

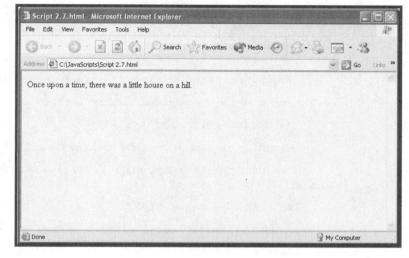

Figure 2.4

This example demonstrates how to concatenate two-strings together.

object is created automatically in every JavaScript and JScript, so you do not have to create an instance of it as you do with the `String` object. You can simply refer to the `Math` object when you need to. Like other objects, the `Math` object has properties and methods associated with it.

The `Math` object's properties contain mathematical constants. For example, the `Math` property `PI` stores the value of pi. The `Math` object's methods contain built-in mathematical functions. There are methods that round numbers up and down, generate random numbers, and return the absolute value of a number.

The following example demonstrates how to use several of the `Math` object's properties and methods:

```
<HTML>

  <HEAD>

    <TITLE>Script 2.8 - Example of working with the Math
object</TITLE>

  </HEAD>

  <BODY>

    <SCRIPT LANGUAGE="JavaScript" TYPE="Text/JavaScript">

    <!-- Start hiding JavaScript statements
```

```
//Generate a random number between 0 and 1
document.write("<B>Random number between 0 - 1 = </B>", +
   Math.random(), "<BR>");
//Generate a random number between 0 and 10
document.write("<B>Random number between 0 - 10 = </B>", +
   Math.random() * 10, "<BR>");
//Rounding a number to the nearest whole number
document.write("<B>Rounding 6.777 = </B>",
Math.round(6.777), "<BR>");
//Getting the value of PI
document.write("<B>Value of PI = </B>", Math.PI, "<BR>");
//Getting the absolute value of a number
document.write("<B>Absolute value of -55 = </B>",
Math.abs(-55));
// End hiding JavaScript statements -->
</SCRIPT>
</BODY>
</HTML>
```

NOTE

You may have noticed that I slipped the `<B>` and `</B>` HTML tags into my JavaScripts to add bold formatting to my text. The key when using HTML tags is to keep them within the quotation marks. I could just as easily have inserted any of the other HTML tags within my script using the same technique.

The first three `document.write()` statements use the `Math` object's `random()` and `round()` methods. The fourth `document.write()` statement does not use a `Math` method. Instead, it accesses the `Math PI` property as evidenced by the lack of parentheses. The last of the `document.write()` statements demonstrates the `Math abs()` method, which returns the absolute value of any given number. Figure 2.5 shows the results of loading this page using Netscape Communicator.

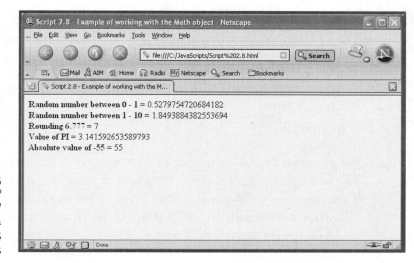

Figure 2.5

An example of how to access the `Math` object's properties and methods

Take a Break

Okay, let's take a break. We have covered quite a bit of material since breakfast. Why don't you give yourself a few minutes to let it sink in. When you return, you will review examples of the programming statements that make up the JavaScript and JScript languages. A solid understanding of these statements will enable you to begin writing more powerful scripts. We'll also go over objects built in to JavaScript and JScript.

JavaScript and JScript Statements

JavaScripts and JScripts consist of a series of statements. These *statements* are the programming instructions, or logic, that you write to tell the scripts what you want them to do.

Using Conditional Statements to Alter Script Flow

Conditional statements enable you to test for various conditions and take action based on the results of the test. Specifically, conditional statements execute when the tested condition proves to be `true`. Conditional statements include the `if`, `if...else`, and `switch` statements.

The if Statement

The `if` statement checks whether a logical condition is `true`; if it is, it then executes one or more statements. The basic syntax of the `if` statements is shown here:

```
if (condition)
  statement
```

For example, the following pair of statements shows a simple `if` statement. The first line sets up a conditional test. If the test proves `true` (for example, if the `counter` variable is currently less than 10), the statement immediately following is executed. In this example, the current value of the variable `counter` is then incremented by 1.

```
if (counter < 10)
  counter++;
```

There will be times when executing a single statement is just not enough. In this case, you can write your `if` statement using the following format:

```
if (counter > 10) {
 counter++;
 window.alert("This is a test");
}
```

The preceding example shows an `if` statement where the condition is followed immediately by the { sign and terminated with the } sign. Between the braces can be any number of script statements.

The following sample script uses the two types of `if` statements you just looked at plus a third variation:

```
<HTML>
  <HEAD>
    <TITLE>Script 2.9 - Demonstration of if statements</TITLE>
  </HEAD>
  <BODY>
```

```
<SCRIPT LANGUAGE="JavaScript" TYPE="Text/JavaScript">

<!-- Start hiding JavaScript statements

    var accountStatus = open;   //assume all accounts are
open by default

    //Prompt the user for an account name

    var accountName = window.prompt("Enter your account
name:");

    //Test whether the supplied account name equals
Morganstern

    if (accountName == "Morganstern")

        document.write("The account number for this account
is 12321. <BR>");

    //Set accountStatus equal to warning if the account
name equals Davidson

    if (accountName == "Davidson") {

        document.write("The account number for this account
is 88844. <BR>");

        accountStatus = "warning";

    }

    //Display one of two messages based on the value of
accountStatus

    if (accountStatus != "warning") {

        document.write("You may accept new orders from this
customer.");

    }

    else {

        document.write("Do not accept new orders for this
account.");

    }

    // End hiding JavaScript statements -->

    </SCRIPT>

  </BODY>

</HTML>
```

This example starts by displaying a prompt dialog box asking the user to input the name of a business account using the `window.prompt()` method. Next, it executes three `if` statements, each of which compares the user's input against three separate criteria. Any conditional test that proves `true` results in some action. As you can see, the `if` statement enables you to create different logical flows based on user input.

The third `if` statement adds a new twist by adding an `else` statement. In the event that the `if` statement's conditional test proves `true`, the statements following the `if` statement are executed, and the `else` statement is skipped. But if the `if` statement proves `false`, the logic in the `else` statement is processed. The `else` statement enables you to provide an alternative course of action for any conditional test.

Figures 2.6 and 2.7 show the logical flow of the script when the user inputs the account name of Morganstern.

Figure 2.6

The `window.prompt()` method enables you to create a dialog box that gathers user input interactively.

Figure 2.7

Here is what happens when the user types in a valid business account name.

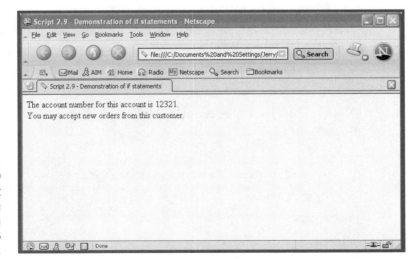

Before I move on, there is one final variation of the if statement I want to mention. This is the *nested* if *statement*. A nested if statement is a series of two or more if statements nested or embedded within one another. The following example shows a nested if that is two if statements deep. The second if statement is executed only if the first if statement proves true:

```
if (accountStatus != "warning") {

  if (accountNumber > 10000) {

    document.write("You may accept new orders from this
customer.");

  }

  else {

    document.write("Invalid account number. Notify bank
security.");

  }

}

Else {

  document.write("This Account has been marked with a
warning.");

}
```

The switch Statement

The switch statement evaluates a series of conditional tests or cases and executes additional statements based on whether the case proves true. The syntax of the switch statement is shown here:

```
switch (expression) {

  case label:

    statements;

  break;

      .

      .

      .
```

```
case label:
   statements;
break;
default:
   statements;
}
```

The switch statement compares the result of the expression against the label for each case. The statements for the first case that proves true are executed. If no case proves true, the statements associated with the default statement are executed if the optional default statement was included.

The break statement at the end of each case is optional. Its purpose is to tell the script to exit the switch statement as soon as the statements in the first matching case are executed and to proceed with the next script statement following the switch statement. If you remove the optional break statements, the script will continue to examine each case and execute the statements of any case that matches the expression.

In the following example, the user is prompted to type the name of a business account. Starting with the first case statement, the script compares the value assigned to the accountName variable to the label assigned to the first case statement. If the condition proves true (that is, if there is a match), the statements for that case statement are executed, and the break at the end of the case statement tells the script to jump to the first statement after the switch statement, which in this example happens to be an if statement. If none of the case statements proves true, the statement associated with the default statement executes, stating that the account name the user typed is not registered. Figure 2.8 shows what this example looks like when it's executed.

```
<HTML>
  <HEAD>
    <TITLE>Script 2.10 - Demonstration of the switch
statement</TITLE>
  </HEAD>
```

```
<BODY>

   <SCRIPT LANGUAGE="JavaScript" TYPE="Text/JavaScript">

   <!-- Start hiding JavaScript statements

      var accountStatus = "None";

      var accountName = window.prompt("Enter your account
name:");

      switch (accountName) {

        case "Morganstern":

           document.write("The account number for this
account is 12321.");

           accountStatus = "approved";

           break;

        case "Davidson":

           document.write("The account number for this
account is 88844.");

           accountStatus = "warning";

           break;

        default:

           document.write("The account is not registered in
this system.");

           accountStatus = "error";

      }

      if (accountStatus == "warning") {

        document.write(accountStatus);

        window.alert("Contact the on-duty supervisor");

      }

   // End hiding JavaScript statements -->

   </SCRIPT>

  </BODY>

</HTML>
```

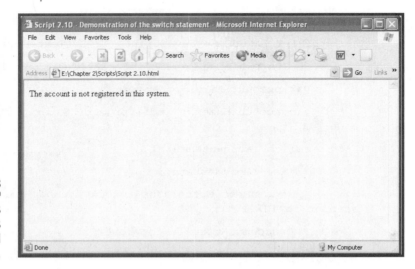

Figure 2.8

The script flags
`Paterson` as
an invalid
account name.

Adding Comments for Clarity

Comment statements have no effect on the logical performance of the script. However, they can be used to make scripts easier to understand by providing you with a means of internally documenting your scripts. You can place a comment in your scripts in either of two ways. To place a single comment line within the body of your script, type `//` followed by your comment, as shown here:

```
//This is an example of a script comment
```

You can also add a comment at the end of script statements as demonstrated here.

```
document.write("Hello World");  //Write a message to the current
Window
```

If one line isn't enough space for you to write out a complete comment, you may always add additional comments as demonstrated below.

```
//The following statement writes a message in the currently
open browser window
```

```
//using the document object's write4() method.
```

```
document.write("Hello World");
```

Alternatively, you may create multiline comments by placing them inside the /* and */ characters as demonstrated in the following example.

```
/* The following statement writes a message in the currently
open browser window

using the document object's write4() method. */

document.write("Hello World");
```

Comments are not always for other people; they are for you as well. For example, you might have a large script, several pages long, that allows customers to fill in a form and place orders for some type of product. If the tax rate changes, you'll have to find the portion of the script that does this calculation and change it. If you had added a comment that identifies the line of code where the tax calculation is performed as demonstrated below, it would make it easier to modify the script years later.

```
//Compute the amount of tax to apply to the order

totalOrder = totalOrder + (totalOrder * .05);
```

The following script provides an example of how you might document your own scripts:

```
<HTML>


  <HEAD>

    <TITLE>Script 2.11 - Comment Example</TITLE>

  </HEAD>


  <BODY>


    <SCRIPT LANGUAGE="JavaScript" TYPE="Text/JavaScript">

    <!-- Start hiding JavaScript statements


      //Define a variable representing the cost of a customer
order
```

```
        var totalOrder = 100;


        //Compute the amount of tax to apply to the order

        totalOrder = totalOrder + (totalOrder * .05);   //Tax
rate = 5%


        /*The following statement simply demonstrates the use
of the document statement to write

        a message on the current browser window.*/

        document.write(totalOrder);


    // End hiding JavaScript statements -->

    </SCRIPT>


  </BODY>

</HTML>
```

NOTE Another technique for making scripts easier to read is the insertion of blank lines between different groups of statements.

Declaring and Assigning Data to Variables

We already examined variable declaration and assignment statements at the beginning of this session. Most assignments are performed using the equal sign (=), but you can use any of the assignment operators listed in Table 2.3.

Optimizing Code with Looping Logic

A *loop* is a series of statements that executes repeatedly, allowing you to perform iterative operations within your script. JavaScript and JScript statements that support looping logic include the for, while, do...while, `label`, `break`, and `continue` statements. The nice thing about loops is that they enable you to write just a few line of code and then to execute them repeatedly, making your scripts easier to write and maintain.

The for Statement

The `for` statement executes until a condition becomes `false` and uses a variable to control the number of times the loop executes. The `for` loop is comprised of three parts: a starting expression, a test condition, and an increment statement. The syntax of the `for` statement is shown here:

```
for (expression; condition; increment) {
  statements;
}
```

For example, the statement `for (i=0; i<5; i++)` establishes a `for` loop that has an initial count of 0, that runs as long as `i` is less than 5, and that increments the value of `i` by one upon each iteration. All the statements within the starting and ending brackets are executed with each execution of the `for` loop.

The following example shows how the `for` statement can be used to set up a loop that iterates five times. When the script begins to execute, the value of `i` is 0. Each time the loop executes, the value of `i` is incremented by 1 (in the `i++` clause). Although this example displays just five lines of text that show the value of `i` as it grows, I think you can see that it can be easily modified to do just about anything, such as repeatedly prompting the user for input and iteratively processing that input.

```
<HTML>
  <HEAD>
    <TITLE>Script 2.12 - Demonstration of a for loop</TITLE>
  </HEAD>
  <BODY>
    <SCRIPT LANGUAGE="JavaScript" TYPE="Text/JavaScript">
    <!-- Start hiding JavaScript statements
```

```
       for (i=0; i<5; i++) {
            document.write("Watch as the variable grows with each
    iteration: ",i,"<BR>");
          }
       // End hiding JavaScript statements -->
       </SCRIPT>
     </BODY>
   </HTML>
```

Figure 2.9 shows the result of loading the previous example. If you run this script yourself, you should take note just how quickly the scripts executes.

The while Statement

The while statement executes a loop as long as a condition is true. The syntax of the while statement is shown here:

```
while (condition) {
  statements;
}
```

For example, you might write a while loop that looks like this:

```
while (counter > 0) {
  counter++;
  document.write("counter = ", counter , "<BR>");
}
```

In the next example, I set up a loop that runs as long as the value assigned to a variable named counter is greater than 0. As soon as counter becomes 0 or less, the loop terminates. To control the termination of the loop, I decremented the value of counter by 1 each time through the loop. When working with while loops, be sure that you set them up so that they will properly break out of the loop; otherwise, they will run forever, leaving the user no option other than to close the HTML page or terminate the execution of your JScript.

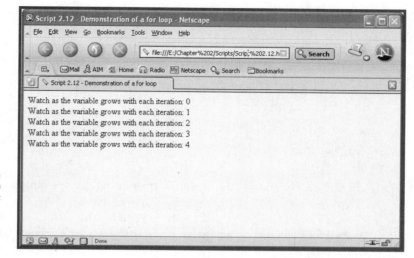

Figure 2.9

An example of using a `for` loop to perform iterative processes

This is because the `while` loop is designed to iterate for as long as the tested condition remains `true`, as demonstrated in the following example.

```
<HTML>

  <HEAD>

    <TITLE>Script 2.13 - Demonstration of the while
statement</TITLE>

  </HEAD>

  <BODY>

    <SCRIPT LANGUAGE="JavaScript" TYPE="Text/JavaScript">

    <!-- Start hiding JavaScript statements


      var counter = 10;


      document.write("<B>Watch me count backwards!</B><BR>");


      while (counter > 0) {

        counter-;
```

```
        document.write("counter = ", counter , "<BR>");

    }


    // End hiding JavaScript statements -->

    </SCRIPT>

  </BODY>

</HTML>
```

Figure 2.10 shows the results of loading this example using Internet Explorer.

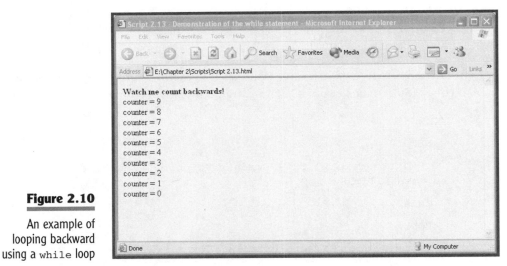

Figure 2.10

An example of looping backward using a `while` loop

The do...while Statement

The `do...while` statement executes a loop until a condition becomes `false`. The syntax of the `do...while` statement is outlined below:

```
do {

  statements;

} while (condition)
```

The difference between the do...while loop and the while loop is that the do...while loop always executes at least once. This is because the condition is checked at the end of the first execution of the loop instead of at the beginning. However, you can use either style to achieve the same end, as demonstrated in the next example.

```
<HTML>

  <HEAD>

    <TITLE>Script 2.14 - Demonstration of the do...while
statement</TITLE>

  </HEAD>

  <BODY>

    <SCRIPT LANGUAGE="JavaScript" TYPE="Text/JavaScript">

    <!-- Start hiding JavaScript statements


      var counter = 10;


      document.write("<B>Watch me count backwards!</B><BR>");

      do {

        counter—;

        document.write("counter = ", counter , "<BR>");

      } while (counter > 0)


    // End hiding JavaScript statements -->

    </SCRIPT>

  </BODY>

</HTML>
```

The results of running this script are exactly the same as those that were displayed in Figure 2.11.

NOTE You may have noticed my use of commas in the `document.write()` statement located in the preceding example. In this context, commas are used to separate a list of arguments used by the `document.write()` statement. For example, in `document.write("counter = ", counter , "<BR>");`, three arguments are passed. The first argument is a text message surrounded by double quotes, the second argument is a variable named `counter` whose value will be displayed when the statement is executed, and the final argument is a HTML line break tag.

The label Statement

The `label` statement lets you specify a reference point in your script. Typically, the `label` statement is associated with loops. A `label` statement can be referenced by either the `break` or `continue` statement. The syntax of the `label` statement is shown here:

```
label:
  statements;
```

In the following example, I have created a `label` called `CounterLoop`. When the script executes the first time, the `label` statement is ignored. Within the `while` loop, I set up a test that checks to see whether the value of `counter` is equal to 5. If it is, the script executes the `continue` statement, which tells the script to skip the rest of the statements in the `while` statement and continue with the next execution of the loop.

```
<HTML>
  <HEAD>
    <TITLE>Script 2.15 - Demonstration of the label statement </TITLE>
  </HEAD>
  <BODY>
    <SCRIPT LANGUAGE="JavaScript" TYPE="Text/JavaScript">
    <!-- Start hiding JavaScript statements

      var counter = 10;
```

```
document.write("<B>Watch me count backwards!</B><BR>");


CounterLoop:


while (counter > 0) {
  counter--;
  if (counter == 5 ) continue CounterLoop;
  document.write("counter = ", counter , "<BR>");
}


  // End hiding JavaScript statements -->
  </SCRIPT>
</BODY>
</HTML>
```

When you load this script, you will see that the `continue` statement has the effect of skipping the display of the fifth statement.

The break Statement

The `break` statement lets you terminate a label, switch, or loop. The script then continues processing with the statement that follows the `label`, `switch`, or `loop` statement that was broken out of.

The following example shows how to use the `break` statement to terminate the execution of a `while` loop. In this case, the `break` statement terminates the loop when the value of `counter` becomes equal to 5. Because there are no other statements following the `while` loop, script execution stops when it processes the `break` statement.

```
<HTML>
  <HEAD>
    <TITLE>Script 2.16 - Demonstration of the break
statement</TITLE>
  </HEAD>
```

```
<BODY>
  <SCRIPT LANGUAGE="JavaScript" TYPE="Text/JavaScript">
  <!-- Start hiding JavaScript statements

    var counter = 10;

    document.write("<B>Watch me count backwards!</B><BR>");

    while (counter > 0) {
      counter-;
      document.write("counter = ", counter , "<BR>");
      if (counter == 5 ) break;
    }

  // End hiding JavaScript statements -->
  </SCRIPT>
</BODY>
</HTML>
```

The continue Statement

The continue statement is similar to the break statement. However, instead of terminating the execution of the loop, it merely terminates the current iteration of the loop.

The following example demonstrates how the continue statement can be used to terminate a given iteration of a loop. In this example, the loop examines four different cases as part of a switch statement. The result is that the iteration of the loop that occurs when the value assigned to the counter variable is equal to 8, 6, 4, or 2 is skipped, but processing of the loop does not terminate as would be the case when using a break statement. Instead, the loop simply continues with the next iteration.

```
<HTML>

  <HEAD>

    <TITLE>Script 2.17 - Demonstration of the continue
statement</TITLE>

  </HEAD>

  <BODY>

    <SCRIPT LANGUAGE="JavaScript" TYPE="Text/JavaScript">

    <!-- Start hiding JavaScript statements


      var counter = 10;


      document.write("<B>Watch me count backwards!</B><BR>");


      CounterLoop:


      while (counter > 0) {
        counter—;
        switch (counter) {
          case 8:
            continue CounterLoop;
          case 6:
            continue CounterLoop;
          case 4:
            continue CounterLoop;
          case 2:
            continue CounterLoop;
        }
        document.write("counter = ", counter , "<BR>");
      }
```

```
    // End hiding JavaScript statements -->

    </SCRIPT>

  </BODY>

</HTML>
```

Manipulating Objects

As I have already stated, JavaScript and JScript enable you to create scripts that work with objects. You can think of objects as being similar to variables except that objects can contain multiple values known as its properties. Objects also can contain built-in functions, which are collections of predefined script statements that are designed to work with the object and its data. Examples of browser objects include browser windows and form elements. Examples of WSH objects include printers and drives.

There are a number of JavaScript and JScript statements that provide you with the ability to manipulate properties associated with objects. These statements include the for...in and with statements. The for...in statement enables you to access all the properties for a specified object, and the with statement provides easy access to specific object properties and methods.

The for...in Statement

The for...in statement is used to iterate through all the properties belonging to a specified object. The syntax of the for...in statement is listed below:

```
for (variable in object) {

  statements;

}
```

This statement works by creating a variable that is used to iterate through all of an object's properties. The following example shows how to loop through all the properties belonging to the navigator object. The navigator object contains information about the type of browser being used to view the HTML page containing the JavaScript.

```
<HTML>

  <HEAD>

    <TITLE>Script 2.18 - Demonstration of the for...in statement
</TITLE>

  </HEAD>

  <BODY>

    <SCRIPT LANGUAGE="JavaScript" TYPE="Text/JavaScript">

    <!-- Start hiding JavaScript statements


      for (i in navigator) {

        document.write(i,"<BR>");

      }


    // End hiding JavaScript statements -->

    </SCRIPT>

  </BODY>

</HTML>
```

Figure 2.11 shows the result of loading the preceding page using Internet Explorer. By modifying this example, you can easily view all the properties for any object. However, I'd recommend that you save yourself the trouble of modifying this example and refer to Appendix A, "A Brief JavaScript and JScript Object Reference," to get information about the various properties of any object.

The with Statement

The with statement is a convenient way of saving a few keystrokes when writing your scripts. It enables you to set a default object for a group of statements. The syntax of the with statement is listed below.

```
with (object) {

  statements;

}
```

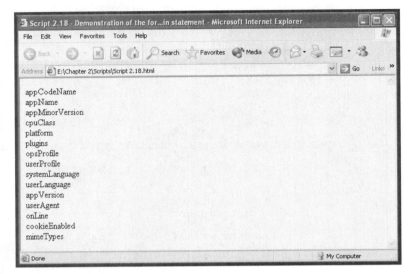

Figure 2.11

Using the
`for...in`
statement to loop
through the screen
object's properties

The following example shows how you can use the `with` statement to set the
`document` object as the default object and then apply all the statements contained within the opening and closing braces to that object. As you can see,
by using this shortcut statement, I was able to type `write()` in place of
`document.write()`. Although this did not save me much work in this
example, it could certainly save a lot of time in situations where you need to
work a lot with a given object.

```
<HTML>

  <HEAD>

    <TITLE>Script 2.19 - Demonstration of the with statement
</TITLE>

  </HEAD>

  <BODY>

    <SCRIPT LANGUAGE="JavaScript" TYPE="Text/JavaScript">

    <!-- Start hiding JavaScript statements


    with (document) {
```

```
            write("The with statement saved me a few keystrokes.
<BR>");

            write("Its use is purely discretionary!");

        }


        // End hiding JavaScript statements -->
        </SCRIPT>
     </BODY>
  </HTML>
```

Streamlining Your Scripts with Functions

A *function* is a collection of statements that performs a given task. Most functions are defined in the head section of HTML pages. Putting your functions in the head section is a good idea for two reasons: The first is that you'll always know where your functions are because they're in a common location. The second reason is that the head section always executes first, ensuring that functions are available when needed later in the script. If a JavaScript statement attempts to call a function before the browser has loaded it, an error will occur because the function is technically still undefined. I also recommend putting your functions in a common location in your WSH JScript files.

 NOTE You may be wondering what the difference is between a function and a method. The answer is not much. Methods are simply functions that have been predefined. Methods are associated with specific objects, meaning that each object provides its own collection of methods that you can call from within your scripts.

Defining a Function

The first step in working with a function is to define it, which is accomplished using the syntax outlined below.

```
function FunctionName (p1, p2,....pn) {
```

```
   statements;
return
}
```

The `function` statement defines a new function with the name you specify. The function's name is followed by a pair of parentheses that may contain a list of optional arguments that the function can use as input. Commas separate multiple arguments. All `function` statements are placed within the curly braces `{}`. Functions can end with an optional `return` statement, which enables optional information to be returned to the statement that called the function.

For example, the following example shows a function named `SayHello()` that accepts a single argument, a person's name. It then uses the name argument to display a welcome message with the user's name. The `return` statement returns control of the script to the script statement that called the function.

```
function SayHello(visitorName) {
  window.alert("Hello and welcome, " + visitorName);
return
}
```

Defining a function in a script does not cause it to execute. Functions must be called by another script statement in order to execute. The nice thing about functions is that you can call them repeatedly as needed.

Calling Functions

Now that you know what a function is and how to define one, the question remains: How do you call it? The calling statement can take either of two forms. The first form calls the function but does not accept any returned results from the function. The following two function calls demonstrate this form of call. The first example calls a function named `SayHello()` without passing any arguments. The second example calls a function named

SayGoodbye() and passes a single argument. When the function finishes executing, control is returned to the statement immediately following the function call.

```
SayHello();
SayGoodbye("William");
```

 NOTE It's up to you to make sure that the function is capable of handling the number of arguments that are passed to it.

Alternatively, you can make a call to a function in the form of an expression. This enables the function to return a value to the calling statement. For example, the following statement calls a function named GetUserName() and stores the result returned by the function in a variable named UserName.

```
UserName = GetUserName();
```

The following example shows a function named SayHello() in the head section of the HTML page. It is executed by a SayHello() statement in the body section of the HTML page and receives a single argument called name. The name argument is a variable established by the statement that precedes the function call. The function takes the name argument and uses it to display a greeting message to the user in a pop-up dialog. The script pauses until the user clicks on OK, at which time the function terminates and returns control to the statement that immediately follows the function call in the body section.

```
<HTML>
  <HEAD>
    <TITLE>Script 2.20 - A simple function</TITLE>
    <SCRIPT LANGUAGE="JavaScript" TYPE="Text/JavaScript">
    <!-- Start hiding JavaScript statements

      function SayHello(visitorName) {
```

```
          window.alert("Hello and welcome, " + visitorName);
      }


   // End hiding JavaScript statements -->
   </SCRIPT>
</HEAD>
<BODY>
   <SCRIPT LANGUAGE="JavaScript" TYPE="Text/JavaScript">
   <!-- Start hiding JavaScript statements


     var name;


     name = window.prompt("What is your name?","");
     SayHello(name);


   // End hiding JavaScript statements -->
   </SCRIPT>
   </BODY>
</HTML>
```

Figures 2.12 shows how the script interacts with the user when it executes.

Figure 2.12

Using the user's
name as part of the
dialog message

The following example shows how to write a function that returns a value to the calling statement. This example is actually just a rewrite of the previous example, and the results are the same. The only difference is that the function call does not supply an argument this time and instead receives the name of the user from the function.

```
<HTML>
  <HEAD>
    <TITLE>Script 2.21 - Returning values from
functions</TITLE>
    <SCRIPT LANGUAGE="JavaScript" TYPE="Text/JavaScript">
    <!-- Start hiding JavaScript statements


      var name;
      var result;


      function SayHello() {
        name = window.prompt("What is your name?","");
        return name;
      }


    // End hiding JavaScript statements -->
    </SCRIPT>
  </HEAD>
  <BODY>
    <SCRIPT LANGUAGE="JavaScript" TYPE="Text/JavaScript">
    <!-- Start hiding JavaScript statements


      result = SayHello();


      window.alert("Hello and welcome, " + result);


    // End hiding JavaScript statements -->
    </SCRIPT>
  </BODY>
</HTML>
```

Using Arrays

An *array* is an indexed list of values that can be referred to as a unit. Arrays can contain any type of value. Before you can use an array, you must first declare it. The following example shows how to create an array that will hold 10 strings that contain information about an automobile inventory.

```
Auto = new Array(10);

Auto[0] = 98 Ford Explorer;

Auto[1] = 97 Ford Explorer;

Auto[2] = 85 Plymouth Mustang;

Auto[3] = 96 Plymouth Voyager;

Auto[4] = 90 Honda Civic;

Auto[5] = 97 Honda Civic;

Auto[6] = 96 Plymouth Neon;

Auto[7] = 98 Plymouth Neon;

Auto[8] = 92 Ford Explorer Wagon;

Auto[9] = 95 Honda Civic Hatchback;
```

The first statement uses the new keyword to create an Array object named Auto that will contain 10 entries. The rest of the statements assign string values to the array. As you can see, the array's index starts with 0 and goes to 9.

Defining an Array

The following script uses the preceding array example to demonstrate how to display an array element by using the document.write() statement with the element's array name and index number.

```
<HTML>

  <HEAD>

  <TITLE>Script 2.22 - Sample Array</TITLE>

  </HEAD>

  <BODY>

    <SCRIPT LANGUAGE="JavaScript" TYPE="Text/JavaScript">
```

```
<!-- Start hiding JavaScript statements

    Auto = new Array(10);
    Auto[0] = "98 Ford Explorer";
    Auto[1] = "97 Ford Explorer";
    Auto[2] = "85 Plymouth  Mustang";
    Auto[3] = "96 Plymouth Voyager";
    Auto[4] = "90 Honda Civic";
    Auto[5] = "97 Honda Civic";
    Auto[6] = "96 Plymouth Neon";
    Auto[7] = "98 Plymouth Neon";
    Auto[8] = "92 Ford Explorer Wagon";
    Auto[9] = "95 Honda Civic Hatchback";


    document.write("The first element in the array is a
<B>", Auto[0], "</B>");


// End hiding JavaScript statements -->
    </SCRIPT>
  </BODY>
</HTML>
```

Figure 2.13 shows the results of loading the previous example. In this case, the first array element, Auto[0], is displayed.

Processing Arrays with for Loops

In this next example, we'll use a for loop to traverse the entire array and display all of its contents. The loop begins at the beginning of the array, Auto[0], and uses an increment of 1 to step through the elements of the array until it reaches the end. To determine the end of the array, the script creates a variable called arrayLength and sets its value equal to the array length property, which in this example is 10.

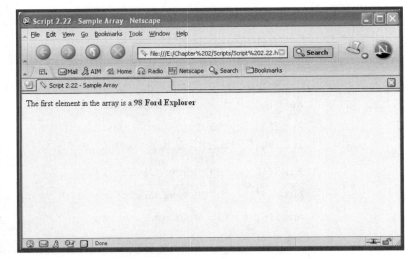

Figure 2.13

Array elements can be individually extracted by referencing their index number in the array.

```
<HTML>
  <HEAD>
  <TITLE>Script 2.23 - Looping through an Array</TITLE>
  </HEAD>
  <BODY>
    <SCRIPT LANGUAGE="JavaScript" TYPE="Text/JavaScript">
    <!-- Start hiding JavaScript statements

      var arrayLength;
      Auto = new Array(10);
      Auto[0] = "98 Ford Explorer";
      Auto[1] = "97 Ford Explorer";
      Auto[2] = "85 Plymouth Mustang";
      Auto[3] = "96 Plymouth Voyager";
      Auto[4] = "90 Honda Civic";
      Auto[5] = "97 Honda Civic";
      Auto[6] = "96 Plymouth Neon";
```

```
Auto[7] = "98 Plymouth Neon";

Auto[8] = "92 Ford Explorer Wagon";

Auto[9] = "95 Honda Civic Hatchback";


arrayLength = Auto.length;


document.write("<B>Current Inventory Listing</B><BR>");


for (var i = 0; i < arrayLength;i++) {
  document.write(Auto[i], "<BR>");
}


// End hiding JavaScript statements -->
</SCRIPT>
</BODY>
</HTML>
```

Figure 2.14 demonstrates how the for loop was able to process every array element.

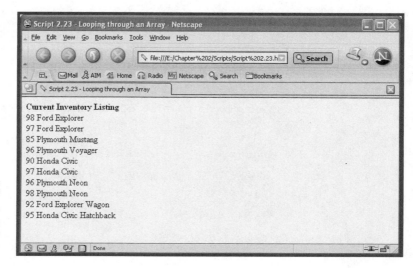

Figure 2.14

A for loop enables you to read the entire contents of an array.

Dense Arrays

You can also create dense arrays. A *dense array* is one that is populated at the time it is declared. This is a very efficient technique for creating small arrays. The following example shows you how to create a dense array named `animals` that consists of five entries. The array will have the following structure:

```
animals = new Array("mice", "dog", "cat", "hamster", "fish");
```

After creating the array, the script prints its contents using a `for` loop and the `Animals.length` property.

```
<HTML>
  <HEAD>
    <TITLE>Script 2.24 - A Dense Array</TITLE>
  </HEAD>
  <BODY>
    <SCRIPT LANGUAGE="JavaScript" TYPE="Text/JavaScript">
    <!-- Start hiding JavaScript statements


      var arrayLength;


      Animals = new Array("mice", "dog", "cat", "hamster",
"fish");


      arrayLength = Animals.length;


      document.write("<B>List of animals in the Zoo</B><BR>");


      for (var i = 0; i < arrayLength;i++) {
        document.write(Animals[i], "<BR>");
      }


    // End hiding JavaScript statements -->
```

```
    </SCRIPT>

   </BODY>

</HTML>
```

Figure 2.15 shows the results of loading this example into your browser. Each array entry is listed beginning at index 0 and going through to the end of the array.

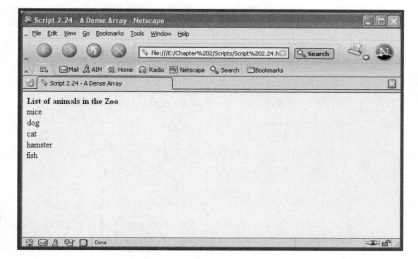

Figure 2.15

The result of a dense array

Sorting Arrays

Arrays have a `sort()` method you can use to sort their contents. The following example shows how to display a sorted list of the contents of an array. The script first defines a dense array with five entries. Next, it displays a heading, and it then uses the `sort()` method inside a `document.write()` statement to display the sorted list. Notice that I did not have to create a `for` loop to step iteratively through the array's index. The `sort()` method took care of this for me.

```
<HEAD>

  <TITLE>Script 2.25 - Sorting an Array</TITLE>

</HEAD>
```

```
<BODY>

  <SCRIPT LANGUAGE="JavaScript" TYPE="Text/JavaScript">

  <!-- Start hiding JavaScript statements


     Animals = new Array("mice", "dog", "cat", "hamster",
"fish");


     document.write("<B>List of animals in the
Zoo</B><BR>");

     document.write(Animals.sort());


     // End hiding JavaScript statements -->

     </SCRIPT>

  </BODY>

</HTML>
```

Figure 2.16 shows the results of loading the previous page into your browser.
Note that the result of the sort() method is a list displayed on a single line,
with the elements in the array separated by commas.

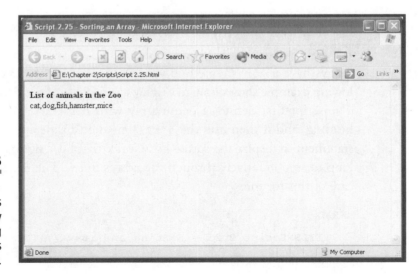

Figure 2.16

The array's sort()
method provides
an efficient way
of sorting
the elements
of the array.

Populating Arrays with Dynamic Data

You can create scripts that enable users to supply them with their data, as opposed to hard coding it into the script. For example, the following script prompts users to type their three favorite things and then creates an array to contain the list.

The script uses a for statement to control program execution. Each time the loop executes, it asks the user to type a response and assigns the response to the array by giving it the next available array index number (as designated by the current value of i).

```
<HTML>

  <HEAD>

    <TITLE>Script 2.26 - Building a dynamic Array</TITLE>

  </HEAD>

  <BODY>

    <SCRIPT LANGUAGE="JavaScript" TYPE="Text/JavaScript">

    <!-- Start hiding JavaScript statements


        document.write("What are your 3 most favorite things?
<BR>");


        NumberArray = new Array(3);


        for (var i = 0; i < 3;i++) {

          var yourNumber = prompt('I like: ', ' ');

          NumberArray[i] = yourNumber;

          document.write(NumberArray[i], "<BR>");

        }


    // End hiding JavaScript statements -->

    </SCRIPT>

  </BODY>

</HTML>
```

TIP

The preceding example shows you how to write a script that enables the user to populate its contents dynamically rather than requiring you to hard code in its contents. Another way to work with an array dynamically is by increasing its length during script execution. You can extend the size of an array by adding new array elements with an index number that is higher than the last index number in the array. For example, if I were to declare an array with an index of 50, I could later expand the array by adding a new array element with an index number of 99. This would increase the size of the array to 100.

Figure 2.17 shows the results of loading the previous example into your browser. As you can see, the heading is displayed followed by the contents of the new array.

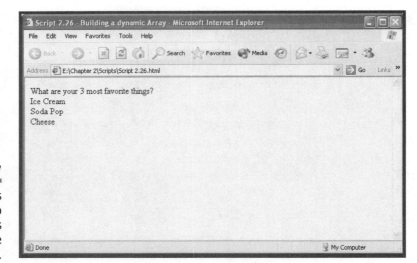

Figure 2.17

Dynamic arrays make it possible to show the contents of an array that the user just populated.

Object-Based Programming

JavaScript and JScript support script execution by providing access to resources by way of objects. Both languages share the same built-in object model, which consists of a small collection of objects. Access to additional objects is provided to scripts by the browser or the WSH, depending on which environment the scripts execute in.

NOTE Not every object has both properties and methods, although most do. For a detailed list of objects, see Appendix A.

Creating Custom Objects

Custom objects are created using the new keyword. For example, you can create a new instance of an `Array` object as demonstrated below.

```
Animals = new Array("mice", "dog", "cat", "hamster", "fish");
```

As you can see, the new keyword is used to create an instance (`Animals`) of the `Array` object.

Working with Built-In Objects

JavaScript and JScript provide access to a collection of built-in objects. These objects are always available regardless of the environment in which your scripts execute. These objects include the `Array`, `Boolean`, `Date`, `Function`, `Math`, `Number`, `Object`, and `String` objects.

NOTE Notice that built-in object names are always capitalized.

The Array Object

I touched on the `Array` object earlier this morning. To work with arrays, you must create an instance of an `Array` object.

An *array* is an indexed list of values that can be referred to as a unit. You can work with array elements by referencing their names and index numbers. An array has a `length` property that tells you how large the array is, as well as an assortment of methods for manipulating its contents. These include methods to sort an array, to concatenate two arrays into a single array, to add or remove elements from the array, and to reverse the order of the array. The first entry in an array is assigned the index 0.

One thing I did not show you earlier is how to create multidimensional arrays; I showed you only single-dimension arrays. An example of a single-dimension array is a list of automobiles. For example, the following list contains three elements and is a single-dimension array:

✿ Ford

✿ Honda

✿ Jeep

A multiple-dimension array can be used to represent data stored in table format. For example, the following information could be stored in a two-dimensional array:

Ford	Red	$4,000
Honda	Blue	$4,888
Jeep	Green	$12,500

The following script demonstrates how to build and display the contents of a multidimensional array:

```
<HTML>
  <HEAD>
    <TITLE>Script 2.27 - Creating a Multi-Dimensional
Array</TITLE>
  </HEAD>
  <BODY>
    <SCRIPT LANGUAGE="JavaScript" TYPE="Text/JavaScript">
    <!--Start hiding JavaScript statements


      var arraySize


      //Part 1 - Prompt user for array size
      arraySize = window.prompt("How many cars do you plan to
list?","");
```

```
      MyArray = new Array(arraySize);


      //Part 2 - Populate the array with user supplied
information
      for (row=0; row < arraySize; row++ ) {
        MyArray[row] = new Array(3);
        MyArray[row][0] = window.prompt("Type of car?","");
        MyArray[row][1] = window.prompt("Color of car?","");
        MyArray[row][2] = window.prompt("Sale price?","");
      }


      //Part 3 - Display the contents of the array
      for (row=0; row < arraySize; row++ ) {
        for (column=0; column < 3; column++ ) {
          document.write(MyArray[row][column] + " ");
        }
        document.write("<BR>");
      }
    // End hiding JavaScript statements -->
    </SCRIPT>
  </BODY>
</HTML>
```

I've used comments to divide this script into three parts, each of which performs a specific activity. In Part 1, I defined a variable called arraySize that contains the number of cars the user wants to enter. I then created an array called MyArray using the values contained in arraySize. If you think of a multidimensional array as a table, then this step defines the table length.

In Part 2, I added a for loop that creates the second dimension of the array. In this case, the for loop starts at 0, incrementing by 1 until it has executed for each element in the array. Again, if you look at the multidimensional array as a table, you can see that this step populates each column in the table as it iterates from top to bottom on a row-by-row basis. In each iteration, the user is asked to enter the type, color, and price of a car. In its first iteration, the script starts at row 0 (`MyArray[0]`) and populates each column in row 0 (`MyArray[0][0]`, `MyArray[0][1]`, `MyArray[0][2]`). On its next iteration, the value of `row` has been incremented by 1 to 1. Again, the script prompts the user for information about the car and populates the cells in the second row (`MyArray[1][0]`, `MyArray[1][1]`, `MyArray[1][2]`). The process repeats as many times as the user has cars to enter.

The result is a multidimensional array that can be represented as a table. In this example, the table is three rows and three columns deep and can be mapped out as shown in Figure 2.18. As Figure 2.19 shows, individuals cells can be referenced.

In Part 3, the script prints out the contents of the multidimensional array using nested `for` loops. The first loop controls the row of the table that is processed. It starts at array element 0 and increments by 1 until the entire array has been processed. The second loop prints the contents of

Figure 2.18

Building a two-dimensional table

0,0	0,1	0,2
1,0	1,1	1,2
2,0	2,1	2,2

myarray[1][2]

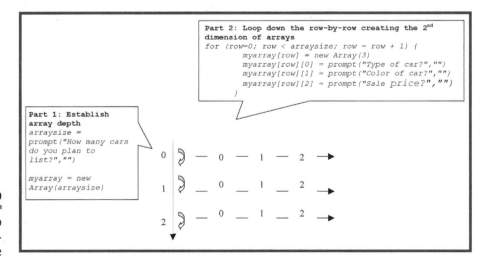

Figure 2.19

A coordinate map of the two-dimensional table

the multidimensional array by executing repeatedly for each row in the table, starting at column 0 and finishing with column 2.

Figure 2.20 shows the results I received when I tested the script.

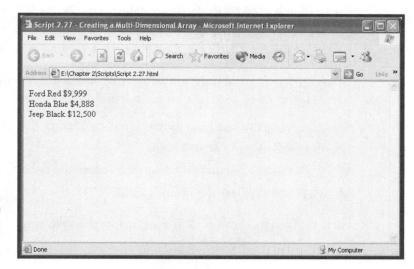

Figure 2.20

An example of a multidimensional array

The Boolean Object

JavaScript and JScript allow you to treat `Boolean` values like objects. You need to use the following syntax to create new `Boolean` objects.

```
BooleanObject = new Boolean(value);
```

In this syntax, `value` must be either `true` or `false`. If you assign a `Boolean` object a value other than `true` or `false`, the value will be converted to a `Boolean` value. If a value of `NaN`, null, undefined, -0, or 0 is found, then the values assigned will be `false`; otherwise the value is converted to `true`.

Following is a list of sample `Boolean` objects:

```
TestObject1 = new Boolean();        //initial value is false

TestObject2 = new Boolean(-0);      //initial value is false

TestObject3 = new Boolean(false);   //initial value is false

TestObject4 = new Boolean(true);    //initial value is true
```

```
TestObject5 = new Boolean("Hello"); //initial value is true
TestObject6 = new Boolean("false"); //initial value is true
```

NOTE There is a distinction between `false` and "`false`" in the last two examples. This is because "`false`" is a string, and `false` is a keyword.

By using `Boolean` objects instead of simple `Boolean` values, you can take advantage of three `Boolean` object methods:

- `toSource()`. Used internally to return a string that represents the `Boolean` object's source code.
- `toString()`. Returns a string that represents the object.
- `valueOf()`. Gets the object's value.

Each of these methods is demonstrated in the following example:

```
<HTML>
  <HEAD>
    <TITLE>Script 2.28 - Working with the Boolean Object</TITLE>
  </HEAD>
  <BODY>
    <SCRIPT LANGUAGE="JavaScript" TYPE="Text/JavaScript">
    <!--Start hiding JavaScript statements

        TestObject = new Boolean(false);    //initial value is
false

        document.write(TestObject.toString() + "<BR>");
        document.write(TestObject.valueOf());
    // End hiding JavaScript statements -->
    </SCRIPT>
  </BODY>
</HTML>
```

The Date Object

JavaScript and JScript do not provide a date value. Instead, you must use the Date object to insert dates and times in your scripts. The Date object does not have any properties but does provide access to a large number of built-in methods.

Date information is based on the number of millions of seconds that have passed since January 1, 1970. You create instances of Date objects using the new operator as demonstrated below.

```
Today = new Date();
document.write(today);
```

This example creates a variable called today and sets it equal to the current date. The second line displays the result of the today variable. If you were to put these statements into a script and run it, you'd get a result similar to the following when processed by Netscape Communicator:

```
Thu Dec 10 12:21:29 GMT-0500 (Eastern Standard Time) 2000
```

As you can see, the default format for the Date object is the day of the week followed by the name of the current month, its numeric date, the current time, the offset from GMT time, time-zone information, and finally the current year.

If this is a bit more information than you want or need, you can use various Date methods to retrieve more specific information. The following example demonstrates some of the more commonly used Date methods. In this script, the result of each method is assigned to an array element in an array named MyDate, the total length of which is eight elements (MyDate[x] = "message = " + TodaysDate.datemethod()). After executing the Date object's methods and loading the array, the script executes a for loop to spin through the array and print its contents. The loop begins with array element 0 (i = 0) and increments by 1 (i = i + 1) with each iteration until it reaches the end of the array (that is, until i < arrayLength is no longer true).

```
<HTML>

  <HEAD>
```

```
    <TITLE>Script 2.29 - Using the Date Object</TITLE>
  </HEAD>
  <BODY>
    <SCRIPT LANGUAGE="JavaScript" TYPE="Text/JavaScript">
    <!-- Start hiding JavaScript statements


      var arrayLength;


      TodaysDate = new Date();


      document.write("<B>Today's date is: </B>" + TodaysDate
  + "<P>");


      MyDate = new Array(8);
      MyDate[0] = "thedate = "    + TodaysDate.getDate();
      MyDate[1] = "theday = "     + TodaysDate.getDay();
      MyDate[2] = "theyear = "    + TodaysDate.getFullYear();
      MyDate[3] = "thehour = "    + TodaysDate.getHours();
      MyDate[4] = "theminute = " + TodaysDate.getMinutes();
      MyDate[5] = "themonth = "   + TodaysDate.getMonth();
      MyDate[6] = "thesecond = " + TodaysDate.getSeconds();
      MyDate[7] = "thetime = "    + TodaysDate.getTime();


      arrayLength = MyDate.length;


      document.write("<B>Array of Date Method Examples</B>
  <BR>");


      for (var i = 0; i < arrayLength; i++ ) {
        document.write(MyDate[i], "<BR>");
      }
```

```
    // End hiding JavaScript statements -->
    </SCRIPT>
  </BODY>
</HTML>
```

Figure 2.21 shows the result of executing this script.

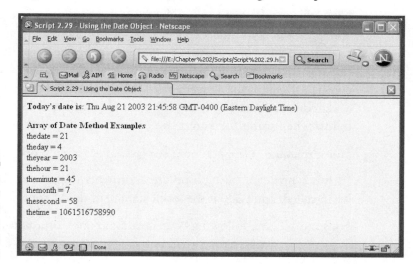

Figure 2.21

Using an array to store and display the results of data gathered using the Date object's methods

 NOTE When working with the Date object's methods, you must use 0 to 59 when representing minutes and seconds, 0 to 23 to represent hours, 0 to 6 to represent days, 1 to 31 when working with dates, and 0 to 11 to represent months. In the example, the date given is Friday, February 23, 1996. Note, however, that the getMonth() method returns 1, not 2, for February as you'd expect. Remember that computer logic makes January month 0, February month 1, and so on.

The Date object also provides a set of methods for setting the value of Date objects, including:

- ⚙ setDate(12)
- ⚙ setFullYear(2000)
- ⚙ setHours(11)

⚙ `setMinutes(30)`

⚙ `setMonth(4)`

⚙ `setYear(2000)`

The Function Object

JavaScript and JScript also enable you to create `Function` objects and provide you with access to `Function` properties and methods that are not available to normal functions. `Function` objects are easier to work with when your functions are composed of a single line of code. However, because of inefficiencies inherent in `Function` objects you are better off sticking with declared functions. The following example outlines the syntax that you must follow when using the `Function` object.

FunctionName = new Function([*p1*, ... *pn*] *body*)

In this syntax, `p1` through `pn` are arguments that `Function` objects receive when called, and `body` is the script statement that is compiled as the function.

For example, the following code creates a `Function` object named `Warn`:

```
Warn = new Function("alert('HI!')");
```

You can call this function as follows:

```
Warn();
```

The preceding `Function` object is equivalent to the following declared function:

```
function Warn() {
  window.alert("Warning: You should not run this script!");
  return;
}
```

NOTE Because the `Function` object is compiled, it is less efficient than using declared functions. Therefore, I recommend that you avoid using compiled functions and the `Function` object.

The following script demonstrates the use of the previous `Function` object examples.

```
<HTML>
  <HEAD>
    <TITLE>Script 2.30 - Working with the Function Object</TITLE>
  </HEAD>
  <BODY>
    <SCRIPT LANGUAGE="JavaScript" TYPE="Text/JavaScript">
    <!--Start hiding JavaScript statements


        Warn = new Function("window.alert('Warning: You should
not run this script!')");

        Warn();


    // End hiding JavaScript statements -->
    </SCRIPT>
  </BODY>
</HTML>
```

Figure 2.22 shows what happens if you load this page.

Figure 2.22

Using the
`Function` object
in place of regular
functions

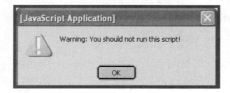

The Math Object

The `Math` object provides mathematical constants in the form of properties. It also provides mathematical functions in the form of methods. Earlier this morning, I demonstrated several `Math` properties and methods. Tables 2.5 and 2.6 provide a review of the `Math` object's major properties and methods.

TABLE 2.5 SUMMARY OF MATH PROPERTIES	
Property	**Description**
E	Euler's constant (2.718)
LN2	Natural logarithm of 2 (2.302)
LN10	Natural logarithm of 10 (.693)
LOG2E	Base 2 logarithm of e (.434)
LOG10	Base 10 logarithm of 10 (1.442)
PI	Ratio of the circumference of a circle to its diameter (3.141549)
SQRT1_2	Square root of ? (.707)
SQRT2	Square root of 2 (1.414)

The Number Object

The Number object lets you treat numbers like objects and store numerical constants as properties. The values of these constants cannot be changed. You will most likely never need to know or work with the Number object, but just in case, Table 2.7 outlines its properties.

You define an instance of the Number object using the new keyword as demonstrated below.

```
MyNumber = new Number(99.99);
```

The Object Object

This is the object on which all other objects are based. This means that all objects inherit this object's properties and methods.

TABLE 2.6 SUMMARY OF MATH METHODS	
Method	**Description**
`abs()`	Returns the absolute value
`cos(),sin(),tan()`	Trigonometric functions
`acos(),asin(),atan()`	Inverse trigonometric functions
`exp(),log()`	Exponential and natural logarithms
`ceil()`	Returns the lowest integer greater than or equal to the argument
`floor()`	Returns the highest integer less than or equal to the argument
`min(x,y)`	Returns either x or y, depending on which is lower
`max(x,y)`	Returns either x or y, depending on which is higher
`pow(x,y)`	Returns the value of x^y
`random()`	Returns a random number between 0 and 1
`round()`	Rounds the argument to the nearest integer
`sqrt()`	Returns the square of the argument

You can create new `Object` objects by specifying an `Array`, `Boolean`, `Function`, `Number`, or `String` object in the `Object()` constructor as shown here:

```
MyNumberObject = new Object(99.99);

MyStringObject = new Object("Testing");
```

TABLE 2.7 SUMMARY OF THE NUMBER OBJECT'S PROPERTIES

Property	Description
MAX_VALUE	Largest possible number
MIN_VALUE	Smallest possible number
NaN	Not a number
NEGATIVE_INFINITY	Positive infinity
POSITIVE_INFINITY	Negative infinity

NOTE   A *constructor* is a function that each object provides that you can use to create instances of objects. For example, to create an instance of a String object named MyString, you would specify the following MyString = new String("Add your message text here.").

You'll probably never see anybody create objects in this manner. Instead, you'll see objects created using constructors specific to each object type, such as these constructors:

- Array()
- Boolean()
- Function()
- Number()
- String()

The String Object

As you have already learned, the String object enables you to work with strings as objects. However, you shouldn't need to use this object because JavaScript and JScript automatically converts simple strings into temporary String objects whenever you use a String object method or property on them.

The String object has just one property, length, which contains the number of characters that comprise the String object. However, the String object has a number of useful methods for manipulating the String object, as outlined in Table 2.8.

TABLE 2.8 COMMLY USED STRING OBJECT METHODS

Method	Description
charAt()	Returns the character at the specified position in the string where the index of a String object begins at zero
concat()	Combines two strings into one new string
fromCharCode()	Creates a string value based on the supplied code set
indexOf()	Returns the position of a specified substring
lastIndexOf()	Returns the last position of a specified substring
slice()	Creates a new string using a portion of the current string
split()	Organizes a string into an array
substring()	Returns the specified portion of a string
toLowerCase()	Returns the string in all lowercase characters
toUppercase()	Returns the string in all uppercase characters

The following example creates two `String` objects and then demonstrates the use of various `String` methods using these `String` objects and displays their results with the `document.write()` method.

```
<HTML>
  <HEAD>
    <TITLE>Script 2.31 - Working with the String Object</TITLE>
  </HEAD>
  <BODY>
    <SCRIPT LANGUAGE="JavaScript" TYPE="Text/JavaScript">
    <!-- Start hiding JavaScript statements


        MyString1 = new String(" He is gone now!");


        MyString2 = new String("Once upon a time there was a
little boy " +
          "who cried wolf.");


        document.write("<B>MyString1 - </B>" + MyString1 +
"<BR>");
        document.write("<B>MyString2 - </B>" + MyString2 +
"<BR>");


        document.write("<B>MyString2.charAt(5) - </B>" +
MyString2.charAt(5) +
          "<BR>");
        document.write("<B>MyString2.charCodeAt(5) - </B>" +
          MyString2.charCodeAt(5) + "<BR>");


        document.write("<B>MyString2.indexOf('little') - </B>" +
          MyString2.indexOf("little") + "<BR>");
        document.write("<B>MyString2.lastIndexOf('who') - </B>" +
          MyString2.lastIndexOf("who") + "<BR>");
```

```
document.write("<B>MyString2.substring(15) - </B>" +
    MyString2.substring(15) + "<BR>");
document.write("<B>MyString2.substring(15,22) - </B>" +
    MyString2.substring(15,22) + "<BR>");


document.write("<B>MyString2.toUpperCase() - </B>" +
    MyString2.toUpperCase() + "<BR>");
document.write("<B>MyString2.toLowerCase() - </B>" +
    MyString2.toLowerCase() +"<BR>");


document.write("<B>MyString2.concat(MyString1) - </B>" +
    MyString2.concat(MyString1) + "<BR>");


document.write("<B>MyString2.slice(' ') - </B>" +
    MyString2.slice(" ") + "<BR>");


// End hiding JavaScript statements -->
</SCRIPT>
</BODY>
</HTML>
```

Figure 2.23 shows the result of loading the page created in this example.

What's Next?

Oh my! I'd call this a full morning's work. Why don't you put this book down for a while, stretch your legs, and go get a bite to eat. Things are starting to get really good, and you need to keep up your strength. When you come back, we'll jump right in and start working with browser-based objects and events. Before the afternoon ends, you will have a solid foundation for object-based programming.

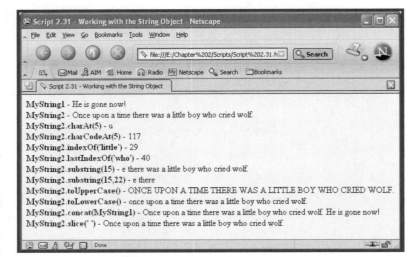

Figure 2.23

A demonstration
of String
object methods

Using JavaScript to Build Better Web Pages

➤ Working with built-in browser objects

➤ Handling browser events

➤ Managing HTML frames and frame content

➤ Validating HTML forms

Welcome back. Hopefully, you have had a good break and are ready for an afternoon full of learning. This afternoon you will learn about built-in browser objects and their properties and methods. By working with these objects, you will be able to create JavaScripts that can control browser navigation, browser window, and content.

Next you'll learn how to create scripts that can react to browser events. This will include learning how to react to events triggered when Web pages are loaded, as well as when visitors point and click their way around your Web site. By the time you make it through this information, you will have mastered all the basic building blocks of JavaScript programming.

You'll end the afternoon by learning how to use JavaScript to manage and control HTML frames and forms. This will include learning how to use JavaScript to load content into frames and to validate the content of forms that you create to collect information from visitors.

Working with Browser-Based Objects

When an HTML page loads a browser such as Netscape Communicator or Internet Explorer, the browser defines a collection of objects based on the content it finds on the page. These objects are created in a top-down order as the page is loaded. As the browser builds the object references, it does so in a hierarchical fashion.

The object organizational hierarchy for a given browser is known as its *object model*. In the early days of Internet browser development, there were many differences in the object models provided by various browsers. In addition, as companies such as Microsoft and Netscape improved their browsers over the years, they continued to add new features and support for new objects. As a result, JavaScripts that were designed to be processed by the latest version of either of these two browsers often didn't work with older browsers, which even today are still used by many people. Even worse, you couldn't count on your JavaScripts running the same way when executed by Internet Explorer or Netscape Communicator. All this made for a very confusing situation.

Because of the number of different versions of Internet Explorer and Netscape Communicator that have been developed over the years, there is no way that I can cover issues specific to each version of both browsers within the confines of this book. There are just too many different objects, and these objects have too many methods and properties to be covered in a single weekend. Therefore, I plan to cover the objects that you'll most likely need to work with. In addition, the scripts provided in this book will be written and tested using the latest versions of Internet Explorer and Netscape Communicator.

A Browser View of Objects

When a browser loads an HTML page, it simultaneously creates a logical view of all relevant objects into a tree-like structure. These objects are related to one another and have parent-child and sibling relationships. For example, consider the following HTML page:

```
<HTML>

  <HEAD>

    <TITLE>Script 3.1 - A Typical HTML page</TITLE>

  </HEAD>
```

```
<BODY>

  <P>Hello.</P>

  <P>Welcome to my Web site.</P>

</BODY>


</HTML>
```

When loaded by a browser, you see the output shown in Figure 3.1.

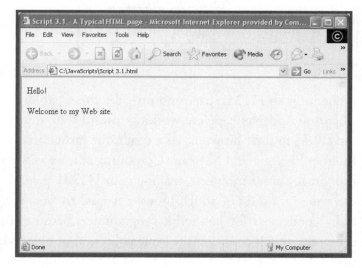

Figure 3.1

From a browser point of view, the content displayed in this Web page consists of objects that are related to one another.

The browser, on the other hand, sees the content of the HTML page a little differently, as depicted in Figure 3.2.

As you can see, the document object resides at the top of this tree. Underneath it are the various HTML tags that define its contents, and under these tasks is the content they contain.

A Brief Overview of Browser Object Models

In an effort to help bring stability to Web development, a group known as the World Wide Web Consortium developed a browser object standard called the *Document Object Model* (DOM). This model defines every

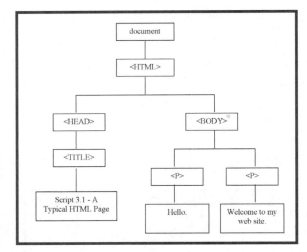

Figure 3.2

Examining the
organizational tree
structure of objects
located on an
HTML page

element on an HTML page and provides the capability to access it. Both Microsoft and Netscape are working toward fully integrated support for the DOM in their browsers. As a result, the most current versions of both Internet Explorer and Netscape Communicator are very consistent in their support for browser objects, making your HTML pages look pretty much the same regardless of which browser is used to view them. This is especially good news for JavaScript programmers because it means that you can pretty much count on the same collection of objects being available.

 NOTE There is no way that this book can completely cover all the ins and outs of the DOM. If you would like to learn more about it, visit www.w3c.org/DOM.

Supporting Older Browser Object Models

As I have already suggested, older versions of both Internet Explorer and Netscape Communicator supported their own particular object models, whereas the most current versions of both browsers provide backward support for old browser object models while simultaneously incorporating support for the DOM.

Because so many people are still surfing the Internet using older browsers, it is important to understand how the older browsers support object access. The uppermost object supported by older browser object models is the `window` object. This object provides access to a number of lower-level or child objects, as listed below.

- **document object**. Provides the capability to access and manipulate the currently loaded HTML page.

- **frames collection**. Provides access to an indexed list of the frames defined in the browser window.

- **history object**. Provides methods that can be used to navigate through the `document` object's history list (e.g. to Web pages previously visited).

- **location object**. Provides access to information about the current URL as well as the capability to load a new URL.

- **navigator object**. Provides access to information about the browser being used to access the HTML page.

Figure 3.3 shows the relationship of these objects to one another.

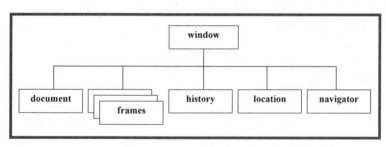

Figure 3.3

The `window` object provides access to multiple child objects.

Of all these objects, the one that you will use the most is the `document` object. The `document` object provides access to a large number of additional objects and collections, as depicted in Figure 3.4.

To support older browsers, you must refer to objects by name. For example, the following statement refers to the `document` object's `write()` method.

```
document.write("Welcome to my Web page!");
```

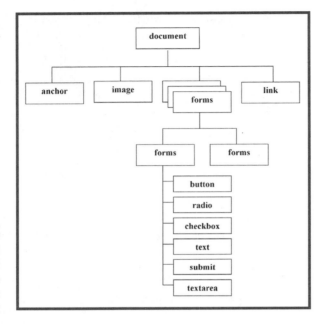

Figure 3.4

Commonly used
objects and
collections
belonging to the
document object

As you work your way through the rest of today, I'll provide you with examples that further demonstrate how to reference objects by name.

Working with the Document Object Model

The latest versions of Internet Explorer and Netscape Communicator support the DOM. Therefore, you have two different ways of accessing browser objects. First, you can access them by name as previously demonstrated. The advantage of using this option is that it helps make your HTML pages and JavaScripts backwardly compatible with older browsers. The disadvantage of this option is that it provides a lot less flexibility when compared to using properties provided by the DOM.

Table 3.1 provides a complete listing of DOM properties that you can use within your JavaScripts in order to access browser objects. These properties provide comprehensive control over all the content located on an HTML page by providing you with the capability to travel up and down the tree without having to hard code in references to specific HTML elements (e.g. via the NAME attribute).

TABLE 3.1 DOM PROPERTIES	
Property	**Description**
firstChild	The first child node belonging to an object
lastChild	An object's last child node
childNodes	A collection (e.g. array) of child objects belonging to an object
parentNode	An object's parent object
nextSibling	The child node following the previous child node in the tree
prevSibling	The child node that comes before the current child node
nodeName	The name assigned to an object's HTML tag
nodeType	Identifies the type of HTML element (tag, attribute, or text) associated with the object
nodeValue	Retrieves the value assigned to a text node
data	Retrieves the value for the specified text node
specified	Determines whether an attribute has been specified
attributes	A collection (e.g. array) made up of all an object's attributes

To demonstrate how to use the DOM properties listed in Table 3.1 to access and manipulate HTML content, take a look at the following example.

```
<HTML>

    <HEAD>
      <TITLE>Script 3.2 - DOM Navigation and Access
Example</TITLE>
    </HEAD>
```

```
<BODY ID="bodyTag">

   <P ID="Tag1" Name="helloTag">Hello.</P>

   <p ID="Tag2" NAME="welcomeMsg"> Welcome to my Web
site.</P>

   </BODY>


</HTML>
```

Graphically, this script can be represented as shown in Figure 3.5. The
`document` object sits at the root of the tree and has just one child object,
`documentElement`. `documentElement` represents the HTML page's
opening `<HTML>` tag.

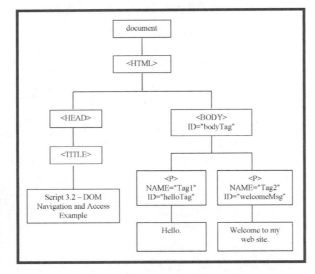

Figure 3.5

An illustration of
the HTML page's
layout from a DOM
standpoint

Now modify the previous script so that it looks exactly like the example
shown below.

```
<HTML>


   <HEAD>
     <TITLE>Script 3.3 - DOM Navigation and Access Example
   </TITLE>
```

```html
</HEAD>


<BODY ID="bodyTag">


  <P ID="Tag1" NAME="helloTag">Hello.</P>
  <P ID="Tag2" NAME="welcomeMsg"> Welcome to my Web
site.</P>


  <SCRIPT LANGUAGE="JavaScript" TYPE="Text/JavaScript">
  <!-- Start hiding JavaScript statements


    window.alert("The ID assigned to the 1st HTML tag is: " +
      document.documentElement.firstChild.tagName);
    window.alert("The ID assigned to the 2nd HTML tag is: " +
      document.documentElement.lastChild.tagName);
    window.alert("The ID assigned to the child of the 1st
HTML tag is: " +

document.documentElement.firstChild.firstChild.tagName);
    window.alert("Click on OK to dynamically modify the
value of Tag2");

document.getElementById("Tag2").firstChild.nodeValue="Welcome
to " +
      "my new and improved Web site.";


  // End hiding JavaScript statements -->
  </SCRIPT>


</BODY>


</HTML>
```

The first JavaScript statement displays the tag name of the first HTML tag that exists under the document object (e.g. the <HEAD> tag), as shown in Figure 3.6.

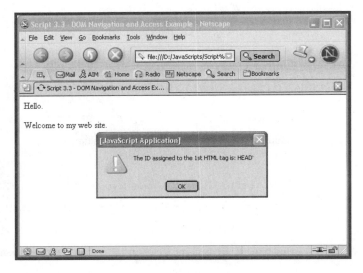

Figure 3.6

Using DOM properties to navigate and reference different elements on an HTML page

Take a look at the tree hierarchy shown in Figure 3.5 and compare it to the components that make up this statement. Next, the JavaScript uses the lastChild property to reference the <BODY> tag. Then the script references the <TITLE> tag, which happens to be the first tag located under the first tag in the script. The next statement displays a message stating that the script is about to rewrite the value assigned to the HTML page's second tag. Finally, the last statement in the script, shown below, rewrites a portion of the text displayed on the screen. It accomplishes this task by using the GetElementById() method to establish a reference to Tag2. This establishes a reference to the HTML page's second <P> tag. The statement then references the nodeValue of the tag's firstChild (e.g. the tag's content) and assigns it a new value.

```
document.getElementById("Tag2").firstChild.nodeValue="Welcome
to " +

        "my new and improved Web site.";
```

Figure 3.7 shows how the HTML page looks after its content has been changed dynamically.

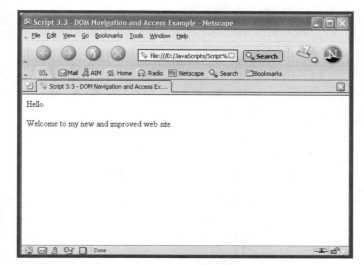

Figure 3.7

Dynamically
modifying
HTML content

The DOM provides the capability to reference any element located on an HTML page. It provides the capability to navigate the HTML page without having to reference hard coded tag names and to modify content dynamically. However, the price for this flexibility is complexity.

Unfortunately, the DOM is not supported by versions of the Internet Explorer browser prior to version 5, nor is it supported by versions of Netscape Communicator prior to version 6. Therefore, many visitors to your Web pages may be using browsers that do not support it.

Browser Objects

Internet browsers provide access to a large collection of browser objects. In the next several sections I will introduce you to some of the more commonly used browser objects and demonstrate how to work with them using JavaScript.

The window Object

The window object is the ancestor of all other objects on the page. Multiple windows can be opened at the same time. The window object has dozens of objects and methods associated with it, many of which you have already worked with. For example, you've used the window.alert() method to display messages in the alert dialog box, window.prompt() to retrieve user input, and window.confirm() to seek user permission before taking action.

Depending on which browser you use, there are also methods for controlling navigation. For example, Netscape Communicator supports window.back(), window.forward(), and window.home(). However, Internet Explorer does not support these methods. This points out one small area of difference between the two browsers. The following example demonstrates the use of these window object methods when processed by Netscape Communicator.

```
<HTML>


  <HEAD>

    <TITLE>Script 3.4 - Working with the Window Object -
1</TITLE>

  </HEAD>


  <BODY>

    <FORM NAME="form1">

      <INPUT TYPE="button" VALUE="Back" onClick="window.back()">

      <INPUT TYPE="button" VALUE="Home" onClick="window.home()">

      <INPUT TYPE="button" VALUE="Forward"
onClick="window.forward()">

    </FORM>

  </BODY>


</HTML>
```

The script defines a form that contains three buttons. Clicking on a button causes its onClick event to execute. In the case of the button labeled Back, the onClick event executes the window.back() method, causing the browser to load the previous Web page. Clicking on the Forward button causes the exact opposite action, while clicking on the Home button reloads the current page. Don't worry about the onClick event handler right now; you'll cover event handlers at the end of the afternoon. For now, just know that event handlers enable you to associate JavaScript statements and functions with user actions such as mouse clicks on objects.

Figure 3.8 shows how the preceding looks when loaded by Netscape Communicator. Clicking on the Home button tells the browser to load the URL that the user has set up as the default home page. Clicking on the Back or Forward button produces the same effect as clicking on the browser's Back or Forward button.

Figure 3.8

Creating your own navigation buttons

The following script gives you another example of working with the window object's methods. In this example, the browser opens a second window as soon as the Web page loads, using the window object's open() method. The window is named window1.

```
<HTML>

  <HEAD>

    <TITLE>Script 3.5 - Working with the Window Object - 2
</TITLE>

  </HEAD>

  <BODY>

    <SCRIPT LANGUAGE="JavaScript" TYPE="Text/JavaScript">
    <!-- Start hiding JavaScript statements
      window1=window.open();
    // End hiding JavaScript statements -->
    </SCRIPT>

    <FORM NAME="form1">
      <INPUT TYPE="button" VALUE="Close the window"
onClick="window1.close()">
      <INPUT TYPE="button" VALUE="Resize"
onClick="window1.resizeTo(300,400)">
    </FORM>

  </BODY>

</HTML>
```

NOTE

You have doubtlessly seen many Web sites in which multiple windows open when you click on links. Usually, the other windows appear in the form of smaller windows that try to sell you a product or point you to other links.

The script contains a form that defines two buttons, each of which contains an `onClick` event handler. If you click the first button, labeled Close the Window, the `window` object's `close()` method is executed. In order for the browser to know which window you want to close, you must specify the window's name (in this case, it's `window1`).

The second button in the form, Resize, executes the `window` object's `resizeTo()` method. This method tells the browser to change the size of the `window1` window object to a pixel size of 300 by 400.

Figure 3.9 demonstrates what you'll see when you first load this page using Internet Explorer. Two windows are opened. The first window displays the form containing the script, and the second window is opened as a result of the script's `window1=window.open()` statement.

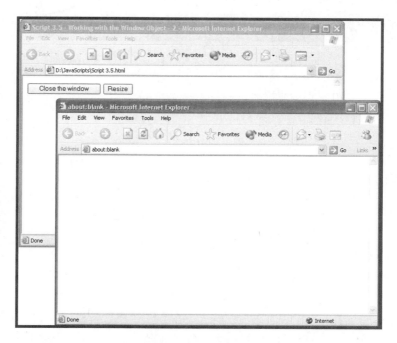

Figure 3.9

Opening and controlling browser windows

The `window` object's `open()` method enables you a great deal of control over the appearance of the window. For example, you can control whether the window has certain features such as a menu bar, toolbar, scroll bar, and status bar, as well as whether the window can be resized.

Figure 3.10 shows the location of these features on the browser window.

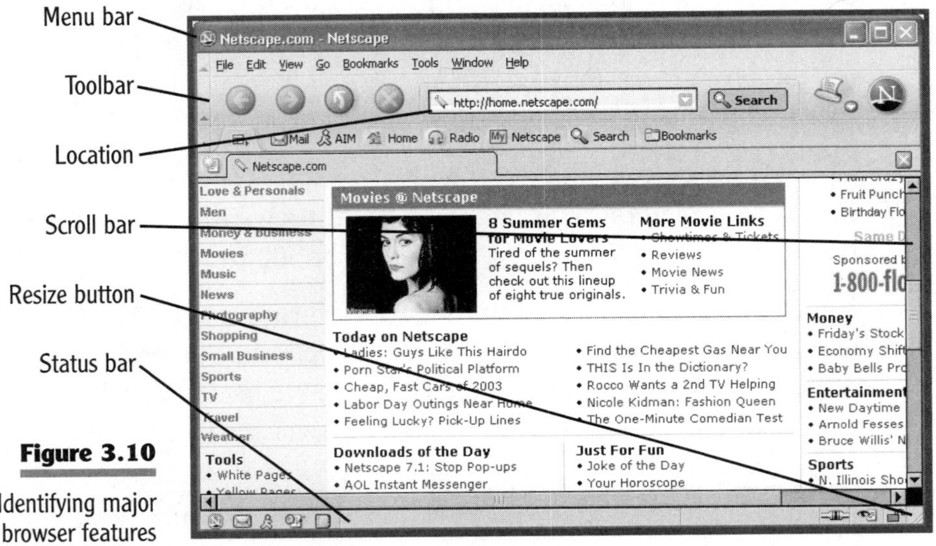

Menu bar

Toolbar

Location

Scroll bar

Resize button

Status bar

Figure 3.10

Identifying major
browser features

The example that follows demonstrates how to control each of these window features:

```
<HTML>


  <HEAD>
    <TITLE>Script 3.6 -Working with the Window Object - 3
</TITLE>
  </HEAD>


  <BODY>


    <SCRIPT LANGUAGE="JavaScript" TYPE="Text/JavaScript">
    <!-- Start hiding JavaScript statements
      window.open("", "Window1", "menubar=no,toolbar=yes," +
        "scrollbar=yes,resizable=yes,status=yes,
location=yes");
      // End hiding JavaScript statements -->
```

```
</SCRIPT>


</BODY>
```

By default, all the window features are enabled. To control them, you would rewrite the statement containing the `open()` method as follows:

```
window.open("", "Window1",

    "menubar=no,toolbar=yes,scrollbar=yes,resizable=yes,
    status=yes,location=yes");
```

When written this way, the `open()` method accepts three sets of parameters. The first parameter is the URL that should be opened in the new window. In the preceding example, I left this parameter blank, causing the browser to open an empty window. The second parameter is the name you are assigning to the window. You must assign a name to the window so that you can reference it from other parts of your script. The final parameter is comprised of one or more arguments separated by commas. Each argument identifies a window feature and assigns it a value of `yes` or `no`. A value assignment of `yes` tells the browser to include that option when creating the window. A value of `no` tells the browser to eliminate the specified feature. By default, all features are enabled. Therefore, I can get the same results by writing the statement to look like the following:

```
window.open("", "Window1, " menubar=no")
```

However, by writing the statement the way I did originally, it's easier to come back and change things later; I also think it makes things easier to understand. Figure 3.11 shows what the second window looks like when you load this example using Internet Explorer.

The document Object

The `document` object is the heart and soul of JavaScript. Each Web page can contain a single `document` object. You have already used it extensively to write output to the screen using the `document.write()` method.

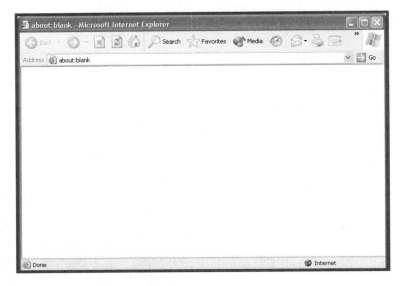

Figure 3.11

Preventing the display of the menu bar on a new window

The properties of the `document` object depend on the content of the page's HTML. For example, if a Web page contains images, then the document properties for the page will contain an `images[]` array that lists every image on the page.

The `document` object has a host of properties you can use to control the appearance of the page and to gather information about its contents. For example, the `document` object stores property values for the following arrays:

- **`anchors[]`**. An array containing a list of all anchors in the document
- **`applets[]`**. An array containing a list of all applets in the document
- **`embeds[]`**. An array containing a list of all embedded objects in the document
- **`forms[]`**. An array containing a list of all forms in the document
- **`images[]`**. An array containing a list of all images in the document
- **`links[]`**. An array containing a list of all links in the document
- **`plugins[]`**. An array containing a list of all plug-ins in the document

Other `document` object properties enable you to affect appearance:

- **`bgColor`**. Specifies the document background color
- **`fgColor`**. Specifies the color of document text
- **`linkColor`**. Specifies the color of links
- **`alinkColor`**. Specifies the color of active links
- **`vlinkColor`**. Specifies the color of visited links

Here is a partial list of other useful document properties:

- **`cookie`**. Lets you get and set cookie values
- **`lastModified`**. A string that shows the date and time at which the document was last changed
- **`referrer`**. A string showing the URL the user came from
- **`title`**. A string containing the contents of the HTML `<TITLE>` tags
- **`URL`**. A string containing the document's URL

The following example demonstrates the use of two document properties. The first statement in the script prints the title located in the HTML `<TITLE>` tags, using the `document.title` property. The second statement displays the last modification date and time for the page, using the `document.lastModified` property. Figure 3.12 shows the results of loading this example in Netscape Communicator.

```
<HTML>

  <HEAD>

    <TITLE>Script 3.7 - Setting the Modification Date and
Time</TITLE>

  </HEAD>

  <BODY>

    <SCRIPT LANGUAGE="JavaScript" TYPE="Text/JavaScript">
```

```
<!-- Start hiding JavaScript statements

    document.write("<B>Document Title:</B> " +
document.title + "<BR>");

    document.write("<B>Last Modified on:</B> " +
document.lastModified);

    // End hiding JavaScript statements -->

    </SCRIPT>


    </BODY>


</HTML>
```

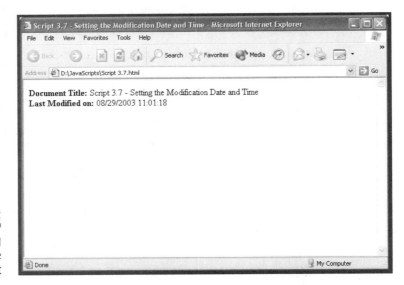

Figure 3.12

Displaying
properties of the
document object

The form Object

Later this afternoon, I will dedicate a substantial portion of text to exploring
the control of forms using JavaScript. Consider the information provided in
this section to be a sneak preview of the form object.

The document object's forms[] array maintains a list of every form on a
page, starting with form[0] and incrementing by 1 for each additional

form. You can refer to individual forms using their `forms[]` array index number or by name.

For example, the following code creates a form called `form1` that contains a single button:

```
<FORM NAME="form1">

  <INPUT TYPE="button" NAME="backButton" VALUE="Back"
onClick="window.back()">

</FORM>
```

Assuming that this is the only form on the page, you can refer to it either as `document.forms[0]` or as `document.form1`. Forms can contain many elements, such as text boxes and buttons. To manage these form elements, each `form` object contains its own array, named `elements[]`. The first element in the form is stored as `element[0]`, the second element is stored as `element[1]`, and so on.

The location Object

The `location` object is relatively simple. Its properties contain information about its own URL. For example, `location.href` specifies the URL of the page, and `location.pathname` specifies just the path portion of the URL. If you make changes to the `location` object, the browser automatically attempts to load the URL again.

The `location` object has just two methods: The `reload()` method enables you to force a reload of the page, and `replace()` lets you specify a new URL to load. Because the `replace()` method writes a new entry to the history list on top of the current entry, this method prevents the user from using the browser's Back button to return to the previous page.

The following script shows how you can use the `location` object to force the browser to reload the current page or to load a new URL. First, the script defines a variable called `myUrl` and sets it equal to the value of `location.href` (that is, to the URL of the current page).

Then it defines a form with two buttons. The onClick event handler has been assigned to the first button. When the user clicks on this button, the location.replace() method instructs the browser to load http://www.netscape.com. When the user clicks on the second button, the location.reload() method instructs the browser to reload the current Web page. Figure 3.13 shows the result of loading this example.

```
<HTML>

  <HEAD>
    <TITLE>Script 3.8 - Working with the location object</TITLE>
  </HEAD>

  <BODY>

    <SCRIPT LANGUAGE="JavaScript" TYPE="Text/JavaScript">
    <!-- Start hiding JavaScript statements
      myUrl= location.href;
      document.write("myUrl = " + myUrl + "<BR>");
    // End hiding JavaScript statements -->
    </SCRIPT>

    <FORM NAME="form1">
      <INPUT TYPE="button" VALUE="go to www.netscape.com"

onClick="location.replace('http://www.netscape.com')">
      <INPUT TYPE="button" VALUE="Reload this page"
        onClick="location.reload()">
    </FORM>

  </BODY>

</HTML>
```

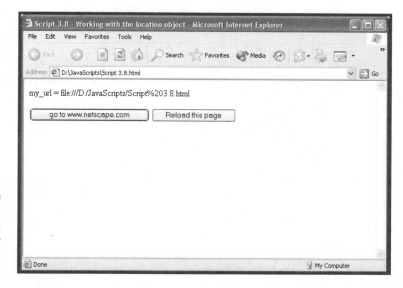

Figure 3.13

Using the
`location` object
to control browser
navigation and
page reload

The history Object

The `history` object maintains a list of URLs that the browser has visited
since it began its current session. One useful property of this object is the
`length` property, which you can access using the following syntax:

```
history.length
```

The `history` object has three methods:

- The `back()` method loads the previously visited URL in the
  history list. This is the same as clicking on the browser's Back
  button.

- The `forward()` method loads the next URL in the history list.
  This has the same effect as clicking on the browser's Forward
  button.

- The `go()` method loads the specified URL in the history list.
  For example, `history.go(4)` loads the URL four entries ahead
  in the history list, `history.go(-4)` loads a URL four entries back in
  the history list, and `history.go(0)` reloads the current URL.

The following example demonstrates the use of the `history` object's `back()`, `go()`, and `forward()` methods. It defines a form with three buttons, each of which is assigned one of the methods. The `onClick` event handler is used to associate one of the methods with each button.

```
<HTML>

  <HEAD>
    <TITLE>Script 3.9 - Using History Object Methods for
Navigation</TITLE>
  </HEAD>

  <BODY>
    <FORM NAME="form1">
      <INPUT TYPE="button" VALUE="Back"
        onClick="history.back()">
      <INPUT TYPE="button" VALUE="Reload"
        onClick="history.go(0)">
      <INPUT TYPE="button" VALUE="Forward"
        onClick="history.forward()">
    </FORM>
  </BODY>

</HTML>
```

Figure 3.14 shows the results of loading this example using Internet Explorer. Clicking on the three form buttons has the same effect as clicking on the Back, Forward, and Reload buttons on the browser's toolbar.

The navigator Object

The `navigator` object is a top-level object like the `window` object. This means that the `navigator` object is not below any other object in the

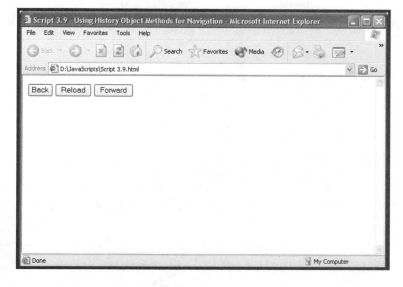

Figure 3.14

Adding navigation
buttons to your
Web pages

object hierarchy. It contains information about the browser that loaded the Web page. Both Netscape Navigator and Internet Explorer support this object, even though Internet Explorer's use of the object might seem a little funny. Some of the useful properties of the `navigator` object include the following:

- `navigator.appCodeName`. Contains the code name of the browser
- `navigator.appName`. Contains the name of the browser
- `navigator.appVersion`. Contains the version number of the browser

Your scripts can use the values of these properties to determine the browser (and its version number) that is loading the Web page. You can then use this information to direct the browser to a JavaScript you have written to work with that particular browser.

The following example shows you how to create variables and assign them the values of `navigator` object properties. This script then prints the values of the variables. However, you could add additional logic to this script to interrogate the value of these variables and then direct the user's browser to a Web page you have designed to work with that particular browser.

```
<HTML>

  <HEAD>

    <TITLE>Script 3.10 - Displaying navigator object properties
</TITLE>

    </HEAD>


  <BODY>

    <SCRIPT LANGUAGE="JavaScript" TYPE="Text/JavaScript">
<!-- Start hiding JavaScript statements

      document.write("<B>navigator.appCodeName = </B>" +
navigator.appCodeName + "<BR>");

      document.write("<B>navigator.appName = </B>" + navigator.
appName + "<BR>");

      document.write("<B>navigator.appVersion = </B>" +
navigator.appVersion + "<BR>");

      // End hiding JavaScript statements -->

    </SCRIPT>

  </BODY>


</HTML>
```

Figure 3.15 shows the result when I loaded this script in Netscape
Communicator.

Creating Custom Objects

In addition to core JavaScript objects and browser-based objects,
JavaScript provides you with the capability to build your own objects.

Three basic steps are required to create an instance of an object:

1. Define its structure

2. Assign its properties

3. Assign functions that will act as object methods

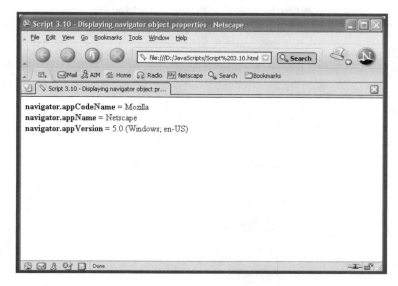

Figure 3.15

Viewing browser information

There are two ways to create a new object. The first is to write a function that defines the format of the new object and then to use the new operator to instantiate a new object. For example, the following function defines a new object that contains two properties and one method:

```
function Customer(name, phone) {
        this.name = name;
        this.phone = phone;
        this.ShowAlert = ShowAlert;
}
```

The first line defines a function that accepts two arguments. The next two lines use these arguments to establish property attributes. The last line assigns a method named ShowAlert. Notice that there is no associated argument with the defined method.

The ShowAlert method is itself just a function. As shown here, ShowAlert() displays an alert prompt that reveals the name and phone properties of a customer object:

```
function ShowAlert() {
        window.alert("Customer: " + this.name + " - Phone: "
+ this.phone)
}
```

The following line of code can then be used to instantiate a new object using the `customer()` function:

```
Customer1 = new customer("Robert Robertson", 8043334444)
```

This statement creates a new object called `Customer1` that has the following properties:

```
Customer1.name
Customer1.phone
```

You can call the function again and again to create other new objects. The `Customer1` object also has a single method that can be invoked using the following statement:

```
Customer1.ShowAlert()
```

If you put this whole example together, you'll end up with the following script:

```
<HTML>

  <HEAD>
    <TITLE>Script 3.11 - Creating a custom object</TITLE>

    <SCRIPT LANGUAGE="JavaScript" TYPE="Text/JavaScript">
    <!--Start hiding JavaScript statements

      function Customer(name, phone) {
        this.name = name;
```

```
            this.phone = phone;

            this.ShowAlert = ShowAlert;

        }


        function ShowAlert() {

            window.alert("Customer: " + this.name + " - Phone: "
+ this.phone);

        }


    // End hiding JavaScript statements -->

    </SCRIPT>


  </HEAD>


  <BODY>


    <SCRIPT LANGUAGE="JavaScript" TYPE="Text/JavaScript">

    <!--Start hiding JavaScript statements

        Customer1 = new Customer("Robert Robertson",
8043334444);

        Customer1.ShowAlert();

    // End hiding JavaScript statements -->

    </SCRIPT>


  </BODY>

</HTML>
```

Figure 3.16 shows what you will see when you run this script.

Figure 3.16

Displaying your
custom object's
property values

Creating Objects with an Object Initializer

An alternative to writing a function to create new instances of objects is to take advantage of an *object initializer*. In this case, you create the object in the form of an expression by placing properties and methods inside a pair of curly braces, separating the property or method name from its value with a colon. For example, the following statement could be used to create an object called `Customer1`:

```
Customer1 = {name:"Robert Robertson", phone:8043334444,
showAlert:showAlert};
```

The first two entries inside the braces define the following pair of properties and set their values:

```
Customer1.name = "Robert Robertson";
Customer1.phone = 8043334444;
```

The last entry defines a method:

```
Customer1.ShowAlert();
```

If you use an object initializer, you can rewrite the code in the preceding example as shown here:

```
<HTML>

  <HEAD>

    <TITLE>Script 3.12 - Another way to create a custom
object</TITLE>

    <SCRIPT LANGUAGE="JavaScript" TYPE="Text/JavaScript">
    <!--Start hiding JavaScript statements
      function ShowAlert() {
        window.alert("Customer: " + this.name + " - Phone: "
+ this.phone);
```

```
        }
    // End hiding JavaScript statements -->
    </SCRIPT>


  </HEAD>


<BODY>


    <SCRIPT LANGUAGE="JavaScript" TYPE="Text/JavaScript">
    <!--Start hiding JavaScript statements
        Customer1 = {name:"Robert Robertson", phone:8043334444,
ShowAlert:ShowAlert};

        Customer1.ShowAlert();
    // End hiding JavaScript statements -->
    </SCRIPT>


    </BODY>


</HTML>
```

Deleting Your Object

JavaScript provides a `delete` operator you can use to delete any objects you no longer want. You can add the following line of code to delete the `Customer1` object you've just created:

```
delete Customer1;
```

You can also use the `delete` operator to delete individual object properties or methods without deleting the entire object. For example, to delete the `name` property of the `Customer1` object, type the following:

```
delete Customer1.name;
```

Expanding Object Definitions

You can add additional properties to an object by any of three means:

○ Rewrite the function to accommodate the new object property

○ Use the prototype property to add an additional property to all instances of the object

○ Add a new property to an individual object without affecting other objects

Rewriting the function to accommodate new properties is an obvious option. The *prototype property* can be used to add a new property to all object instances. For example, to add a property named `nickname` to all objects of type `customer`, you can write the following statement:

```
customer.prototype.nickname=null;
```

You can then populate an individual object's `nickname` property using the following statement:

```
Customer1.nickname="Leeman";
```

To add a new property to an individual object without adding the property to other instances of the object, type the name of the object, a period, and then the name of the new property and assign its value as shown in the following example. Here a new property, `zipcode`, has been created for the `Customer1` object and assigned a value of `23116`.

```
Customer1.zipcode = 23116;
```

Handling Events

Until now, most of the JavaScripts you have seen have executed in a top-to-bottom manner. By this, I mean that the browser begins executing your script as soon as the page loads, beginning with the first JavaScript statement and moving on to the succeeding statements until the last statement is processed.

The one exception to this was the use of functions placed in the head section of the page or at the top of the body section and executed by functions calls later in the script. In some cases, the addition of an `if...then` statement or a `switch` statement might have made the execution of a statement or function optional. But even in these cases where multiple logical paths of script execution exist, the script statements execute logically in a serial fashion.

Defining Events

In JavaScript, an event occurs within the confines of the browser. Events include such activities as mouse clicks, mouse movement, pressing keyboard keys, the opening and closing of windows and frames, and the resizing of windows. Browsers recognize events and perform default actions when those events occur. For example, when a user clicks on a link, the `onClick` event occurs, and the browser's default action is to load the Web page or image specified by the link.

To make your Web pages really interactive, you must add another tool to your scripting skill set: event handlers. An *event handler* is a trap that recognizes the occurrence of a particular type of event. You can add code to your scripts that alters the browser's default response to events. For example, instead of automatically loading the URL specified by a link, you could display a confirmation dialog box that asks the user to agree to certain terms before proceeding.

NOTE The names of event handlers are based on the events that trigger them. Placing the word `on` in front of the event name creates the event handler's name. For example the event handler for the `click` event is `onClick`.

Each event is associated with a specific object. When an event occurs for a given object, its event handler executes (assuming that you have written one). For example, the `click` event occurs whenever a user clicks on a button, document, check box, link, radio option, reset button, or submit button.

Event handlers are surprisingly easy to define considering their power. You place them within HTML tags that define the object. For example, you can define an event to occur whenever a Web page is loaded by placing an onLoad event handler inside the first HTML <BODY> tag as shown here:

```
<BODY onLoad="window.alert('Web page loading: Complete.')">
```

In this example, an alert dialog appears when the page finishes loading. Notice that the event handler comes immediately after the tag and that its value is placed within quotation marks. You can use any JavaScript statement as the value for the event handler. You can even use multiple statements, provided that you separate them with semicolons. Alternatively, you can use a function call, which enables you to perform more complex actions in response to the event.

You will see plenty of examples of how and where to place event handlers in various types of HTML tags throughout the rest of this session.

 NOTE See Appendix B, "A Summary of JavaScript Events and Event Handlers," for a complete list of events, event handlers, and objects to which specific events apply.

The event Object

The event object is populated on every occurrence of an event. The information in its properties can be referenced by event handlers, giving your script access to detailed information about the event.

For example, the event.modifiers property specifies any modifier keys that were associated with a mouse or keyboard event. If the user pressed the Alt key while clicking the mouse button, the event.modifiers property contains the value Alt. The event.type modifier contains a string representing the type of event that occurred, and the event.which modifier contains a number that specifies the mouse button that was pressed or the ASCII value of the keyboard key that was pressed.

Types of Events

JavaScript currently supports 24 different events and event handlers. These events can be broadly divided into a few categories:

- ✪ Window and frame events
- ✪ Mouse events
- ✪ Keyboard events
- ✪ Error events

A number of these events and their associated event handlers are demonstrated in the scripts that follow. For a complete list of events and event handlers, see Appendix B.

Window and Frame Events

Events that affect `window` and `frame` objects include the `load`, `resize`, `unload`, and `move` events. The event handlers for these events are `onLoad`, `onResize`, `onUnload`, and `onMove`. These event handlers are placed inside the `<BODY>` tag. The following script uses the `alert()` method to demonstrate how to execute JavaScript statements in response to occurrences of these events:

```
<HTML>

  <HEAD>

    <TITLE>Script 3.13 - onLoad, onResize, onUnload & onMove
Example</TITLE>

  </HEAD>

  <BODY onLoad="window.alert('Web page loading: Complete.')"

    onResize="window.alert('What is the matter with my current
size?')"

    onUnload="window.alert('Oh no, I am melting......')"

  </BODY>

</HTML>
```

The first thing you will see when you run this script is a prompt notifying you that the Web page has finished loading (see Figure 3.17). This message is triggered when the onLoad event handler executes in response to the load event.

If you resize the window, the reload event will cause the onReload event handler to execute and display an alert message. Likewise, resizing the window results in a similar alert message. The unLoad event handler does not execute until you close the window or load it with another URL.

Figure 3.17

Using the onLoad event handler to notify a user that the entire page has completed loading

Mouse Events

Mouse events execute whenever you do something with the mouse. This includes any of the following:

- The MouseOver event occurs when the pointer is moved over an object.
- The MouseOut event occurs when the pointer is moved off an object.
- The MouseDown event occurs when a mouse button is pressed.
- The MouseUp event occurs when a mouse button is released.
- The MouseMove event occurs whenever the mouse is moved.
- The Click event occurs whenever you single-click on an object.
- The DblClick event occurs whenever you double-click on an object.

The following script demonstrates the use of the onMouseOver/onMouseOut and onMouseDown/onMouseUp events. This script defines two links. Clicking on either link instructs the browser to load the Web page at www.microsoft.com. By adding the onMouseOver and onMouseOut event handlers to the first HTML link tag, I instructed the browser to change the document's background to red when the pointer passes over the link. The onMouseOut event handler then changes the background to white when the pointer moves off the link.

The onMouseDown and onMouseUp event handlers associated with the second link instruct the browser to change the document's background to red when the user clicks on the link (that is, when the user presses down on the mouse button) and to change the background color to white when the user releases the mouse button. Neither the onMouseDown nor the onMouseUp event handler alters the default action of the link. Therefore, if you click on the second link, the Web page at www.microsoft.com is still loaded.

```html
<HTML>

  <HEAD>

    <TITLE>Script 3.14 - Mouse Event Handler Example</TITLE>

  </HEAD>

  <BODY>

    <A HREF="http://www.microsoft.com"

      onMouseOver='document.bgColor="red"';

      onMouseOut='document.bgColor="white"';>

      onMouseOver and onMouseOut example</A><P>

    <A HREF="http://www.microsoft.com"

      onMouseDown='document.bgColor="red"';

      onMouseUp='document.bgColor="white"';>

      onMouseDown and onMouseUp example</A><P>

  </BODY>

</HTML>
```

Figure 3.18 shows the appearance of the browser window when the pointer is not positioned over the first link or the second link.

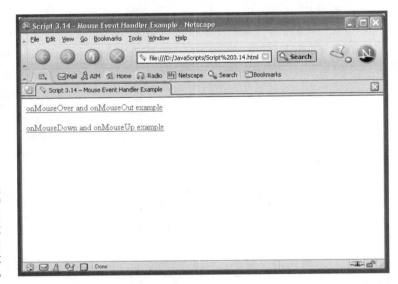

Figure 3.18

Controlling
document
properties using
mouse event
handlers

NOTE One use of the `onMouseOver` and `onMouseOut` event handlers is to create a *rollover effect*, in which a button changes its appearance when the mouse pointer passes over it. You have doubtless seen this effect on many Web sites. I will show you how to create your own button rollover script later this afternoon.

The following script demonstrates the use of the `onClick` and `onDblClick` event handlers. This script creates a form with two buttons. The `onClick` event is assigned to the `<INPUT>` tag of the first button; the `onDblClick` event handler is assigned to the `<INPUT>` tag of the second button.

```
<HTML>

  <HEAD>
    <TITLE>Script 3.15 - onClick & onDblClick Example</TITLE>
  </HEAD>
```

```
<BODY>

  <FORM>

  <INPUT TYPE="button" VALUE="Click on me!"

     onClick="window.alert('You single-clicked.')">

  <INPUT TYPE="button" VALUE="Double-Click on ME"

     onDblClick="window.alert('You double-clicked!')">

  </FORM>

  </BODY>

</HTML>
```

When you load this page and click on one of the buttons, a prompt appears, informing you which button you clicked (see Figure 3.19).

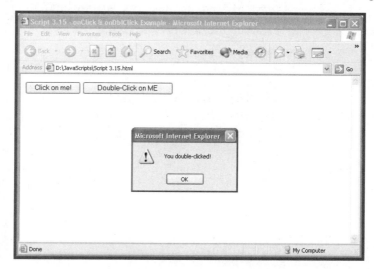

Figure 3.19

Demonstrating onClick and onDblClick event handling

Keyboard Events

Keyboard events are like mouse events in that they occur whenever the user presses or releases a keyboard key. There are three keyboard events: KeyDown, KeyUp, and KeyPress. The following example demonstrates how you can use the onKeyDown event handler to trap keyboard information from Netscape Navigator.

```
<HTML>

  <HEAD>
    <TITLE>Script 3.16 - onKeyDown Example</TITLE>

    <SCRIPT LANGUAGE="JavaScript" TYPE="Text/JavaScript">
    <!-- Start hiding JavaScript statements
      var totalKeyStrokes = 0;
    // End hiding JavaScript statements -->
    </SCRIPT>

    <SCRIPT LANGUAGE="JavaScript" TYPE="Text/JavaScript">
    <!-- Start hiding JavaScript statements
      function CountKeyStrokes() {
        totalKeyStrokes = ++totalKeyStrokes;
      }
    // End hiding JavaScript statements -->
    </SCRIPT>


  </HEAD>

  <BODY>

    <P>Type a few characters and then click on the
button:</P>

    <FORM>
      <TEXTAREA ROWS="4" COLS="70"
onKeyDown="CountKeyStrokes()"></TEXTAREA>
        <P></P>
```

```
    <INPUT TYPE="button" VALUE="Count Keystrokes" +
        onClick="window.alert('Total # of keystrokes = ' +
totalKeyStrokes)">

    </FORM>


    </BODY>


</HTML>
```

The script defines a simple form that consists of two elements: a TEXTAREA field and a button. The onKeyDown event handler is used to keep track of the total number of keystrokes typed by the user in the TEXTAREA field. The onKeyDown event is set to trigger each time the user types a new keystroke. It calls the CountKeyStrokes() function, which adds 1 to a variable called totalKeyStrokes. This variable stores a running total of the current number of keystrokes made by the user. When the user clicks on the form's button, a pop-up dialog is displayed that shows the total number of keystrokes entered so far by the user.

NOTE The event object's event.which property specifies the ASCII value of the key pressed or the ASCII value of the mouse button that was clicked.

Figure 3.20 demonstrates what happens when you run the script, enter a few words in the TEXTAREA field, and then click on the form's button.

Error Events

An error event occurs whenever your JavaScripts run into an error. Error events automatically trigger the onerror event. By adding an onerror event handler to your scripts, you can intercept these errors and suppress them. After they are suppressed, you then can either attempt to fix them programmatically or display a customized error message.

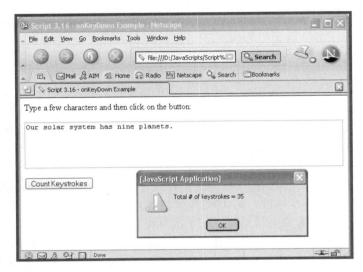

Figure 3.20

Using the
onKeyDown
event handler to
count keystrokes

NOTE Unlike other event handlers, the onerror event handler is spelled in all lowercase.

The onerror event handler automatically receives three arguments when
it is triggered: the error message itself, the URL of the Web page, and the
line number in the script where the error occurred. You can use the
onerror event handler to respond to the error. For example, you can
display an alert prompt, redirect the user to another Web page, call a
function, advise the user to upgrade the browser or get a specific plug-in,
and so on.

The onerror event handler works a little differently than other event
handlers and has the following syntax.

```
window.onerror=FunctionName
```

Note that the spelling of the onerror event handler is in all lowercase and
that it is not embedded within HTML tags like other event handlers.
Instead, it is defined within the <SCRIPT> </SCRIPT> tags as a JavaScript
statement. When triggered, the onerror event handler calls a function.

However, the matching pair of parentheses are left off of the end of the function call. When used, the `onerror` event handler is set up in the head section of the HTML page, along with its associated function.

The following script demonstrates how to use the `onerror` event handler to display error information using a function called `ErrorTrap()`. This function accepts three arguments that map to the three arguments passed to the `onerror` event handler. The function uses these arguments to format three lines of text that present the error information. To produce an error on the page, I deliberately added an s to the end of the word `window` in the HTML page's body tag. `windows` is a not a valid browser object.

```
<HTML>

  <HEAD>
    <TITLE>Script 3.17 - onError Example</TITLE>


    <SCRIPT LANGUAGE="JavaScript" TYPE="Text/JavaScript">
    <!--Start hiding JavaScript statements


      function ErrorTrap(msg,url,line_no) {

        document.write("<P>An error has occurred in this
script.</P>");

        document.write("Error = " + msg + " on line " +
line_no + "<BR>");

        document.write("URL = " + url + "<BR>");

        return true;

      }



      onerror=ErrorTrap;


    // End hiding JavaScript statements -->
    </SCRIPT>
```

```
        </HEAD>

        <BODY onLoad="windows.alert('Hi')">

          Welcome to my Web page.

        </BODY>


        </HTML>
```

NOTE

Note the `return true;` statement at the end of the `ErrorTrap` function in the previous example. This statement tells the browser to suppress the error.

Figure 3.21 shows the results of loading this script using Internet Explorer. As you can see, the message written to the window tells you what the error was, where in the Web page the error occurred, and where the page is located.

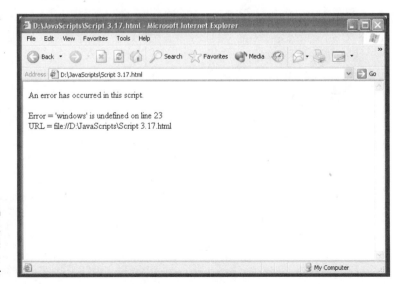

Figure 3.21

Trapping errors with the `onerror` event handler

The onerror event hander can also be used within HTML tags. By placing the onerror event handler within a particular HTML tag, you can define different actions for error events on an object-by-object basis. For example, the following JavaScript uses this technique to create an error message in the event that the specified graphic file cannot be found.

```
<HTML>


  <HEAD>

    <TITLE>Script 3.18 - Another onError Example</TITLE>

  </HEAD>


  <BODY>

    <IMG NAME="xxxx" SRC="xxxx.jpg"
onError="window.alert('Unable to load image!')">

  </BODY>


</HTML>
```

Figure 3.22 shows the results of loading the previous script. An alert prompt is immediately displayed when the browser fails to locate the specified xxxx.jpg image file.

Using the onClick Event as a Decision Point

Before wrapping up the first half of this afternoon, I want to show you a neat little trick using links and the onClick event handler. In the example that follows, I defined a link to a Web site to which I added the onClick event. Inside the event handler, I used the window.confirm() method to ask the user for confirmation before enabling the browser to load the link. The window.confirm() prompt gives the user two options. Clicking on OK returns a value of true, which enables the browser to load the Web page; clicking on Cancel returns a value of false, which prevents the browser from loading the specified URL.

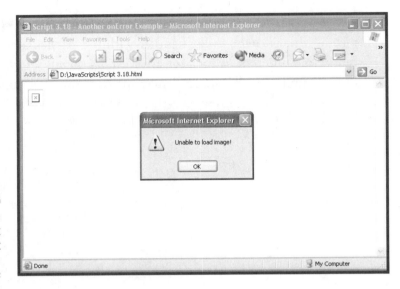

Figure 3.22

Using the
onerror event
handler to report
problems when
loading an image

```
<HTML>

  <HEAD>

    <TITLE>Script 3.19 - Age Verification Example</TITLE>

  </HEAD>


  <BODY>

    <A HREF="http://www.ptpmagazine.com"

      onClick="return(window.confirm('You must be older than
30 to visit ' +

      'this site. Are you?'))";> ptpmagazine.com</A>

  </BODY>


</HTML>
```

TIP

You can use a variation of this example to ask users whether they are sure they want to
leave your Web site when they click on links.

Figure 3.23 shows what happens if you load the preceding page.

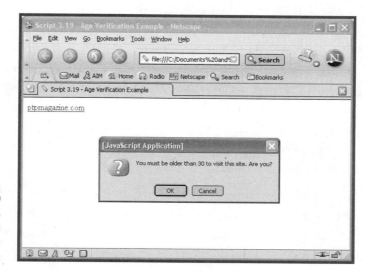

Figure 3.23

Verifying a user's age before allowing him into your Web site

Take a Break

Okay, let's take a break. Maybe you should take a walk to stretch out or turn on the TV for a while to catch up on the news. When you return, we'll take at look at how to use JavaScript to control HTML frames and forms. You will learn how to control frames and display content in them. You will also learn how to validate form contents in order to ensure that visitors to your Web sites provide you with the information that you require on your forms.

Using JavaScript to Manage Frames

So far, every HTML page that I have shown you has been based on the `window` object. In other words, all the Web pages you have worked with have the `window` object at the top of the page's object hierarchy. In addition, every HTML page so far has contained a head and a body section. You have embedded JavaScripts in both of these sections.

Modern browsers provide an alternative approach to organizing and presenting data within the browser. Using *frames*, HTML pages can divide a window into multiple smaller windows, each of which is its own entity with its own URL. In fact, as far as JavaScript is concerned, a frame is simply a variation of the `window` object. So even though there is a JavaScript `frame` object, this object is really just a convenient way of referring to a specialized `window` object. Because a frame is a `window` object, `frame` objects support the same methods and properties that `window` objects do. When you use frames, you will have one `frame` object for every frame defined on the page.

Frames are created using the HTML `<FRAMESET>` and `<FRAME>` tags. The `<FRAMESET>` tag replaces the body section in an HTML page. This tag defines how your frames will be laid out and how space is allocated to each frame.

A Typical Frames Example

In its simplest form, an example using frames involves three different HTML pages. The first page contains the `<FRAMESET>` and `<FRAME>` tags and defines the layout in which the other pages will be displayed. These pages provide the content that is loaded into the frames; each of these pages is composed of HTML and JavaScript statements.

The following example can be used to create a HTML page using frames. This HTML page contains two `<FRAME>` tags inside a single `<FRAMESET>` tag. The `<FRAMESET>` tag defines two frames using the `COLS="*,*"` attribute, which instructs the browser to assign all available space to the frames. The first frame is named `left` and loads the specified page. Because the frameset used the `COLS` attribute to define two column frames, the first frame is the left column. The second frame is named `right` and is assigned a different page to load.

```
<HTML>

    <HEAD>
```

```
     <TITLE>Script 3.20 - Building your first frame </TITLE>
   </HEAD>


<FRAMESET COLS="*,*">
   <FRAME SRC="Script3.21b.html" NAME="left">
   <FRAME SRC="Script3.21c.html" NAME="right">
</FRAMESET>


</HTML>
```

Creating Frame Content Using JavaScript

You can use JavaScript to control frames and frame content. JavaScript provides you with the capability to control more than one frame at a time. This is something that cannot be accomplished with HTML.

Before you can take advantage of JavaScript's capability to control frames, you must first understand something about how the browsers build a frame hierarchy into your Web pages. Every frame belongs to a frameset that can be referred to as the frame's parent or top. Each frame in the frameset is listed in an array named frames[], based on the order in which the page is loaded. The first frame in the array is frames[0], the second is frames[1], and so on.

For example, the following page defines a simple two-frame display:

```
<HTML>


  <HEAD>
    <TITLE>Script 3.23 - Using JavaScript to add dynamic
content to frames</TITLE>
  </HEAD>


  <FRAMESET COLS="*,*">
```

```
    <FRAME SRC="Script 3.24.html" NAME="left">
    <FRAME SRC="Script 3.25.html" NAME="right">
  </FRAMESET>


</HTML>
```

The top or parent frameset is at the top of the hierarchy, and each frame in the frameset is listed in the order in which it is defined. Now that you understand how the browser creates this frame hierarchy, you can use JavaScript to reference and control frames. For example, parent.frames[0] and top.frames[0] both refer to the first frame; parent.frames[1] and top.frames[1] reference the second frame.

As you may have noticed, an array is automatically created that contains an entry for each frame on the Web page, beginning with an index of 0 based on the order in which the frames are defined.

NOTE   If you add the NAME="" attribute to the <FRAME> tag, you can also refer to individual frames by their assigned names. In the preceding example, which names the frames left and right, you could reference the first frame in the hierarchy as either parent.left or top.left.

One of the benefits of using JavaScript with frames is that you can provide dynamic content on a frame. In other words, you can write directly to a frame instead of loading a Web page into it. The following example demonstrates this technique.

The previous example showed a Web page that defined two frames. The following example shows the HTML page that is loaded into the left frame.

```
<HTML>


  <HEAD>
    <TITLE>Script 3.24 - Writing dynamic content</TITLE>
```

```
    </HEAD>

    <BODY>
      <FORM>
        <INPUT TYPE="button" NAME="button1" VALUE="Click Me"
          OnClick="top.right.document.write('<H3>Hello
world!</H3>')">
      </FORM>
    </BODY>

  </HTML>
```

This HTML page defines a form containing a button that, when clicked, executes the JavaScript statement `top.right.document.write('Hello world!')` and, as a result, displays the message `Hello world!` in the `right` frame. You might remember that the `top` or `parent` reference represents the top of the frame hierarchy. The `top.right` call refers to the frame named `right` in the same frameset as the `left` frame (its "sibling" frame, and the frame that contains the `top.right` statement). Had you left the `top.right` reference off the `document.write()` statement, the message would have been written in the `left` frame.

The following page shows you the HTML page that is loaded initially into the Web page's `right` frame.

```
<HTML>

  <HEAD>
    <TITLE>Script 3.25 - The initial content displayed in the
right frame</TITLE>
  </HEAD>

  <BODY>
    <H3>This is the right frame.</H3>
```

```
</BODY>
```

```
</HTML>
```

Figure 3.24 shows how things look after you load the first HTML page and click on the Click Me button.

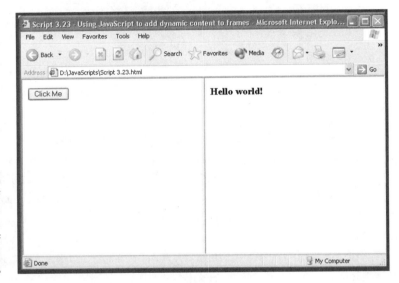

Figure 3.24

An example of using JavaScript to post messages onto frames instead of unloading and loading new pages

Controlling Frames with JavaScript

You already know that you can load Web pages into target frames using the HTML link tag as shown here:

```
<A HREF="link1.html" TARGET="right">Sample Link 1</A>
```

Alternatively, you can use JavaScript to load pages into your frames. Because of JavaScript's programming logic, you can exercise greater control over how and when the frames are unloaded and loaded. The following example shows how you can replace your HTML links with JavaScript to manage your frames. The example consists of four pages.

The first page contains the <FRAMESET> and <FRAME> tags and defines the overall structure of the Web site. In this case, two frames are defined and named left and right; both are assigned 50 percent of the available display area in the browser.

```
<HTML>


  <HEAD>

    <TITLE> Script 3.26- Controlling frames with
JavaScript</TITLE>

  </HEAD>


  <FRAMESET COLS="*,*">

    <FRAME SRC="Script 3.27.html" NAME="left">

    <FRAME SRC="Script 3.28.html" NAME="right">

  </FRAMESET>


</HTML>
```

The left frame contains a form that defines a button named button1 that displays the text Click Me. When clicked, the button's onClick event handler is executed. Using the browser hierarchy, the JavaScript statement in the event handler first references the top (or parent) of the hierarchy. Next, the statement specifies the frame in which the new page will be loaded. Instead of referencing the frame as parent.right, the frame is identified using its location in the frames[] array. Because the target frame is the second frame that was defined and the frames[] array starts with an index value of 0, parent.frames[1] is used to reference the second frame. Next, the location property is added. Finally, the HTML page that is to be loaded is specified.

```
<HTML>


  <HEAD>
```

```
<TITLE> Script 3.27- Adding the JavaScript control</TITLE>
  </HEAD>

  <BODY>
    <FORM>
      <INPUT TYPE="button" NAME="button1" VALUE="Click Me"
        onClick="parent.frames[1].location='Script
3.29.html'">
    </FORM>
  </BODY>

</HTML>
```

The page that is initially loaded into the `right` frame is very straightforward and is shown below.

```
<HTML>
  <HEAD>
    <TITLE> Script 3.28 - Initial content loaded into the
right frame </TITLE>
  </HEAD>
  <BODY>
    <H3>This is the right frame.</H3>
  </BODY>
</HTML>
```

The page that will be loaded into the `right` frame when the button is clicked is equally straightforward, containing a single message formatted as an HTML heading as shown below.

```
<HTML>

  <HEAD>
    <TITLE> Script 3.29 - The new page</TITLE>
```

```
</HEAD>

<BODY>

  <H3>This is the new frame you just loaded!</H3>
</BODY>

</HTML>
```

Figure 3.25 shows the result of loading this example and clicking on the Click Me button. In the next example, I will show you how to use JavaScript to do something that HTML alone cannot do: controlling more than one frame at a time.

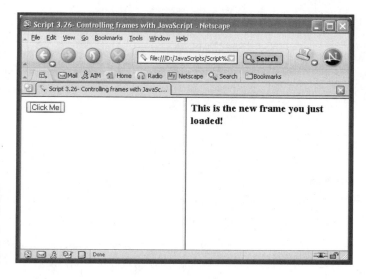

Figure 3.25

An example of loading pages under the control of JavaScript

Controlling More than One Frame at a Time

The next example shows how easy it is to use JavaScript to control more than one frame at a time. In this example, I have modified the form in the left frame from the previous example. As you can see, the onClick event handler now specifies a second JavaScript statement. I was able to add the second statement to the event handler by placing a semicolon at the end of the first statement. Had I wanted to add yet another statement to the event handler, I probably would have elected to create a function, placed all the statements within the function brackets, and then called the function from within the onClick event handler.

```
<HTML>


  <HEAD>
    <TITLE> Script 3.27a- Controlling more than one frame at
a time with JavaScript</TITLE>
  </HEAD>


  <BODY>
    <FORM>
      <INPUT TYPE="button" NAME="button1" VALUE="Click Me"
        onClick="parent.frames[0].location='Script3.30.html';
          parent.frames[1].location='Script3.29.html'">
    </FORM>
  </BODY>


</HTML>
```

The structure of the second statement is the same as that of the first statement except that it references a different frame (the parent.frame[1] frame or the right frame).

Displaying Other Web Sites Using Frames

Many people like to add links to other Web sites on their HTML pages. One of the disadvantages of providing your visitors with links to other Web sites is that they may follow them and never come back to your site. However, if you use frames, you can provide links to other Web pages without actually sending your visitors away. All that you have to do it load the other Web site into a frame located on your HTML page. In addition to keeping your visitors at your site and providing a very slick interface, you can give even a small Web site the appearance of being a huge megasite by doing nothing more than loading other URLs into your frames.

The following example creates a Web site using frames. The frame on the left provides a navigation menu; the frame on the top right displays your Web site's title or other useful information. The remaining frame is used to display the URLs of other Web sites.

The first page defines the layout of the frames. In this case, a <FRAMESET> tag divides the display into two columns, assigning 15 percent of the space to the first column and the remaining 85 percent to the second column. Next, a <FRAME> tag specifies the page that will serve as the navigation index. A second nested <FRAMESET> tag divides the space allocated to the second column into two rows and assigns 8 percent to the first row and the remaining 92 percent to the second row. Two frames are then defined. The first loads a local Web page into the small top frame, and the second loads the URL for a popular Internet search engine, www.yahoo.com, into the larger frame.

```
<HTML>


  <HEAD>

    <TITLE> Script 3.31- Loading other URLs into your
frames</TITLE>

  </HEAD>


  <FRAMESET COLS="15%,85%">

    <FRAME SRC="Script 3.32.html" NAME="left"
SCROLLING="auto">

    <FRAMESET ROWS="8%,92%">

      <FRAME SRC="Script 3.33.html" NAME="right1"
SCROLLING="auto">

      <FRAME SRC="http://www.yahoo.com" NAME="right2"
SCROLLING="auto">
```

```
      </FRAMESET>

    </FRAMESET>


</HTML>
```

The navigation page loaded into the left frame defines several links to other popular Internet search engines. In this case, since the links to these URLs are all loaded into the same frame, I chose to use HTML link tags with the target attribute:

```
<HTML>


  <HEAD>

    <TITLE> Script 3.32- Using the left frame as a navigation
page</TITLE>

    </HEAD>


  <BODY>

    <P><B>Search Engines:</B></P>

      <A HREF="http://www.excite.com"
TARGET="right2">Excite</A><BR>

      <A HREF="http://www.alta-vista.com"
TARGET="right2">AltaVista</A><BR>

      <A HREF="http://www.yahoo.com"
TARGET="right2">Yahoo</A><BR>

    </BODY>


</HTML>
```

The page shown below is loaded into the top frame and is used to display the name of the Web site; this frame helps to give a polished look and feel to the Web site.

```
<HTML>
```

```
<HEAD>

    <TITLE> Script 3.33- Adding a title frame to your Web
site</TITLE>

    </HEAD>


<BODY>

    <CENTER>

    <H2>Welcome to my Internet Search Engine Web Site.</H2>

    </CENTER>

    </BODY>


</HTML>
```

Figure 3.26 shows what the initial display looks like when you first load this example. As you can see, by using frames and three simple scripts, you can create a Web site that provides users with access to a collection of popular URLs.

Figure 3.26

Using JavaScript to control multiple frames simultaneously

NOTE

There are lots of ways to make money on the Internet. One way is to join associate programs with various Internet companies. In these programs, you get paid for every customer you lead to their Web site who then makes a purchase. For example, using a modified version of the previous example, you could easily create your own online bookstore with several pages that highlight books you think will attract customers; then you provide links to other online bookstores whose affiliate programs you have joined. Visitors to your site can purchase books or anything else that the other online company sells. In fact, tomorrow morning, I'll demonstrate how to build such a bookstore.

Frames—No Thank You

Although you might appreciate how easy it is to load other URLs into your frames, you may not want to have your own Web pages show up in other people's frames, especially if your pages are loaded into frames that are too small, making your site look bad. That's where this next example comes in handy. It shows you how to prevent other people from loading your Web pages into their frames, using just a couple lines of JavaScript.

```
<HTML>

  <HEAD>

    <TITLE>Script 3.34 - Blocking frames from loading your
Web page</TITLE>

    <SCRIPT LANGUAGE="JavaScript" TYPE="Text/JavaScript">

    <!-- Start hiding JavaScript statements

      if (top.frames.length!=0) {

        top.location=self.document.location;

      }

    // End hiding JavaScript statements -->

    </SCRIPT>

  </HEAD>
```

```
<BODY>

  <CENTER>

    <H1>Welcome to my page!</H1><BR>

    <H3>Thanks for visiting!!!</H3>

  </CENTER>

</BODY>


</HTML>
```

I placed the script inside the head section of the page so that it would execute as soon as possible. The first line in the script is an `if` statement that checks to see whether somebody is trying to load the page into a frame by checking the value of `top.frames.length`. If the condition is 0 or `true`, then the statement `top.location=self.document.location` tells the browser to set the page's `location` property to itself, thus preventing it from being loaded into a frame.

Anyone who tries to load this Web page into his frame will be surprised to see that your page not only is not loaded, but also that it has completely replaced his own Web page.

Using JavaScript to Manage Forms

Within the context of an HTML page, a form is created using the `<FORM>` tags. Within the `<FORM>` tags, individual form elements such as check boxes or text fields are defined.

You can use the power of forms on your Web pages without using JavaScript. However, JavaScript provides powerful validation capabilities and enables you to interact with visitors as they fill out the forms.

The form Object

The browser creates a `form` object for every form element defined by `<FORM>` tags. You can assign a name to each element using the optional

NAME="" attribute for each element, or you can use the forms[] array, which contains an index listing of every form element on the page, beginning with an index of 0. In addition, each form contains its own elements[] array that contains an entry for each form element on that particular form. For example, the fourth form element on a form called myForm can be referenced as myForm.elements[3].

Form Properties and Methods

The form object has a number of properties, many of which are objects in their own right. You can use these properties, listed below, to access and manipulate form contents.

- **action**. Created based on the <FORM> tag's ACTION attribute.
- **button**. An object that users can click to initiate an action.
- **checkbox**. An object that enables users to select or clear an option by clicking on it.
- **elements[]**. An array of all the form elements.
- **encoding**. Created based on the <FORM> tag's ENCTYPE attribute.
- **fileUpload**. An object used to specify a file that can be included as form data.
- **hidden**. An object that does not appear on the form but that you can programmatically fill with data.
- **length**. A property that specifies the number of elements in the forms[] array.
- **method**. Created based on the <FORM> tag's METHOD attribute.
- **name**. Created based on the <FORM> tag's NAME attribute.
- **password**. An object that masks any text that is typed into it.
- **radio**. An object that is organized into a collection of similar objects, only one of which can be selected.
- **reset**. A button object that enables you to clear and reset a form to its default values.
- **select**. An object that provides a list of selectable options.

- **submit**. A button object that enables you to submit the form for processing.
- **target**. Created based on the <FORM> tag's TARGET attribute.
- **text**. An object used to hold a single line of text.
- **textarea**. An object similar to the text object except that it accepts multiple lines of text.

The form object also has several methods that can be applied to it:

- **handleEvent()**. Enables you to simulate a specific event on the specified object such as click or dblclick events.
- **reset()**. Enables you to clear and reset a form to its default values programmatically.
- **submit()**. Enables you to submit a form programmatically for processing.

NOTE Of the three form methods, only the form handleEvent() method enables you to pass it an argument. For example, handleEvent(click).

Form Events

In addition to event handlers supplied by individual form elements, the form object provides the following two event handlers:

- The onReset event handler enables you to execute JavaScript statements or call a function before the form is reset.
- The onSubmit event handler enables you to execute JavaScript statements or call a function before the form is submitted.

These event handlers enable you to execute commands or call subroutines before performing the reset or submit actions requested by the visitor. As the examples that follow will demonstrate, this provides you with the opportunity to create warning messages that inform the visitor of the consequences of his actions or to validate form contents and assist the visitor in properly filling out the form, while at the same time making sure only valid data is provided.

The following list identifies which events are associated with each form element and can be used as a reference to see what events each form element enables you to use when you are developing your forms:

Event	Form Elements Affected
Click	button, checkbox, radio, reset, submit
Blur	button, checkbox, fileUpload, password, radio, reset, select, submit, text, textarea
Focus	button, checkbox, fileUpload, password, radio, reset, select, submit, text, textarea
Select	fileUpload, password, text, textarea

In the next section, I'll show you how to take advantage of event handlers so that you can trigger validation of user input on your forms.

Other form Related Methods

Most form elements provide a number of methods you can use to work with the elements programmatically. These methods enable you to invoke events without depending on the visitor. For example, you might create a form that includes several text fields and a reset button. In the event that the user decides to click on the reset button and start filling out the form all over again, you could add the focus() method to the reset button's onClick event and assist the visitor by placing the cursor back in the first text field. A list of methods supported by form elements includes:

- ✿ The click() method has the same affect as though the user clicked on the object.
- ✿ The blur() method moves the focus away from the object.
- ✿ The focus() method places the focus on the object.

○ The select() method highlights the text in the form elements that contain text.

Form Validation

The real benefit of using JavaScript with your forms is to validate visitor input. Form validation enables you to ensure that the visitor has filled in all required fields and that valid data has been entered in those fields. When the visitor makes a mistake, you can display alert messages explaining the error and ask the visitor to correct the problem before submitting the form again.

The following example creates a form for a bicycle shop that enables Internet customers to place online orders for new bikes. Customers are given a list of options to choose from and are asked to specify what method of payment they plan to use when they pick up their new bikes.

First, I will show the full example, and then I will break it down and explain it piece by piece:

```
<HTML>

  <HEAD>
    <TITLE>Script 3.35- A form validation example</TITLE>

    <SCRIPT LANGUAGE="JavaScript" TYPE="Text/JavaScript">
    <!-- Start hiding JavaScript statements
      function ValidateOrder() {
        if (document.myForm.firstName.value.length < 1) {
          window.alert("Missing First name! Please correct");
          return;
        }
        if (document.myForm.lastName.value.length < 1) {
          window.alert("Missing Last name! Please correct");
```

```
      return;
   }
   if (document.myForm.address.value.length < 1) {
      window.alert("Missing Address! Please correct");
      return;
   }
   option_selected = "no";
   for (i=0; i < document.myForm.radio_option1.length; i++) {
      if (document.myForm.radio_option1[i].checked) {
         option_selected = "yes";
      }
   }
   if (option_selected == "no") {
      window.alert("Please specify a bike model!");
      return;
   }
   window.alert("Your order looks good. Click on Submit!");
 }
// End hiding JavaScript statements -->
</SCRIPT>


</HEAD>


<BODY>
  <CENTER>
     <H2>Welcome to Jerry's Custom Bike Shop</H2>
     <H5>Payment due at pickup</H5>
  </CENTER>
  <FORM NAME="myForm" METHOD="post" ACTION="cgi-bin/myscript">
     <B>First name:</B> <INPUT NAME="firstName" TYPE="text"
SIZE="15"
```

```
            MAXLENGTH="20"><BR>

      <B>Last name:</B> <INPUT NAME="lastName" TYPE="text"
SIZE="15"

            MAXLENGTH="20">

      <P><B>Mailing Address:</B> <INPUT NAME="address"
TYPE="text"

            SIZE="30" MAXLENGTH="50"></P>

      <P><B>Select the bike you wish to order:</B></P>

      10 Speed Deluxe: <INPUT NAME="radio_option1"
TYPE="radio"

            VALUE="10Speed"><BR>

      15 Speed Racer: <INPUT NAME="radio_option1"
TYPE="radio"

            VALUE=15Speed"><BR>

      <P><B>Additional Comments: (Optional)</B></P>

      <TEXTAREA NAME="myTextarea" TYPE="textarea" ROWS="4"

         COLS="40"></TEXTAREA>

      <P><B>Please specify method of payment:</B>

      <SELECT NAME="myList">

         <OPTION SELECTED VALUE="check">Personal Check

         <OPTION VALUE="creditCard">Credit Card

         <OPTION VALUE="moneyOrder">Money Order

      </SELECT></P>

      <INPUT TYPE="reset" VALUE="Reset Form">

      <INPUT TYPE="submit" VALUE="Submit Order"
onClick="window.alert('Your' +

         ' bike will be ready in 5 days')">

      <INPUT TYPE="button" VALUE=Validate Order"
onClick="ValidateOrder()">

    </FORM>

  </BODY>


</HTML>
```

Start out by examining the contents of the body section of the page. This section begins with two headers and defines the form that will use the `post` method to send the form's contents to a CGI program named `myscript`. Because the CGI `ACTION` attribute does not specify a URL or path, you know that the program must reside in the same location as the example page.

```
<FORM NAME="myForm" METHOD="post" ACTION="cgi-bin/myscript">
```

NOTE *CGI* stands for *Common Gateway Interface.* CGI is not a programming language. It is a specification that is used by languages such as PERL to run programs on Web servers. In this example it is assumed that the client-side JavaScript is supposed to pass the form's contents off to a Web server for further processing.

TIP You do not have to have access to the CGI or server-side scripts and programs on a Web server to be able to collect the contents of forms that visitors to your Web site fill out. You can always use e-mail to retrieve the contents of your forms. The trick to making this work is to modify the `<FORM>` tag as shown here:

```
<FORM NAME="myForm" ACTION="mailto:jlf04@yahoo.com" ENCTYPE="text/plain">
```

The `ACTION="mailto:jlf04@yahoo.com"` attribute setting tells the browser to submit the form's contents in an e-mail message to the e-mail address specified by the `mailto:` setting. The `ENCTYPE="text/plain"` attribute sends the text in a plain non-encoded format.

The browser will always require confirmation from the visitor before it will attempt to submit the form's contents in an e-mail message. Once confirmed, the contents of the form are sent to the specified e-mail account as the body of the e-mail message.

Next, three `text` fields are defined in order to collect the visitor's first name, last name, and address information. The two name fields are 15 characters wide, and each can collect up to 20 characters of information. The address field is 30 characters long and can contain up to 50 characters.

```
<INPUT NAME="firstName" TYPE="text" SIZE="15" MAXLENGTH="20">
<INPUT NAME="lastName" TYPE="text" SIZE="15" MAXLENGTH="20">
<INPUT NAME="address" TYPE="text" SIZE="30" MAXLENGTH="50">
```

A pair of radio buttons is then defined and grouped using the group name radio_option1.

```
<INPUT NAME="radio_option1" TYPE="radio" VALUE="10Speed">
<INPUT NAME="radio_option1" TYPE="radio" VALUE=15Speed">
```

The next form element is a textarea. It can contain up to 160 characters of additional information regarding the bicycle order:

```
<TEXTAREA NAME="myTextarea" TYPE="textarea" ROWS="4"
COLS="40"></TEXTAREA>
```

A drop-down list named myList defines three options for payment.

```
<SELECT NAME="myList">
   <OPTION SELECTED VALUE="check">Personal Check
   <OPTION VALUE="creditCard">Credit Card
   <OPTION VALUE="moneyOrder">Money Order
</SELECT>
```

The final form elements are three buttons. The first button is a reset button that clears the form and restores all its default settings. The second button is a submit button. Before submitting the form for processing, the submit button's onClick event handler displays an alert message telling the customer that the selected bike will be ready for pick up in five days. The form is submitted when the customer clicks on OK. The last button enables the customer to validate the order before submitting it. When clicked, this button calls the function ValidateOrder().

```
<INPUT TYPE="reset" VALUE="Reset Form">

<INPUT TYPE="submit" VALUE="Submit Order"
onClick="window.alert('Your bike will be

   ready in 5 days')">

<INPUT TYPE="button" VALUE=Validate Order"
onClick="ValidateOrder()">
```

The `ValidateOrder()` function consists of a series of `if` statements that check the value of specific form elements to ensure that they have been properly completed.

The first `if` statement checks the value of the `length` property for the form's `firstName` text field. If this field contains no character information, an alert pop-up dialog box appears, instructing the user to fill in that field. The `return` statement that follows the `alert()` statement prevents further processing of the `ValidateOrder()` function.

```
if (document.myForm.firstName.value.length < 1) {

   window.alert("Missing First name! Please correct");

   return;

}
```

The next section of the `ValidateOrder()` function checks to see whether one of the `radio` options has been selected to specify the kind of bike being ordered. You might have noticed that when the form defined the `radio` elements, it did not set one of them as the default answer; it is possible that the customer might forget to select one of these two options. To check all the `radio` elements on the form, a `for` loop is set up that loops through all `radio` elements beginning at 0 and incrementing by 1 until all the `radio` options have been processed. The `length` property of the `radio_option1` object specifies the total number of radio buttons that are a part of the group and provides this upper limit.

For each iteration of the loop, an `if` statement checks each radio button to see whether its CHECKED property has been set; if it has, a variable named `option_selected` is set equal to `yes`. Otherwise, this variable remains set equal to no. After every radio element has been examined, another if statement checks to see whether the value of option_selected was ever set to yes; if this is not the case, an alert pop-up dialog box appears, instructing the user to pick one of the radio options. This if statement also ends with a return statement that prevents further processing of the ValidateOrder() function.

```
option_selected = "no"

for (i=0; i < document.myForm.radio_option1.length; i++) {

  if (document.myForm.radio_option1[i].checked) {

    option_selected = "yes";

  }

}

if (option_selected == "no") {

  window.alert("You must select the bike model that you wish
to order! Please correct");

  return;

}
```

The final statement in the ValidateOrder() function is executed only if all of the function's preceding validation logic finds that the form has been correctly filled in. This last statement displays a pop-up dialog box informing the customer that the order is ready for processing.

```
alert("Your order looks good. Click on Submit!")
```

Figure 3.27 shows what the form looks like when you load the page.

Of course, depending on the customer to initiate the validation of his order might not be the best course of action. Instead, you probably want to execute the ValidateOrder() function automatically when the user clicks on the submit button. You can accomplish this by modifying the <FORM> to include a call to ValidateOrder() using the onSubmit event handler:

```
<FORM NAME="myForm" METHOD="post" ACTION="cgi-bin/myscript"

  onSubmit="return ValidateOrder();">
```

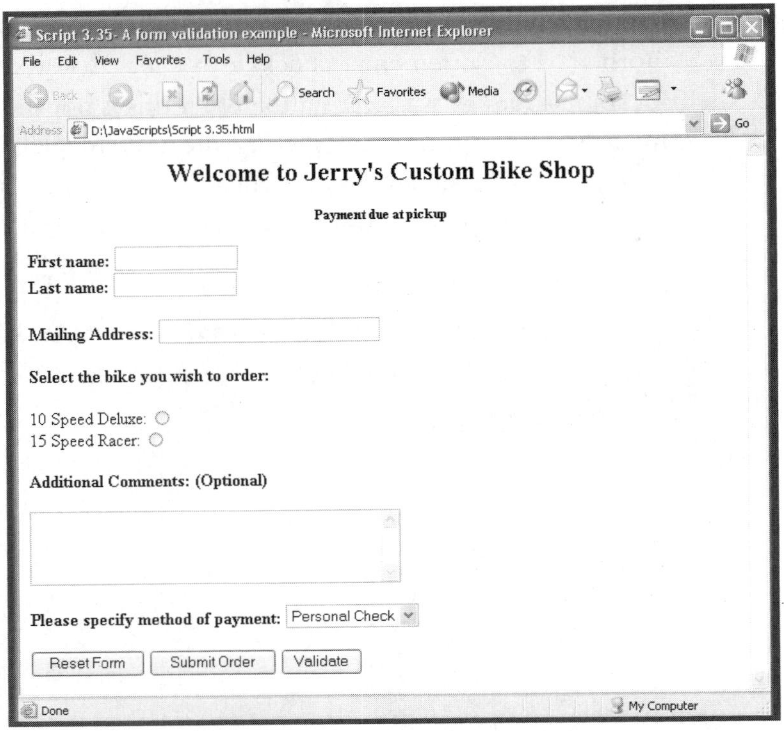

Figure 3.27

An example of validating the contents of a form before allowing it to be submitted for processing

For this validation technique to work, you also must modify the return statement on all the `if` statements in the function to say `return false`, as shown in the following example. This modification not only stops the processing of the `ValidateOrder()` function as soon as a validation error is discovered, but also prevents the `submit` event from executing.

```
if (document.myForm.firstName.value.length < 1) {
  window.alert("Missing First name! Please correct");
  return false;
}
```

Another validation technique you might want to consider is to validate each form element as the customer completes it. To use this technique, you must understand the concepts of *focus* and *blur*. When a cursor has been placed in a text field, that field is said to have the document's focus.

Any keystroke that is typed is sent to that field. If you then move the cursor to a different location in the form, the text field loses focus, a situation known as *blur*. Selecting a form element executes its focus event, and moving the focus to another form element executes the blur event for the form object that has lost focus.

In the following example, the `onBlur` even handler has been added to an `<INPUT>` tag that defines a `text` object. The `ValidateOrder()` function executes after the customer selects the `text` field and then changes the form's focus to another object. Of course, if the customer forgets to fill in this field and never selects it, this validation technique will not help.

```
<INPUT NAME="firstName" TYPE="text" SIZE="15" MAXLENGTH="20"
VALUE=""

    onBlur="ValidateOrder()">
```

TIP One validation technique you can use to make things as easy as possible for your users is to add a statement that places the focus on the form object that has not been properly completed. For example, you might modify the `if` statement that validates the customer's first name as shown here:

```
if (document.myForm.firstName.value.length < 1) {

  window.alert("Missing First name! Please correct");

  document.myForm.firstName.focus();

}
```

What's Next?

Okay, time for another break. Why don't you go get a little dinner before you start this evening's chapter. When you return, I'll show you how to use JavaScript to take control of the browser's status bar. You will also learn how to control browser navigation and interact with visitors using pop-up dialogs. While you are at it, you will find out how to create graphical effects using JavaScript. Finally, you will look at how to spruce things up by adding graphic animation.

Doing Really Cool Things with Your Web Pages

- ➤ Adding message content to the browser status bar
- ➤ Using JavaScript to enhance navigation
- ➤ Using the power of dialog boxes
- ➤ Detecting and working with different types of browsers
- ➤ Working with graphics and animation

Now that you have had a break, I hope you are ready to jump back into things. You have spent all day learning the basics about JavaScript statements, programming logic, syntax, and so on. Starting tonight, you are going to get the chance to start having fun and put all this practical knowledge to use.

This evening, you will see example after example of how to apply JavaScript to your Web pages. The emphasis will be on applying what you know to create scripts that are really useful. After all, that's why you started reading this book. Of course, I will have tidbits of new information for you to digest along the way, but the emphasis this evening is more on doing than on learning.

Controlling the Status Bar

One of the simplest and most powerful tricks you can do with JavaScript is to take control of the browser's status bar. You can do this using the `window` object's `status` property. In the next four sections, I will show you examples that include how to post a message to the status bar, how to post a blinking message, how to post a message and have it scroll over and over again, and finally how to use the status bar as a tool for displaying link descriptions.

TIP

Don't get carried away when working with the browser's status bar. You may have seen examples of Web designers going a little overboard with their use of the status bar. Like anything, use this information in moderation.

Posting a Message to the Status Bar

Ordinarily, browsers use the status bar to display either the URL of the currently selected link or a description of the selected browser toolbar or menu option. However, as the following example shows, you can change this default behavior.

```
<HTML>


  <HEAD>

    <TITLE>Script 4.1 - Posting a message in the status
bar</TITLE>


    <SCRIPT LANGUAGE="JavaScript" TYPE="Text/JavaScript">

    <!-- Start hiding JavaScript statements

      function PostMsg() {

        window.status = "You should see the new message in
the status bar"

      }

    // End hiding JavaScript statements -->

    </SCRIPT>


  </HEAD>


  <BODY onLoad="window.status = 'Welcome to my status bar script!'">

    <FORM>

      <INPUT NAME="myButton" TYPE="button" VALUE="Post Status
Bar Message"

        onClick="PostMsg()">

    </FORM>

  </BODY>


</HTML>
```

The first thing this example does is create a script in the head section that defines a function named PostMsg(). This function is used to display information in the browser's status bar. The function contains a single statement that uses the window object's status property to post a message on the status bar as shown below.

```
function PostMsg() {
  window.status = "You should see the new message in the
status bar"
}
```

Note that in this HTML page the <BODY> tag has been modified to include the onLoad event handler as shown here.

```
onLoad="window.status = 'Welcome to my status bar script!'"
```

This statement uses the window.status property to place a message on the browser's status bar as soon as the page loads. The script next defines a form that contains a single button named myButton. When the user clicks on the button, the button's onClick event handler executes the PostMsg() function, which then writes its message on the browser's status bar.

When you load this page and click on the Post Status Bar Message button, you will see the results as shown in Figure 4.1.

Figure 4.1

Manually posting a message in the status bar

Posting a Blinking Message to the Status Bar

The following example shows you how to get just a bit fancier with the messages you post to the status bar. In this script, you are going to post a message in the status bar that blinks every second. You can use this technique to attract the visitor's attention to messages that otherwise might be missed.

```
<HTML>


  <HEAD>
    <TITLE>Script 4.2 - Posting a blinking message in the
status bar</TITLE>


    <SCRIPT LANGUAGE="JavaScript" TYPE="Text/JavaScript">
    <!-- Start hiding JavaScript statements
      window.status="";
      msg_on = "yes";
      function CycleStatusbar() {
        if (msg_on == "yes") {
          msg_on = "no";
          window.status="This message should be blinking in
your status bar!";
        }
        else {
          msg_on = "yes";
          window.status="";
        }
        setTimeout("CycleStatusbar();",1000);
      }
    // End hiding JavaScript statements -->
    </SCRIPT>


  </HEAD>
```

```
<BODY onLoad="CycleStatusbar()">

  <H3>Blinking Status bar Example</H3>

</BODY>


</HTML>
```

The bulk of the work in this script occurs in the head section. First, the status bar is cleared of any existing messages by the `window.status=""` statement. Next, a variable named `msg_on` is assigned an initial value of `yes`. The `CycleStatusbar()` function that follows toggles the value of this variable from `yes` to `no` with each execution.

As its name implies, the `CycleStatusbar()` function displays and removes a message over and over again in the status bar to produce a blinking effect. When first called, the function checks the value of `msg_on`; because the variable equals `yes`, the function writes its message on the browser's status bar. The function then passes control to the next statement in the script.

The `setTimeout("CycleStatusbar();",1000);` statement tells the browser to run the `CycleStatusbar()` function again in 1000 milliseconds (one second). Once it's activated, the `setTimeout()` method executes the `CycleStatusbar()` function again. This time when it runs, the value of `msg_on` will equal `no`, so the function executes the `window.status=""` statement (clearing the status bar of any text) and toggles the value of `msg_on` back to `yes`. As you can see, the combination of the `CycleStatusbar()` function and the `setTimeout()` method creates a loop that writes and clears the message from the status bar.

NOTE The `setTimeout()` method belongs to the `window` object. Its purpose is to automate the execution of JavaScript statements or functions after a specified number of milliseconds has passed. This method does not force the script to wait until it executes. Instead, it enables the browser to continue processing.

The page's `<BODY>` tag has been modified with the addition of `onLoad="CycleStatusbar()`, which initiates the loop in the head section of the page.

If you run this example, you will see that the message appears in and disappears from the browser's status bar once every second. Figure 4.2 shows what the status bar looks like during an interval in which the message is displayed.

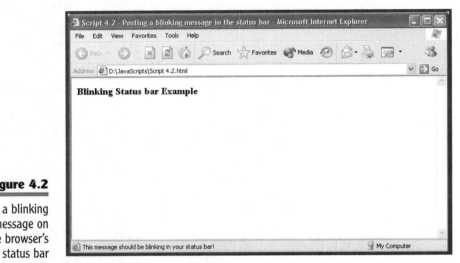

Figure 4.2

Posting a blinking message on the browser's status bar

Scrolling a Message in the Status Bar

Whereas the previous example used the `window.setTimeout()` method to produce a blinking effect in the browser's status bar, this next JavaScript uses the same method to display a message that scrolls across the status bar. The message appears and then moves off the screen, only to reappear again.

```
<HTML>

    <HEAD>

        <TITLE>Script 4.3 - Scrolling a message in the status
bar</TITLE>
```

```
<SCRIPT LANGUAGE="JavaScript" TYPE="Text/JavaScript">

<!-- Start hiding JavaScript statements

    msg = "                         Let me hypnotize you with
this message.... " +

          "                ";

    i = 0;

    function CycleMsg() {

        window.status = msg.substring(i, msg.length) +
msg.substring(0, i);

        i++;

        if (i > msg.length) {

          i = 0;

        }

        window.setTimeout("CycleMsg()",200);

    }

    // End hiding JavaScript statements -->

    </SCRIPT>


  </HEAD>


<BODY onLoad="CycleMsg()">

  <H3>Scrolling Status Bar Message Example</H3>

</BODY>


</HTML>
```

As with the preceding examples, the only code in the body section of this page is an onLoad statement that calls a function named CycleMsg():

```
<BODY onLoad="CycleMsg()">
```

This function initiates a loop in the HTML page's head section that manages the scrolling message. The first statement in the script defines a variable named `msg` and assigns it the text message to be scrolled. Note that I added a number of blank spaces in front of and following the message text itself as shown below. These spaces create a longer message field, enabling the message to remain displayed in its entirety for a longer period before it begins to disappear off the left side of the status bar.

```
msg = "                         Let me hypnotize you with this
message.... " +
       "                   ";
```

The script then sets a variable named `i` equal to 0. The `CycleMsg()` function uses this variable to control the movement of the message across the status bar. The first statement in the function displays the message; it uses the `msg.substring()` method to display a portion of the message beginning at position 0 and ending with position `msg.length` (a number representing the total length of the message). On the first iteration, the entire message is displayed beginning with position 0 and going through the last character in the message (position `msg.length`). Appended to this string is a substring of the message that begins with position 0 and ends with position 0 on this first iteration.

```
function CycleMsg() {
  window.status = msg.substring(i, msg.length) + msg.sub-
string(0, i);
  i++;
  if (i > msg.length) {
    i = 0;
  }
  window.setTimeout("CycleMsg()",200);
}
```

After displaying this initial message, the function increments the value of `i` by 1. It also checks to see whether the function has been executed enough times for the value of `i` to exceed the value stored in `msg.length`.

When this occurs, the function sets `i` back to 0 so that the whole process can start over. Before it completes its first execution, the function schedules itself to execute again in .2 seconds with the `window.setTimeout ("CycleMsg()",200)` statement.

When the function next executes, the value of `i` equals 1. When the `window.status` property is set this time, the first `msg.substring()` method contains one less character because it starts at character position 1 instead of 0. The second `msg.substring()` method contains an additional character beginning at 0 and going through to 1. As you can see, with each iteration, the leading character of the message is stripped from the first substring and placed into the second substring. This has the effect of bringing the message's initial character around to the back of the displayed message, creating the scrolling effect. After the entire message has been processed, the value of `i` is reset to 0, the script is back at its starting point, and everything is repeated.

If you load this page, you will see that the message appears and then slowly scrolls from right to left until it begins to disappear off the left side of the status bar, only to begin reappearing again on the right side of the status bar. Figure 4.3 shows what the message looks like partway through the scroll.

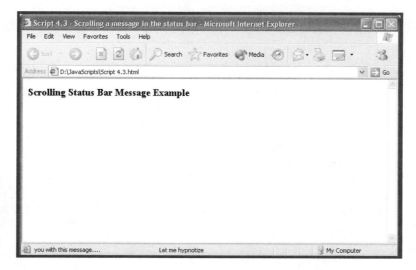

Figure 4.3

Posting a scrolling message on the browser's status bar

Providing Link Descriptions in the Status Bar

This final status bar example shows you how to post descriptive phrases for the links on your Web pages on the browser's status bar whenever a visitor moves the mouse pointer over the links.

```
<HTML>

  <HEAD>
    <TITLE> Script 4.4 - Providing link descriptions in the
status bar</TITLE>

    <SCRIPT LANGUAGE="JavaScript" TYPE="Text/JavaScript">
    <!-- Start hiding JavaScript statements
      function PostMsg(msg) {
        window.status = msg;
      }
      function ClearMsg() {
        window.status="";
      }
    // End hiding JavaScript statements -->
    </SCRIPT>

  </HEAD>
  <BODY>

    <A HREF="http://www.netscape.com"
onMouseOver="PostMsg('Visit Netscape');
      return true;" onMouseOut="ClearMsg();"> Netscape's Web
site</A><P>

    <A HREF="http://www.microsoft.com"
onMouseOver="PostMsg('Visit Microsoft');
      return true;" onMouseOut="ClearMsg();"> Microsoft's Web
site</A><P>
```

```
</BODY>
</HTML>
```

This script contains two functions in the head section. One displays a message that is passed to it as an argument in the status bar, and the other function clears the message:

```
function PostMsg(msg) {
  window.status = msg;
}
function ClearMsg() {
  window.status="";
  }
```

Two links in the body section of the script execute the onMouseOver and onMouseOut events in order to call the status bar functions. When visitors move the mouse pointer over a link, its associated onMouseOver event handler calls the PostMsg() function, passing it a message that describes the link. When visitors move the mouse away from the link, the link's onMouseOut event handler calls the ClearMsg() function and clears the browser's status bar.

```
<A HREF="http://www.netscape.com" onMouseOver="PostMsg('Visit
Netscape');

     return true;" onMouseOut="ClearMsg();"> Netscape's Web
site</A><P>


   <A HREF="http://www.microsoft.com"
onMouseOver="PostMsg('Visit Microsoft');

     return true;" onMouseOut="ClearMsg();"> Microsoft's Web
site</A><P>
```

Figure 4.4 shows the result of loading this page and moving the pointer over the Microsoft link. Clicking on the link instructs the browser to load the associated URL for that link.

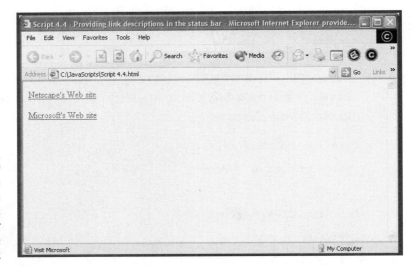

Figure 4.4

Posting descriptive
messages on the
browser's status
bar when a visitor
moves the mouse
pointer over a link

Improving Browser Navigation

Earlier this afternoon, I showed you how to create browser navigation
buttons that enable you to imitate the Back, Forward, Reload, and Home
buttons on the browser's toolbar. The following sections add a host of
new tricks to your tool bag that will enable you to create sophisticated
navigation tools for your visitors. You will learn how to do the following:

- ✪ Create a URL field
- ✪ Enable users to jump to places in your Web site or other Web sites using drop-down lists
- ✪ Add buttons that enable users to scroll or jump quickly to other positions within lengthy pages
- ✪ Add rollover effects to your links and graphics

Creating Your Own URL Field

As the following example shows, it does not take a lot of code to create a
URL field on your Web page. All that you need is a form with a text field,
a button, and the onClick event handler.

```
<HTML>

  <HEAD>

    <TITLE> Script 4.5 - Creating your own URL field</TITLE>

  </HEAD>

  <BODY>

    <H3>Enter a URL and click on Load URL!</H3>

    <FORM NAME="myForm">

      <INPUT NAME="URL_Field" TYPE="text" VALUE="http://"
SIZE="30">

      <INPUT NAME="GoButton" TYPE="button" VALUE="Load URL"

        onClick="window.location=myForm.URL_Field.value">

    </FORM>

  </BODY>


</HTML>
```

The following HTML statements define a form called myForm that contains a text field called URL_Field and a button named GoButton. As you can see, I added an initial value in the text field by adding the VALUE="http://" clause to the <INPUT> tag:

```
<FORM NAME="myForm">

  <INPUT NAME="URL_Field" TYPE="text" VALUE="http://"  size="30">

  <INPUT NAME="GoButton" TYPE="button" VALUE="Load URL"

    onClick="window.location=myform.URL_Field.value">
```

NOTE The window.location statement automatically loads any assigned URL. Unless you preface the URL with http://, the scripts will not be able to load the URL. Make sure you do not remove the http:// text that is appended to the beginning of the URL_Field or else the example will not work.

Adding `onClick="window.location=myform.URL_Field.value"` as the event handler for the button takes the value located in the text field (in this case, `myform.URL_Field.value"`) and assigns it to the `window` object's `location` property. Any time a change is made to `window.location`, the browser immediately tries to load the URL.

Figure 4.5 shows what this URL script looks like when it has been loaded in a browser. By completing the URL address and clicking on the Load URL button, the user can load any Web page into the current window.

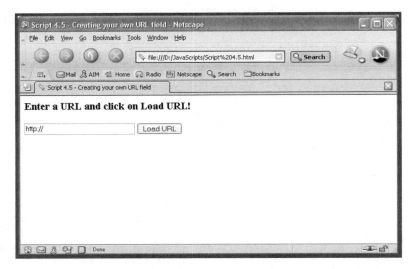

Figure 4.5

Building a custom URL form

Creating an Automatic Drop-Down Navigation Menu

At times you may want to offer visitors to your Web site a large number of links to choose from. Creating each one individually can be tiresome and can result in a page that is overly crowded and unattractive. A simple solution to this problem is to use a drop-down list, as shown in this example:

```
<HTML>

    <HEAD>
        <TITLE> Script 4.6 - Creating a drop-down menu - 1</TITLE>
```

```
</HEAD>


<BODY>

  <FORM NAME="myForm">

    <SELECT NAME="myList" onChange="window.location=

document.myForm.myList.options[document.myForm.myList.selected
Index].value">

      <OPTION SELECTED VALUE="javascript:void(0)">-- Pick One --

      <OPTION VALUE="http://www.microsoft.com"> Microsoft

      <OPTION VALUE="http://www.netscape.com"> Netscape

      <OPTION VALUE="http://www.myopera.com"> Opera

      </SELECT>

  </FORM>

  </BODY>


</HTML>
```

In the body section of the HTML page, a single form called myForm is defined. Within it, a list called myList is declared. The onChange event handler is used to set the window.location property to the value specified by the following statement:

```
document.myForm.myList.options[document.myForm.myList.selected
Index].value"
```

Each option in the list has an implicit index number. Roughly translated, the preceding statement takes the index number of the option you select from the list (the value in document.myForm.myList.selectedIndex) and uses it to assign the value of the selected option to window.location.

If you look at the <OPTION> tags within the form, you will notice that the first tag looks different. I used VALUE="javascript:void(0)" to put an entry into the list that, if selected, is ignored. This trick enables me to add an instruction at the top of the list that otherwise has no effect. The rest of the options are straightforward. Each `<OPTION>` tag contains a `VALUE` that holds the URL; if this option is selected, the specified URL is opened. Note that each `VALUE` entry is followed by a description that identifies the entry within the list.

Figure 4.6 shows how the list looks when you load this page. Selecting the `-- Pick One --` entry has no effect. Selecting any other entry causes the browser to load the URL associated with that selection.

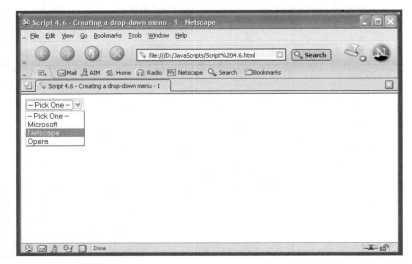

Figure 4.6

Helping users navigate with a drop-down list

Creating a Drop-Down Menu with a Button Control

The following example builds on the one in the previous section by providing the user with an additional level of control. The following script enables the user to select an entry from a drop-down list without having that entry automatically processed (as was the case in the preceding example). Delaying the processing of a selection is appropriate on forms that require the user to complete a number of activities before the form is processed.

The following code is similar to the code in the preceding section. Note, however, that I removed the `onChange` event handler from the list, which prevents the form from automatically processing the selected option. Instead, I added the onClick event handler to the form's button. When the user clicks on the button, the onClick event handler sets the window.location property to the value of the selected list option, causing the appropriate URL to load.

```
<HTML>

  <HEAD>
    <TITLE> Script 4.7 - Creating a drop-down menu - 2</TITLE>
  </HEAD>

  <BODY>
    <FORM NAME="myForm">
      <SELECT NAME="myList">
        <OPTION SELECTED VALUE="javascript:void(0)">-- Pick
One --
        <OPTION SELECTED VALUE="http://www.microsoft.com">
Microsoft
        <OPTION VALUE="http://www.netscape.com"> Netscape
        <OPTION VALUE="http://www.myopera.com"> Opera
      </SELECT>
      <INPUT NAME="Load_URL" TYPE="button" VALUE="Load URL"
        onClick="window.location=
        document.myForm.myList.options[document.myForm.
myList.selectedIndex].value">
    </FORM>
  </BODY>

</HTML>
```

Figure 4.7 shows how the list looks when you load this page. Selecting the `-- Pick One --` entry still has no effect. Selecting any other option no longer causes that option to be loaded. Instead, the `Load URL` button gives the user control over when and if the entry selected from the list is processed.

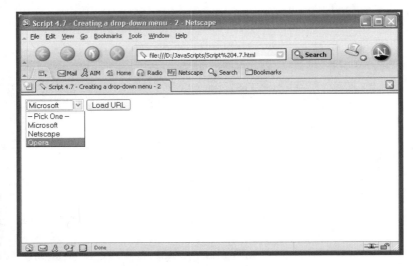

Figure 4.7

Enabling visitors to load pages from a list of predefined URLs

Scrolling and Jumping

Depending on their content, Web page can sometimes grow rather large in size. JavaScript provides the ability to scroll or jump to a predefined location within the page. In addition to making the page easier to navigate, giving the user the ability to jump also can produce a stunning visual effect, as demonstrated by the following example.

```
<HTML>


  <HEAD>

    <TITLE> Script 4.8 - Scrolling and jumping example</TITLE>


    <SCRIPT LANGUAGE="JavaScript" TYPE="Text/JavaScript">
```

```
<!-- Start hiding JavaScript statements

   function ScrollDown(){
     for (i=1; i<=600; i++) {
       parent.scrollTo(1,i);
     }
   }


   function ScrollUp(){
     for (i=600; i>=1; i--) {
       parent.scrollTo(1,i)
     }
   }


   function JumpDown(){
     parent.scrollTo(1,600);
   }


   function JumpUp(){
     parent.scrollTo(1,1);
   }


// End hiding JavaScript statements -->
</SCRIPT>

</HEAD>

<BODY>
  <FORM NAME="myForm">
```

```
        <INPUT TYPE="button" VALUE="Scroll Down"
onClick="ScrollDown()">

        <INPUT TYPE="button" VALUE="Jump Down"
onClick="JumpDown()">

    </FORM>

    <BR><BR><BR><BR><BR><BR>

    <H3>This is an example...</H3>

    <BR><BR><BR><BR><BR><BR>

    <H3>of scrolling and jumping...</H3>

    <BR><BR><BR><BR><BR><BR>

    <H3>from the top to the bottom of a page...</H3>

    <BR><BR><BR><BR><BR><BR>

    <H3>and back again!!</H3>

    <FORM>

        <INPUT TYPE="button" VALUE="Scroll Up"
onClick="ScrollUp()">

        <INPUT TYPE="button" VALUE="Jump Up"
onClick="JumpUp()">

    </FORM>

  </BODY>


</HTML>
```

Four functions are defined in the head section of the page. Two of these functions manage the scrolling effect, and the other two manage the jump affect. Take the ScrollDown() function as an example. The function starts by setting up a for loop that is controlled by a variable called i. The variable i is initially set to a value of 1 and then incremented by 1 until it reaches 600. With each iteration, the loop executes the window object's ScrollTo() method. This method scrolls the window's viewing area to the location specified by the coordinates x and y. In effect, the for loop executes 600 times and scrolls down the display by 1 pixel position on each occurrence. The ScrollUp() function does the same thing in reverse.

```
function ScrollDown(){
  for (i=1; i<=600; i++) {
    parent.scrollTo(1,i);
  }
}
```

The JumpDown() function skips the scroll effect altogether by simply specifying the destination coordinate. The JumpUp() function does the same thing in reverse.

```
function JumpDown(){
  parent.scrollTo(1,600);
}
```

Two forms are placed at the top and the bottom of the page's body section. These forms define two buttons that call the functions. The buttons in the top form use the onClick event handler to execute the ScrollDown() and JumpDown() functions; the buttons in the bottom form use the onClick event handler to execute the ScrollUp() and JumpUp() functions.

Between the two forms, I placed text to make the page long enough to provide an effective demonstration. Loading this page displays the window shown in Figure 4.8. Clicking on either the Scroll Down or Jump Down button scrolls or jumps the viewing area down to the bottom of the page, where the Scroll Up and Jump Up buttons have been placed.

Working with Rollovers

My personal favorite JavaScript effect is the rollover. A *rollover* is an image that changes when the mouse moves the pointer over it. All the rollover really does is use the onMouseOver and onMouseOut event handlers to toggle between two similar links or images, giving the appearance that they are changing. This very popular technique has become common on the Web.

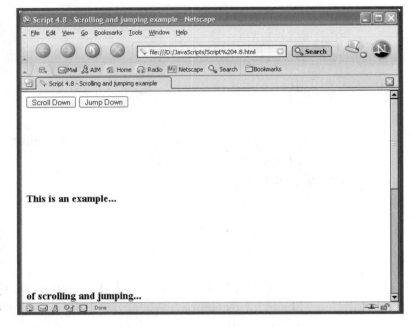

Figure 4.8

Adding scroll and jump buttons to help visitors navigate your Web page faster

 NOTE Make sure that both copies of the rollover images you use are the same size. Otherwise, the effect is lost because the second image will look distorted.

In the following script, you will see an example of how to use the rollover affect to animate three images. While the images appear to the user to be text, they actually are graphic images.

```
<HTML>

  <HEAD>
    <TITLE> Script 4.9 - Working with rollovers</TITLE>

    <SCRIPT LANGUAGE="JavaScript" TYPE="Text/JavaScript">
    <!-- Start hiding JavaScript statements
        netscape1      =new Image;
```

```
            netscape2      =new Image;
            microsoft1     =new Image;
            microsoft2     =new Image;
            opera1          =new Image;
            opera2          =new Image;
            netscape1.src  ="netscape1.jpg";
            netscape2.src  ="netscape2.jpg";
            microsoft1.src ="microsoft1.jpg";
            microsoft2.src ="microsoft2.jpg";
            opera1.src     ="opera1.jpg";
            opera2.src     ="opera2.jpg";
    // End hiding JavaScript statements -->
    </SCRIPT>

 </HEAD>

 <BODY>
   <A HREF="http://www.netscape.com"
      onMouseover="document.mybutton1.src=netscape2.src"
      onMouseout="document.mybutton1.src=netscape1.src">
      <IMG SRC="netscape1.jpg" BORDER="0" NAME="mybutton1">
</A><P>
   <A HREF="http://www.microsoft.com"
      onMouseover="document.mybutton2.src=microsoft2.src"
      onMouseout="document.mybutton2.src=microsoft1.src">
      <IMG SRC="microsoft1.jpg" BORDER="0" NAME="mybutton2">
</A><P>
   <A HREF="http://www.myopera.com"
      onMouseover="document.mybutton3.src=opera2.src"
      onMouseout="document.mybutton3.src=opera1.src">
      <IMG SRC="opera1.jpg" BORDER="0" NAME="mybutton3"></A>
```

```
</BODY>


</HTML>
```

The trick to making your rollovers work is to preload the images into cache on your visitor's computers so that when they are referenced in the script, they can be displayed instantly. The script in the head section of the page does this. The rollover menu is comprised of three images, each of which requires a second but slightly different version of each of the three images. I must therefore define six images. The following statements define each image object and preload them into cache as soon as the page starts loading.

```
netscape1         =new Image;

netscape2         =new Image;

microsoft1        =new Image;

microsoft2        =new Image;

opera1               =new Image;

opera2               =new Image;

netscape1.src        ="netscape1.jpg";

netscape2.src        ="netscape2.jpg";

microsoft1.src       ="microsoft1.jpg";

microsoft2.src       ="microsoft2.jpg";

opera1.src      ="opera1.jpg";

opera2.src      ="opera2.jpg";
```

When the page is first loaded, three images are displayed. Each of these images is defined by links in the body section. The following HTML tag shows the first link.

```
<A HREF=http://www.netscape.com

  onMouseover="document.mybutton1.src=netscape2.src"

  onMouseout="document.mybutton1.src=netscape1.src">

  <IMG SRC="netscape1.jpg" BORDER="0" NAME="mybutton1"></A><P>
```

As you can see, the onMouseOver event handler automatically loads the other version of the image when the mouse pointer passes over the image; the onMouseOut event handler puts the original image back when the mouse pointer moves away from the image. The other two links are defined in a similar fashion.

Figure 4.9 shows how the page looks after the user has placed the pointer over the Microsoft link. If the user clicks on the link, the URL associated with the link is loaded. Otherwise, when the user moves the pointer away, the original graphic for the Microsoft link is reloaded.

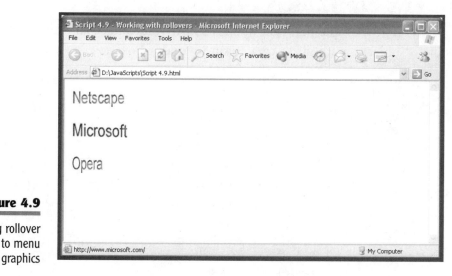

Figure 4.9

Adding rollover effects to menu graphics

 NOTE To really appreciate the rollover example, you need to load it and run it for yourself. It is on the book's accompanying CD-ROM, along with all the other examples that you see in this book.

Taking Advantage of Dialog Boxes

In addition to opening a window and displaying HTML, JavaScript provides you with access to several predefined pop-up dialog boxes you can use to interact with visitors. The three types of dialog boxes are listed here:

- Alert dialog box
- Prompt dialog box
- Confirm dialog box

You have already seen these dialog boxes in use in previous examples. The following sections explain in detail just how you can use the `window` object's `alert()`, `prompt()`, and `confirm()` methods to take full advantage of these dialog boxes.

Testing Pop-Up Dialog Boxes

The example that follows shows how you can use all three of the `window` object's methods to create pop-up dialog boxes:

```
<HTML>

  <HEAD>
    <TITLE> Script 4.10 - Testing pop-up dialog boxes</TITLE>

    <SCRIPT LANGUAGE="JavaScript" TYPE="Text/JavaScript">
    <!-- Start hiding JavaScript statements

      function AlertUsr(msg) {
          window.alert(msg);
      }

      function PromptUsr(msg) {
          age = window.prompt(msg,55);
      }

      function ConfirmUsr(msg) {
          answer = window.confirm(msg);
      }
```

```
    // End hiding JavaScript statements -->
    </SCRIPT>

  </HEAD>

  <BODY>
    <FORM>
      <INPUT NAME="button1" TYPE="button" VALUE="Alert"
        onClick="AlertUsr('This is an alert prompt!')">
      <INPUT NAME="button2" TYPE="button" VALUE="Prompt"
        onClick="PromptUsr('This is a prompt. How old are
you?')">
      <INPUT NAME="button3" TYPE="button" VALUE="Confirm"
        onClick="ConfirmUsr('This is a confirmation!')">
    </FORM>
  </BODY>

</HTML>
```

The script in the head section defines three functions, one for each method. The `AlertUsr()` function executes the `window` object's `alert()` method by passing the message that it receives as an argument. No other arguments are supported.

```
function AlertUsr(msg) {
 window.alert(msg);
}
```

The `PromptUsr()` function executes the `window` object's `prompt()` method and passes it two arguments. The first argument is the message to be displayed in the prompt, and the second argument is a default value that is automatically displayed in the dialog box's text field. If you want to leave the text field empty, you should type empty quotation marks ("")

in place of the argument. If you choose not to include the second argument, the word `undefined` appears in the text field when the dialog box pops up. This is both unattractive and inconvenient for the user.

```
function PromptUsr(msg) {
  age = window.prompt(msg,55);
}
```

The `ConfirmUsr()` function executes the `window` object's `confirm()` method, passing it the message it receives as an argument. No other arguments are supported.

```
function ConfirmUsr(msg) {
  answer = window.confirm(msg);
}
```

To test each function, I next defined a form with three buttons in the body section of the code. I added an `onClick` event handler to each button and assigned the event handler to one of the functions. For example, for the button named `button1`, the `onClick` event handler executes the `AlertUsr()` function and passes it the text `'This is an alert prompt!'` as shown here:

```
<INPUT NAME="button1" TYPE="button" VALUE="Alert"
  onClick="AlertUsr('This is an alert prompt!')">
```

 NOTE Notice the use of the single quotes around the message text in the `onClick` event handler. The single quotes are used because the JavaScript statement assigned to the `onClick` event handler must itself be placed within double quotes. Any time you have quotes inside other quotes, you must differentiate the pairs of quotes. I could have reversed things and used single quotes on the outside and double quotes on the inside; the result would have been the same.

Figure 4.10 shows what the page will look like if you load it using Netscape Navigator.

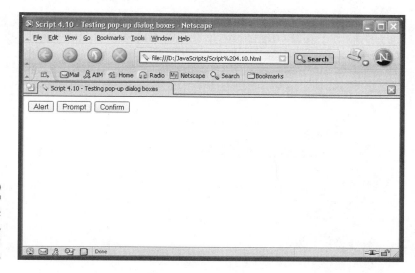

Figure 4.10

Testing the window object's pop-up dialog boxes

Figure 4.11, 4.12, and 4.13 show how each of these pop-up dialogs look when opened by Netscape Communicator.

Figure 4.11

An alert dialog box as it appears in Netscape Communicator

Figure 4.12

A prompt dialog box as it appears in Netscape Communicator

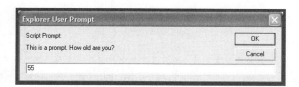

Figure 4.13

A confirm dialog box as it appears in Netscape Communicator

Adding a Welcome Message

One very polite way to make use of the window object's alert() method is to display a welcome message to visitors when they visit your Web page. As the following example shows, this can be done by placing an alert() statement in the body section of the HTML page.

```
<HTML>

  <HEAD>

    <TITLE>Script 4.11 - Adding a simple welcome
message</TITLE>

  </HEAD>

  <BODY>

    <SCRIPT LANGUAGE="JavaScript" TYPE="Text/JavaScript">
    <!-- Start hiding JavaScript statements
      window.alert('Welcome to my Web Site!');
    // End hiding JavaScript statements -->
    </SCRIPT>

  </BODY>

</HTML>
```

NOTE Greeting messages are commonly created by using the onLoad event handler inside the <BODY> tags.

Figure 4.14 shows the result of loading the previous example in Netscape Navigator.

Figure 4.14

Displaying a
generic greeting
when visitors first
access your main
Web page

Using the Visitor's Name in a Message

A more sophisticated greeting involves using the `window` object's `prompt()` method to ask the user to type his name and then to display a greeting that uses that name. The following example demonstrates this technique:

```
<HTML>

  <HEAD>

    <TITLE> Script 4.12 - Using the visitor's name in a
message</TITLE>

  </HEAD>

  <BODY>

    <SCRIPT LANGUAGE="JavaScript" TYPE="Text/JavaScript">

    <!-- Start hiding JavaScript statements

      your_name = window.prompt('Welcome! What is your
name?','');

      window.alert('Thanks for visiting us ' + your_name +

      '.  We hope that you enjoy your experience!');

    // End hiding JavaScript statements -->

    </SCRIPT>

  </BODY>

</HTML>
```

This example uses both the `prompt()` and the `alert()` methods to communicate with the user. The `prompt()` method is used to gather information that is then used by the `alert()` method to thank the user for visiting.

Figure 4.15 shows the first part of the interaction that the user sees when this page loads. Notice that the prompt dialog box does not display an initial message or an undefined message.

Figure 4.15

Using the `window` object's `prompt()` method to collect user input

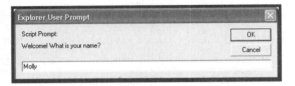

If the user clicks on OK, the alert dialog box appears, as shown in Figure 4.16.

Figure 4.16

Using the `window` object's `alert()` method to send the user an informational message

NOTE Have you ever wondered how it is that some Web sites seem to remember who you are and can greet you by name every time you visit? It's because they have been baking cookies. Tomorrow, I will show you how to bake some cookies of your own. *Cookies* are small, harmless pieces of information you can store on the visitor's computer and retrieve the next time they return. For example, after you collect a visitor's name, you can store that information as a cookie. The next time the visitor returns to your Web page, you can check to see whether the visitor has been to your Web site before by looking to see whether the visitor's computer has stored one of your cookies. If you find the cookie, you can greet the visitor by name. If your script cannot find your cookie, the script can prompt for the visitor's name and save it for the next visit.

Of course, there are many other benefits to asking for the user's name. For example, you can store it in a variable and reference it repeatedly to interact with the user or to thank the user for visiting when the `onUnload` event handler executes to signify that the user is leaving or closing the page. If your page also includes a form, you can use the user's name to fill in a name field and save the user some typing.

Take a Break

Now is as good a time as any to take a break. You've earned it. When you return, I will give you some advice about how to prepare to deal with all the different versions of Internet browsers that are out there. I will also show you how to add a clock to your Web pages and how to set up banners that you can use to advertise your own or other people's Web sites. In addition, you will learn how to create basic animation effects. See you in a few minutes!

Working with Different Types of Browsers

Throughout this book, I have stated again and again that because of the constantly evolving nature of JavaScript and Internet browsers, creating Web pages that everyone can use is a bit of a chore. This task continues to be made more difficult by the appearance of new technologies such as small handheld devices and appliances that are now beginning to access the Internet but that have no JavaScript support whatsoever.

The next two sections describe how to interrogate every visitor's browser for information about its JavaScript capabilities and cover ways in which you might try to support various browsers.

Gathering Browser Information

The following example shows how to determine the type of browser and the version number of the browser that a visitor is using to load your Web page. The script uses the `navigator` object to collect browser-specific information.

```
<HTML>

  <HEAD>
    <TITLE> Script 4.13 - Gathering Browser
information</TITLE>
  </HEAD>


  <BODY>
    <SCRIPT LANGUAGE="JavaScript" TYPE="Text/JavaScript">
    <!-- Start hiding JavaScript statements
      document.write("You are using " + navigator.appName +
"<BR>");
      document.write("Version: " + navigator.appVersion);
    // End hiding JavaScript statements -->
    </SCRIPT>
  </BODY>


</HTML>
```

The script consists of just two statements. The first statement uses the
`document.write()` method to display a message. The message uses the
`navigator.appName` property to display the name of the browser viewing
the page:

```
document.write("You are using " + navigator.appName +
"<BR>");
```

A second `document.write()` statement displays another message using
the `navigator.appVersion` property:

```
document.write("Version: " + navigator.appVersion);
```

When you load this example, you will see results similar to those in Figure
4.17, depending on the browser you are using.

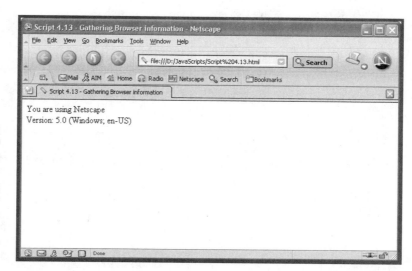

Figure 4.17

Using the
`navigator`
object's properties
to gather
information
about the browser
that loaded your
Web page

A Browser Redirection Example

Once you know how to use the properties of the `navigator` object to
capture browser information, you can write scripts that redirect visitors to
pages you have written to support those particular browsers. The following example shows one manner in which you can do this.

```
<HTML>

  <HEAD>
    <TITLE> Script 4.14 - A browser redirection example</TITLE>
  </HEAD>

  <BODY>

    <SCRIPT LANGUAGE="JavaScript" TYPE="Text/JavaScript">
    <!-- Start hiding JavaScript statements

      if ((navigator.appName=="Microsoft Internet Explorer") ||
```

```
            (navigator.appName=="Netscape")) {

        if (navigator.appName=="Microsoft Internet Explorer") {
          if (navigator.appVersion.indexOf("5") > - 1) {
            window.location = "Default.html";
          } else {
            document.write("Please upgrade to IE version 5
or above.");
          }
        }


        if (navigator.appName=="Netscape") {
          if (navigator.appVersion.indexOf("5") > - 1) {
            window.location = "Default.html";
          } else {
            document.write("Please upgrade to Netscape version
6 or above.");
          }
        }


        } else {
          document.write("This site requires Internet Explorer
5 or above ");
          document.write("or Netscape Communicator 6 and
above.");
        }


    // End hiding JavaScript statements -->
    </SCRIPT>


  </BODY>
</HTML>
```

First the script checks to see if either Microsoft Internet Explorer or Netscape Communicator is being used as shown below.

```
if ((navigator.appName=="Microsoft Internet Explorer") ||
   (navigator.appName=="Netscape")) {
```

If neither or these browsers is being used, the visitor is informed that the Web site requires one of two browsers, as shown below.

```
} else {
   document.write("This site requires Internet Explorer 5 or
above ");
   document.write("or Netscape Communicator 6 and above.");
}
```

Assuming that one of these two browsers is being used to view the HTML page, the following collections of if statements execute.

```
if (navigator.appName=="Microsoft Internet Explorer") {
   if (navigator.appVersion.indexOf("5") > - 1) {
     window.location = "Default.html";
   } else {
     document.write("Please upgrade to IE version 5 or
above.");
   }
}


if (navigator.appName=="Netscape") {
   if (navigator.appVersion.indexOf("5") > - 1) {
     window.location = "Default.html";
   } else {
     document.write("Please upgrade to Netscape version 6 or
above.");
   }
}
```

The first collection of statements executes when Internet Explorer is being used. The second set executes when Netscape Communicator is in use. Both sets perform the same actions, making sure that a specific version of each browser (or higher-level version) is being used. If the correct browser version is being used, the visitor's browser is redirected to an HTML page called `Default.html`. Otherwise, a message is displayed informing the visitor that he needs to upgrade his browser to view your Web page.

Other Neat Stuff

In the next several sections of this chapter, you will learn three very useful tricks. First, I will show you how easy it is to add a clock to your Web pages. A clock is especially useful if you create pages at which visitors are likely to spend a great deal of time. For example, you might write a page that reloads itself every few minutes so that you can provide your visitors with the real-time information you are positing on the Web site. Placing a digital clock on your pages enables your visitors to see how long they have been visiting as well as how current the existing information is.

The second example you will look at shows an option for working around one of JavaScript's main weaknesses: its inability to provide meaningful, password-protected access to your Web pages. This example shows you a way to apply a relatively simple password scheme that will suffice to keep the average unauthorized Web surfer away from your site.

Then I'll show you how to create your own banners. *Banners* provide a great way to advertise other parts of your site or to make money by leasing banner space to people who want to advertise on your Web pages.

Building a JavaScript Clock

Adding a digital clock to your Web pages is a relatively simple task. All it takes is the `Date` object and the `setTimeout()` method. You can create a clock in its most simple form by using the `document.write()` method to display the clock. However, this example adds a finishing touch by displaying the clock inside a form text field.

```html
<HTML>

 <HEAD>
  <TITLE> Script 4.15 - Building a JavaScript Clock</TITLE>

  <SCRIPT LANGUAGE="JavaScript" TYPE="Text/JavaScript">
  <!-- Start hiding JavaScript statements
    function ShowClock() {
      the_time_is = new Date;
      the_minute = the_time_is.getMinutes();
      the_hour = the_time_is.getHours();
      the_second = the_time_is.getSeconds();
      if (the_minute < 10) {
        the_minute = "0" + the_minute;
      }
      if (the_hour < 10) {
        the_hour = "0" + the_hour;
      }
      if (the_second < 10) {
        the_second = "0" + the_second;
      }
      document.myForm.displayTime.value = the_hour + ":"  +
        the_minute + ":" + the_second;
      setTimeout("ShowClock()",1000);
    }
  // End hiding JavaScript statements -->
  </SCRIPT>

 </HEAD>
```

```
<BODY onLoad="ShowClock()">
  <FORM NAME="myForm">
    <B>The time is:</B>
    <INPUT NAME="displayTime" TYPE="TEXT" SIZE="8">
  </FORM>
</BODY>


</HTML>
```

This example places the script in the head section. The first thing the script does is to define a function named ShowClock() that is used to acquire, format, and display the clock's data.

The first thing the ShowClock() function does is to set the value of a variable named the_time_is to the current date. It then uses the getMinutes(), getHours(), and getSeconds() methods of the Date object to extract the individual elements of time:

```
the_time_is = new Date
the_minute = the_time_is.getMinutes()
the_hour = the_time_is.getHours()
the_second = the_time_is.getSeconds()
```

To provide a consistent display, the script examines each element to make sure that it is two digits long. If the minute, hour, or second value is between 0 and 9, the script pads the value with a 0. Therefore 0 hours becomes 00 hours, 6 seconds becomes 06 seconds, and so on.

```
if (the_minute < 10) {
  the_minute = "0" + the_minute
}
if (the_hour < 10) {
  the_hour = "0" + the_hour
}
```

```
if (the_second < 10) {
  the_second = "0" + the_second
}
```

After each element has been properly formatted, the script assembles and displays the elements in the text field `displayTime` on the form `myForm` as shown here:

```
document.myForm.displayTime.value = the_hour + ":"  +
  the_minute + ":" + the_second
```

To keep the clock running, the `ShowClock()` function ends by scheduling its own execution in one second using the `setTimeout()` method:

```
setTimeout("ShowClock()",1000)
```

Figure 4.18 shows what this example looks like when you load the page.

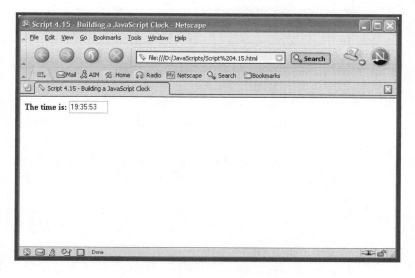

Figure 4.18

Creating a simple digital clock

A Simple Password Script

As I have already stated, client-side JavaScript lacks the capability to implement a true password-protection scheme for a Web site. However, when used in conjunction with a Web server-based program, JavaScript can provide a front end that collects the user's name and password, sends the user's information to the server program, and displays an HTML page that the server returns. Figure 4.19 shows this process. In this example, the server executes a CGI program that validates the user against a database and then returns an HTML page based on the success or failure of the validation process.

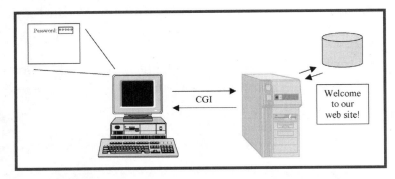

Figure 4.19

A depiction of a typical password validation process

By itself, a client-side JavaScript cannot accomplish this type of password validation. Of course, you could always write a script and embed user names and passwords in the code. Although this approach might stop some unwanted visitors, anyone who knows how to view HTML source code could read it and discover the names and passwords. To be a little more clever, you could place the user names and passwords in an external .js file, which would probably be enough to stop the average unauthorized user.

One trick you can use to provide a measure of password protection for your Web site is to publish an intermediary Web page that requires the visitor to provide a password before loading your site's real home page. The trick is to make the required password the same as the name of your home page.

Figure 4.20 shows an example in which the visitor finds his way to your intermediary page and is confronted by a password form. In this example, the user must enter ivworld in the Password field to gain access to the site. Of course, if users become aware that the password is the name of the site's real home page, they could just as easily load that page instead of opening the intermediary password page and typing the password. However, unless you provide your users with the password, they cannot find the page; if you gave the password to them, then it's probably okay for them to load the page directly anyway.

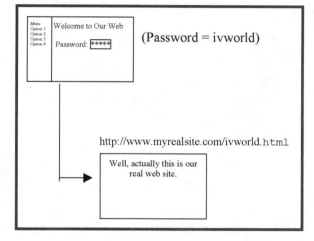

Figure 4.20

Requiring a password to access your Web site

Following is the script required to implement the example presented in Figure 4.21:

```
<HTML>


  <HEAD>

    <TITLE> Script 4.16 - A simple password-protection example
</TITLE>


    <SCRIPT LANGUAGE="JavaScript" TYPE="Text/JavaScript">
    <!-- Start hiding JavaScript statements
      function LoadTheURL() {
        document.location.href = "http://www. xxxxxxxxxx.com/" +
          document.myForm.psswdField.value + ".html";
```

```
        }
     // End hiding JavaScript statements -->
     </SCRIPT>


  </HEAD>


  <BODY>
    <B>Please type your password:</B>
    <FORM NAME="myForm">

       <INPUT NAME="psswdField" TYPE="password" size="15">

       <INPUT NAME="Login" TYPE="button" VALUE="Login"
onClick="LoadTheURL()">

     </FORM>
    </BODY>


  </HTML>
```

NOTE

For the previous example to work, you need to change http://www. xxxxxxxx.com to the URL of a real Web site.

First a function named LoadTheURL() is defined in the head section. The function consists of one statement. The href property of the location object, a child of the document object, is set to the value of a URL address. This address is a concatenated string that includes the value of document.myForm.psswdField.value. This value contains the password typed by the user.

```
function LoadTheURL() {
  document.location.href = "http://www. xxxxxxxxx.com/" +
    document.myForm.psswdField.value + ".html";

}
```

The value of `document.myForm.passwdField.value` is established in the page's form. The form is named `myForm` and contains two elements: The first element is a password field named `passwdField`. This field is similar to the text field you have seen in other form examples except that it automatically hides the characters as the user types them, thus hiding the password from prying eyes. The second form element is a button with an `onClick` event handler that calls the `LoadTheURL()` function when the button is clicked.

```
<FORM NAME="myForm">

  <INPUT NAME="psswdField" TYPE="password" size="15">

  <INPUT NAME="Login" TYPE="button" VALUE="Login"
onClick="LoadTheURL()">

</FORM>
```

The result is that as soon as the script sets the `document.location.href` property, the browser tries to load the target URL. If the user types the wrong password, an error appears; otherwise your home page loads.

NOTE This is a very simple script. In real life, you would probably want to add code that validates the content of the form before processing it. For example, you could make sure that the user does not leave the Password field blank.

Figure 4.21 shows what the preceding script looks like when it is loaded by the browser.

A Rotating Banner Example

This next example shows you one way to create a cycling banner on your Web site. In this case, the script cycles through four banners; the script can be easily modified to accommodate as many or as few banners as you want to display.

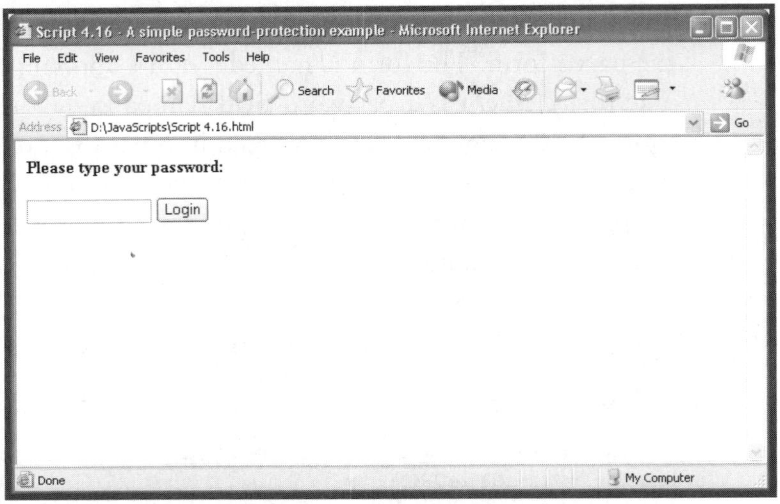

Figure 4.21

Password-
protecting your
Web site

NOTE

An alternative to using JavaScript to create banners is to use a graphics application to create an animated GIF image that automatically cycles through a collection of GIF files. However, creating banners using JavaScript gives you several advantages over using animated GIFs: With JavaScript, you can easily adjust the behavior of the banner. With JavaScript, you can use JPEG files, which produce clearer images and are smaller than their GIF counterparts, making them download faster. You can bet that people who visit your Web site will appreciate that!

```
<HTML>

  <HEAD>
    <TITLE> Script 4.17 - A Rotating Banner Example</TITLE>

    <SCRIPT LANGUAGE="JavaScript" TYPE="Text/JavaScript">
    <!-- Start hiding JavaScript statements

      MyBannerArray = new Array(4);
```

```
        MyBannerArray[0]="banner0.jpg";

        MyBannerArray[1]="banner1.jpg";

        MyBannerArray[2]="banner2.jpg";

        MyBannerArray[3]="banner3.jpg";


        current_banner=0;


        no_of_banners=MyBannerArray.length;


        function CycleBanner() {
            if (current_banner==no_of_banners) {
              current_banner=0;
            }
            document.myBanner.src=MyBannerArray[current_banner];
            current_banner ++;
            setTimeout("CycleBanner()", 5*1000);
        }


    // End hiding JavaScript statements -->
    </SCRIPT>


  </HEAD>


  <BODY onLoad="CycleBanner()">
    <CENTER> <IMG NAME="myBanner" SRC="banner0.jpg"> </CEN-
TER>
    </BODY>


</HTML>
```

The first thing the script does is to define and populate an array named `MyBannerArray` with the four JPEG images files:

```
MyBannerArray = new Array(4);

MyBannerArray[0]="banner0.jpg";

MyBannerArray[1]="banner1.jpg";

MyBannerArray[2]="banner2.jpg";

MyBannerArray[3]="banner3.jpg";
```

Next, two variables are created. The first variable is used to track the currently selected element in the array. The second variable represents the total number of elements in the array:

```
current_banner=0;

no_of_banners=MyBannerArray.length;
```

Then a function called `CycleBanner()` is created. It contains an `if` statement that compares the value of `current_banner` to `no_of_banners`. With each iteration of this function, the value of `current_banner` is increased by 1. When `current_banner` equals `no_of_banners`, every banner will have been displayed. The `if` statement then sets `current_banner` back to 0, thus preparing the next cycle of the banner rotation.

```
if (current_banner==no_of_banners) {

  current_banner=0;

}
```

The script then sets the image source for the `myBanner` image (`document.myBanner.src`) equal to the current banner (`MyBannerArray[current_banner]`). Then it increments the value of `current_banner` to represent the next JPEG in the array:

```
document.myBanner.src=MyBannerArray[current_banner];

current_banner++;
```

The last thing the function does is to use the `setTimeout()` method to call itself again in 5 seconds, thus establishing an indefinite loop:

```
setTimeout("CycleBanner()", 5*1000);
```

NOTE To ensure a smooth and attractive effect as the banners roll by, make sure that all the banner images have the same physical dimensions.

Figure 4.22 shows the result of loading this script in a browser. The first of four banners appears in the body of the page; it will be replaced in five seconds by the second image in the array.

Figure 4.22

Making money by renting banner space on your Web pages

Basic Graphics and Animation

You have already seen examples of how JavaScript can be used to control animation and graphics in a browser. The next three examples further demonstrate ways in which you can use JavaScript to manipulate graphics and animation on your Web pages.

The first example shows how to use JavaScript to create animated effects. The second example demonstrates how you can provide the user with control over a document's background color. The final example sets up an online photo album so that you can share your favorite pictures with the world.

The Blinking Eye

Using JavaScript and a series of like-sized images, you can create basic graphic animations. The next example displays a blinking eye that opens and closes as it stares at your visitors. The actual effect is very simple: First, you need to create a collection of image files that have the same physical dimensions and that are slightly different from each other, as shown in Figure 4.23.

Figure 4.23

The eight images that make up the blinking eye animation example

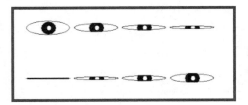

In the following example, I will demonstrate how to create a simple graphic animation using JavaScript. In this example the script will use a series of eight slightly different images to produce the illusion of a blinking eye.

```
<HTML>

   <HEAD>
     <TITLE>Script 4.18 - Blinking eye example</TITLE>

     <SCRIPT LANGUAGE="JavaScript" TYPE="Text/JavaScript">
     <!-- Start hiding JavaScript statements

       current_img = 0;
```

```
function BlinkEye() {
  current_img++;
  if (current_img > images.length - 1) {
    current_img=0;
  }
  document.myEye.src = images[current_img];
  setTimeout('BlinkEye()',100);
}

image1 = new Image; image1.src = "eye1.jpg";
image2 = new Image; image2.src = "eye2.jpg";
image3 = new Image; image3.src = "eye3.jpg";
image4 = new Image; image4.src = "eye4.jpg";
image5 = new Image; image5.src = "eye5.jpg";
image6 = new Image; image6.src = "eye6.jpg";
image7 = new Image; image7.src = "eye7.jpg";
image8 = new Image; image8.src = "eye8.jpg";

images= new Array(8);
images[0] = image1.src;
images[1] = image2.src;
images[2] = image3.src;
images[3] = image4.src;
images[4] = image5.src;
images[5] = image6.src;
images[6] = image7.src;
images[7] = image8.src;
// End hiding JavaScript statements -->
</SCRIPT>
```

```
    </HEAD>

    <BODY>

        <IMG SRC="images[0]" WIDTH="100" HEIGHT="100" BORDER="0"
NAME="myEye">

        <SCRIPT LANGUAGE="JavaScript" TYPE="Text/JavaScript">
        <!-- Start hiding JavaScript statements
            BlinkEye();
        // End hiding JavaScript statements -->
        </SCRIPT>


    </BODY>

</HTML>
```

The first thing the script does is define a variable that tracks the current image:

```
currentImg = 0;
```

Next the script defines a function named BlinkEye() that, when called, increases the current image by 1. The function then sets document.myEye.src equal to the current image (as specified by the array position images[current_img]); this statement has the effect of changing the image displayed in the <IMG> tag named myEye in the body section of the page. The function then sets itself up to execute again in .1 second with the statement setTimeout('BlinkEye()',100).

```
function BlinkEye() {
    current_img++;
```

```
    if (current_img > images.length - 1) {
      current_img=0;
    }
  document.myEye.src = images[current_img];
  setTimeout('BlinkEye()',100);
}
```

To ensure that the graphics load quickly, you should preload them into cache on the visitor's computer. As the following line demonstrates, the script defines an image object for each graphic and then associates it with a graphic. The end result is that all the images are downloaded and placed into the user's cache before the effect begins to execute.

```
image1 = new Image; image1.src = "eye1.jpg";
```

Of course, for the BlinkEye() function to cycle through the images, the images must be loaded into an array:

```
images= new Array(8);
images[0] = image1.src;
images[1] = image2.src;
images[2] = image3.src;
images[3] = image4.src;
images[4] = image5.src;
images[5] = image6.src;
images[6] = image7.src;
images[7] = image8.src;
```

The <IMG> tag in the body section defines the initial graphic that is displayed when the page first loads, as well as its physical dimensions and characteristics. The BlinkEye() statement starts the whole animation process in motion. Figure 4.24 demonstrates the effect of the animation as the eye is beginning to close.

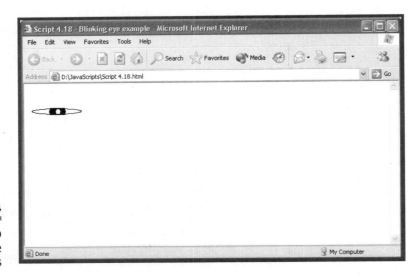

Figure 4.24

Using JavaScript to produce simple animated graphics

The Background Changer

This next example demonstrates how to enable the user to control the document's background color. By adapting this example, you can enable your visitors to customize their views of your pages. If you then combine this approach with the use of cookie technology, you can store this information and retrieve it every time that user visits your Web pages.

This example provides the user with two options for setting background color. The first method is to choose from a list of predefined options, and the second method is to type a color preference.

```
<HTML>

  <HEAD>
    <TITLE>Script 4.19 - Background animation example</TITLE>
  </HEAD>

  <BODY>

    <SCRIPT LANGUAGE="JavaScript" TYPE="Text/JavaScript">
    <!-- Start hiding JavaScript statements
```

```
      function ChangeBackground(color_num) {

        document.bgColor = color_num;

      }

  // End hiding JavaScript statements -->

  </SCRIPT>


  <H3>Select your background preference:</H3>

  <FORM NAME="myForm">

    <SELECT NAME="myList"

      onChange="ChangeBackground(

        document.myForm.myList.options[

        document.myForm.myList.selectedIndex].value)">

      <OPTION VALUE="red"> Red

      <OPTION VALUE="green"> Green

      <OPTION VALUE="yellow"> Yellow

      <OPTION VALUE="blue"> Blue

      <OPTION VALUE="pink"> Pink

      <OPTION VALUE="purple"> Purple

      <OPTION VALUE="orange"> Orange

      <OPTION VALUE="brown"> Brown

      <OPTION VALUE="white"> White

    </SELECT>

    <H3>Or type your own color here:</H3>

    <INPUT NAME="myText" TYPE="text" SIZE="10"
MAXLENGTH="15" VALUE="">

    <INPUT NAME="myButton1" TYPE="button" VALUE="Change"

      onClick="ChangeBackground(document.myForm.myText.
value)">

  </FORM>

  </BODY>


</HTML/>
```

This example defines a function named ChangeBackground() that changes the documents bgColor property to match the argument that it receives:

```
function ChangeBackground(color_num) {

  document.bgColor = color_num;

}
```

The script defines a drop-down list of color options that the visitor can select from and uses the <SELECT> tag's onChange event to call the ChangeBackground() function if the user selects one of the options:

```
onChange="ChangeBackground(

    document.myForm.myList.options[

    document.myForm.myList.selectedIndex].value)"
```

The final portion of the script enables your more discerning visitors to specify their own preferred background color by first defining a text field in which the user can type his color choice and a button that, when clicked, executes the ChangeBackground() function and passes the color the user specified (for example, document.myForm.myText.value).

Figure 4.25 shows how this example looks when first loaded into the browser.

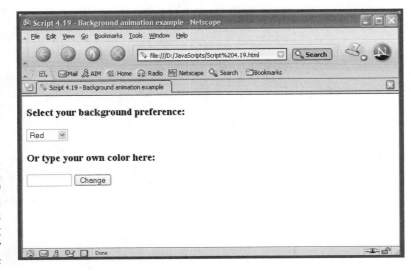

Figure 4.25

An example of a script that enables your visitors to set a background color preference

The Picture Viewer

This final graphic example uses a combination of frames and JavaScript to deliver an impressive but simple online picture viewer. As the following example shows, the JavaScript located in the head section defines and loads all the images into cache on the visitor's computer.

```
<HTML>

  <HEAD>
    <TITLE>Script 4.20 - Example of a picture viewer</TITLE>

    <SCRIPT LANGUAGE="JavaScript" TYPE="Text/JavaScript">
    <!-- Start hiding JavaScript statements
       birthday = new Image(); birthday.src = "birthday.jpg";
       puppydog = new Image(); puppydog.src = "puppydog.jpg";
       stuffed  = new Image(); stuffed.src  = "stuffed.jpg";
    // End hiding JavaScript statements -->
    </SCRIPT>

  </HEAD>

  <BODY>

    <CENTER>
    <TABLE BORDER="10">
      <TR>
        <TD>
          <H3>Hello and welcome to my personal photo
album!</H3>
        </TD>
      </TR>
```

```
        <TR>

          <TD>

            <FORM NAME = myForm>

            <B>Choose a picture:</B>

            <INPUT NAME="myButton1" TYPE="button" VALUE="birthday"
                onClick = "document.myImage.src =
birthday.src">

              <INPUT NAME="myButton2" TYPE="button" VALUE="puppydog"
                  onClick = "document.myImage.src = puppydog.src">

              <INPUT NAME="myButton3" TYPE="button" VALUE="stuffed"
                  onClick = "document.myImage.src = stuffed.src">

            </FORM>

          </TD>

        </TR>

        <TR>

          <TD>

            <IMG NAME="myImage" SRC="welcome.jpg" WIDTH="440"
HEIGHT="292">

          </TD>

        <TR>

      </TABLE>

      </CENTER>

    </BODY>


</HTML>
```

In the body section, a TABLE of one column and three rows is defined.
The first row contains a welcome message formatted with the level 3
HTML header <H3>. The second row contains a form with three buttons,
each of which has an onClick event handler that changes the src property of the image to a different picture.

```
<INPUT NAME="myButton1" TYPE="button" VALUE="birthday"
    onClick = "document.myImage.src = birthday.src">
```

```
<INPUT NAME="myButton2" TYPE="button" VALUE="puppydog"
    onClick = "document.myImage.src = puppydog.src">

<INPUT NAME="myButton3" TYPE="button" VALUE="stuffed"
    onClick = "document.myImage.src = stuffed.src">
```

The last row in the table contains a simple `<IMG>` tag that loads an initial image and defines the display's physical dimensions. Figure 4.26 shows what this example looks like when it is first loaded.

Figure 4.26

By combining JavaScript and frames, you can create very powerful presentations.

What's Next?

Whew! That was a lot to cover in a single session. By now, you should be feeling pretty good about your JavaScript skills. I'll bet that, based on what you have learned so far, you already have plenty of ideas for things you want to try on your Web pages. Tomorrow morning you'll learn how to create JavaScript cookies and to debug your scripts. Then you will wrap up your JavaScript training by working on a project that provides you with the opportunity to put everything you have learned to the test.

Starting tomorrow afternoon, the book will turn its attention to JScript, and you will begin learning how to automate all kinds of tasks on your computer. So go get a good night's sleep, and we'll get started again in the morning.

Advanced
JavaScript Coding

- ➤ Baking your first JavaScript cookie
- ➤ Retrieving your cookie
- ➤ Debugging your JavaScripts
- ➤ Creating a complete Web site project

This morning's chapter will complete this book's JavaScript coverage. It begins by teaching you how to collect, store, and retrieve information about your visitors using cookies. This will provide you with the capability to provide customized content and to provide visitors with a personalized touch.

Next the chapter will provide you with advice and information on how to debug your JavaScripts. You will learn about an assortment of programming tips and tricks. I'll also teach you how to configure Internet Explorer to display error messages so that you will see them automatically when you are testing and debugging your JavaScripts. Then I will show you how to use Netscape Communicator's JavaScript Console as a troubleshooting tool.

Finally, I will wrap up the chapter by walking you through the development of a fictional Web site called the On-line Bookmall. This exercise will give you the opportunity to put your new JavaScript programming skills to work and will provide you with a working example of how to integrate JavaScript into a Web site.

Baking JavaScript Cookies

Cookies are small text strings that you can store on the computers of people that visit your Web site. You can use cookies to store information about visitor activity or preferences. Later, when a visitor returns to your Web site, you can retrieve this information and use it to present customized content. For example, you might use cookies to store and retrieve visitor's names or their preferred color settings.

Cookies are used by virtually every major Web site on the Internet today. Cookies are stored in plain text files on the user's computer. Cookie technology is very limited. Cookies cannot be used to plant viruses on a visitor's computer, nor can they be used to store large amounts of data. In fact, cookies are limited to 4KB in size. Both Internet Explorer and Netscape Communicator limit the number of cookies that can be stored on a computer to 300. In addition, no one Web site is permitted to store more than 20 cookies on a visitor's computer. As a result, the total number of cookies that can be stored on any computer will take up no more than 1.2MB of disk space.

NOTE It is important to understand that your JavaScripts cannot actually store cookies directly on a visitor's computer. Instead, the cookies that your scripts create are stored in the browser's cache. Whether they are ultimately saved on the visitor's computer depends on whether or not the browser has been configured to save them.

Both Internet Explorer and Netscape Communicator provide the capability to block cookies from being stored on computers. However, most users quickly find that disabling cookies is impractical because too many Web sites depend on them in order to provide their content.

Cookies can be retrieved only by the Web site that created them. Therefore any cookie you create is safe from view of other Web sites. This provides a degree of security. However, since cookies are stored as plain text files, they are easily read by anybody working on the computer where they are stored. This makes cookies inappropriate for storing highly sensitive information such as passwords or credit card numbers.

 TIP To learn more than you would ever want to know about cookies, visit www.cookiecentral.com.

Understanding Cookie Syntax

To create and retrieve cookies, you need to know how to work with the `document` object's `cookie` property. By assigning a value to the `document.cookie` property, you create a new cookie. For example, the following statement defines a cookie that stores the visitor's name:

```
document.cookie = "name=" + name + ";expires=" +
expirationDate.toGMTString();
```

The `expires` field is required and tells the browser how long to store the cookie before deleting it. If you forget to add this field, the cookie expires as soon as the current session ends.

In a similar fashion, you can retrieve the cookie the next time the visitor loads your Web page, using the following statement:

```
myCookie = document.cookie;
```

In the examples that follow, I will show you how to create and retrieve your first JavaScript cookie.

Creating a Cookie

This first cookie example displays a form that asks visitors to type their names. It then creates a cookie that includes the visitor's name and an expiration date of one month from the current date.

 NOTE This very simple example does not include logic to first make sure that the visitor does not already have a cookie from you before bothering to ask for his name. The example also does not contain logic to check whether the cookie is about to expire so that it can replace it with a new one. I will leave that code to you to devise.

```
<HTML>


  <HEAD>

    <TITLE>Script 5.1 - Baking your first cookie</TITLE>


    <SCRIPT LANGUAGE="JavaScript" TYPE="Text/JavaScript">
    <!-- Start hiding JavaScript statements
```

```
        expirationDate = new Date;

        expirationDate.setMonth(expirationDate.getMonth() + 1);

        function BakeTheCookie(name) {

            document.cookie = "name=" + name + ";expires=" +
expirationDate.toGMTString();

        }


    // End hiding JavaScript statements -->
    </SCRIPT>


  </HEAD>


  <BODY>
    <H3>Cookie Information Collector</H3>
    <FORM NAME="myForm">
      <B>What is your name? </B>
      <INPUT TYPE="text" NAME="visitorName">
      <INPUT NAME="myButton" TYPE="button" VALUE="Save Cookie"
          onClick="BakeTheCookie(document.myForm.visitorName.
value)">
    </FORM>
  </BODY>


</HTML>
```

This example contains a script in the head section. The first thing the script does is define an object called expirationDate. Next it sets the expiration date for the cookie, using the Date object's setMonth() method to add one month to the current date:

```
expirationDate = new Date;
expirationDate.setMonth(expirationDate.getMonth() + 1);
```

The logic to "bake" the cookie is located in a function named BakeTheCookie(). This function accepts the name of the visitor as an argument:

```
function BakeTheCookie(name) {

  document.cookie = "name=" + name + ";expires=" +
expirationDate.toGMTString();

}
```

The rest of the example is a form that collects the visitor's name and then calls the BakeTheCookie() function.

```
onClick="BakeTheCookie(document.myForm.visitorName.value)"
```

Figure 5.1 demonstrates what the example looks like when it is first loaded into your browser.

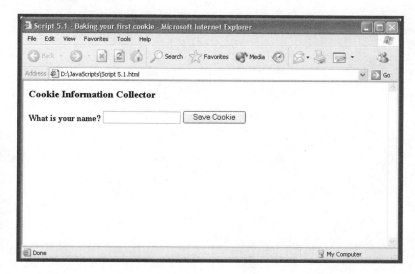

Figure 5.1

You can use a cookie to store information about your visitors that you can reuse every time they visit your Web site.

Viewing Your Cookie

Okay, so you have baked your cookie and saved it on your visitor's computer. What next? The answer is—not much. You just wait for the visitor to return. When the visitor returns, you can check to see whether he has one of your cookies, as demonstrated in the following example.

NOTE

In actual practice, you will want to write a script that combines the cookie logic of this and the previous example so that you first check to see whether the user has one of your cookies before you assign another cookie.

```
<HTML>

  <HEAD>
    <TITLE>Script 5.2 - Retrieving your cookie</TITLE>

    <SCRIPT LANGUAGE="JavaScript" TYPE="Text/JavaScript">
    <!-- Start hiding JavaScript statements

      function CookieCheck() {
        visitorName = "";
        cookieName = "";
       if (document.cookie != "") {
          cookieName = document.cookie.split("=")[0];
          visitorName = document.cookie.split("=")[1];
           window.alert("cookieName = " + cookieName +
"\nCookie Contents = " + visitorName);
        }
        else {
          window.alert("Your cookie was not found!");
        }
      }


      // End hiding JavaScript statements -->
    </SCRIPT>
```

```
    </HEAD>

    <BODY onLoad="CookieCheck()">
    </BODY>


</HTML>
```

The logic that retrieves your cookie is located in a function named Cook-ieCheck(), which is located in a script embedded in the HTML page's head section. The function is called by the onLoad event in the <BODY> tag.

The first thing the script does is check to see whether or not the visitor already has one of your cookies:

```
if (document.cookie != "")
```

If the visitor does not have one of your cookies, the document object's alert() method is used to display a pop-up dialog box stating that a cookie was not found. However, if a cookie *was* found, the script retrieves the value of the cookie using the cookie object's split() method. The split() method breaks the cookie into fields. The first statement sets a variable named cookieName equal to the name the cookie was saved as. The second statement sets another variable named visitorName to the name that is stored in the cookie.

```
cookieName = document.cookie.split("=")[0];

visitorName = document.cookie.split("=")[1];
```

The script then uses the window object's alert() method to display the contents of the cookie:

```
window.alert("cookieName = " + cookieName + "\nCookie
Contents = " + visitorName);
```

NOTE Although this example shows you how to retrieve and display your cookie, a more effective use of this information might be to display a welcome message that greets the visitor by name.

Figure 5.2 demonstrates how the script formats the result when it finds a cookie.

Figure 5.2

By retrieving cookie information, you can avoid having to ask visitors repeatedly for the same information and can greet them by name when they return to your site.

A really good example of how to use cookies when creating your Web site is provided in the On-line Bookmall project presented later in this chapter.

Debugging Your JavaScripts

In programming, there is one universal truth: Everyone makes mistakes. A mistake in a script is referred to as a *bug*. The process of finding and fixing bugs is called *debugging* and is a normal part of the development process. Even if you write a script that seems to work well right from the start, you still should perform a certain amount of testing and debugging to verify that the JavaScript works as expected in different scenarios.

In most cases, the browser will supply you with clues about where problems lie when you test your JavaScripts during script development. However, there will be times when things are not working correctly and the browser will not provide you with any error messages, leaving it totally up to you to locate and resolve the problem. Fortunately, there are a number of steps that you can follow to locate and fix bugs.

Debugging JavaScripts is neither glamorous nor fun, and it always seems to take longer than you anticipate. The bad news is that the longer your program is, the more errors you will see. The good news is that with time, experience, programming discipline, and a sound debugging process you will become proficient at debugging your scripts.

You are going to come across three types of errors when writing JavaScripts, as listed below. Each of these different types of errors is explained in detail in the sections that follow.

- Load-time errors
- Runtime errors
- Logic errors

Load-Time Errors

Load-time errors occur when the browser attempts to load a HTML page that contains an HTML or script error. These errors tend to be fairly obvious and typically involve basic syntax issues. A *syntax error* occurs because the browser is unable to determine what the script is trying to do. Unlike human communications, a small syntactical error in computer code is enough to break down all communications. Remember that JavaScript is case sensitive and that you must be consistent in the manner in which you define and reference variables, functions, objects, methods, properties, and events.

Internet Explorer and Netscape Communicator used to display errors in pop-up dialog boxes that provided you with information about errors when they occurred. The current versions of both browsers now hide error messages from view because the typical user neither needs nor wants to see them. The only person who really needs to see the error messages is the programmer, because after a script has been fully debugged and made available on the Internet, it shouldn't have any errors (and even if there are errors, no one but the programmer can do anything about them anyway). Netscape and Microsoft's philosophy is to minimize the possible impact of a script's bugs on the user. Later this afternoon, I will show you how to view both Internet Explorer and Netscape Communicator error messages.

TIP

The best way to deal with syntax errors is to avoid them in the first place. Type carefully and double-check your scripts before running them to make sure that everything is in order. For example, make sure that you have avoided using reserved words as variable names, and do not forget to match up all opening and closing parentheses and braces. Remember to separate the attributes of the various loop statements with commas (except for the `for` statement, which uses the semicolon to separate its arguments).

Often the error messages tell you everything that you will need to know to find and correct problems. In addition to a brief problem description, the error message may even display the actual portion of code that caused the error. For example, if you attempt to load the following HTML page, an error will occur.

```
1.   <HTML>
2.      <HEAD>
3.         <TITLE>Script 5.3 - Sample syntax error</TITLE>
4.      </HEAD>
5.      <BODY>
6.         <SCRIPT LANGUAGE="JavaScript" TYPE="Text/JavaScript">
7.         <!-- Start hiding JavaScript statements
8.            var testColor = "blue";
9.            if (testColor == "blue" {
10.              document.write("We have a match");
11.           }
12.        // End hiding JavaScript statements -->
13.        </SCRIPT>
14.     </BODY>
15.  </HTML>
```

Can you spot the error by eyeballing the script? The script consists of only a few lines of code, but the error still may not jump out at you. When I loaded this script, Netscape reported the following error message:

```
Error: missing ) after condition
Source File: file:///D:/JavaScripts/Script%205.3.html
Line: 9, Column: 30
Source Code:
        if (testColor == "blue" {
```

Similarly, when I loaded this HTML page using Internet Explorer, the following error occurred.

```
Line: 9

Char: 31

Error: Expected ')'

Code: 0

URL: file://C:\Documents and Settings\Jerry Ford\Desktop\
Script 5.3.html
```

With this information in hand, the job of debugging the script is much easier. As you can see, several very useful pieces of information were provided in the error messages provided by both browsers.

- **Line number on which the error occurred:** line 9
- **Error message itself:** `missing ) after condition` or `Expected ')'`
- **Error text (the actual line of code that generated the error):**
  `if (testColor == "blue" {`

TIP To better show the value of the line number information provided in the error message, I added line numbers to the left of the previous example. These numbers are not part of the sample code that you normally type. When you are looking for a JavaScript editor, you may want to look for one that automatically provides line numbering.

As you can see, the error message indicates that a right parenthesis is missing on line 9. If you look at the error text portion of the error message, you will see where the) should have been inserted, as demonstrated here:

```
if (testColor == "blue" ) {

  document.write("We have a match");

}
```

Runtime Errors

A *runtime error* occurs as a result of an attempt by your script to do something that is against the rules. For example, if a script attempts to reference an undeclared variable or call a function that has not yet been defined, a runtime error will occur. Other examples of runtime errors include using JavaScript commands incorrectly. The following script will produce a runtime error when it is loaded by the Web browser:

```
1.   <HTML>
2.      <HEAD>
3.        <TITLE>Script 5.4 - Sample runtime error</TITLE>
4.      </HEAD>
5.      <BODY>
6.        <SCRIPT LANGUAGE="JavaScript" TYPE="Text/JavaScript">
7.        <!-- Start hiding JavaScript statements
8.          myFunction();
9.          function Myfunction() {
10.             document.write("Hello World!");
11.          }
12.        // End hiding JavaScript statements -->
13.      </SCRIPT>
14.    </BODY>
15. </HTML>
```

If you load this HTML page using Netscape Communicator, the following error will occur:

```
Error: myFunction is not defined
Source File: file:///D:/JavaScripts/Script%205.4.html
Line: 8
```

This error message tells you the line number where the browser thinks the error occurred and gives you a brief description of the error. In the preceding example, I intended to create and call a function named myFunction().

Even though the error message points me to line 8, the actual error is on line 9 where I mistyped the function name as Myfunction().

Logic Errors

Logic errors can be the most difficult type of errors to track down. These errors are not the result of a syntax or runtime error. Instead, they occur when you make a mistake in the logic that drives your script and you do not get the result you expected. Unfortunately, as far as JavaScript is concerned, the script is running well. Therefore, the browser won't generate an error message. The result is that you won't get any help in homing in on where the problem lies.

For example, the following script contains a logic error. The script was supposed to count from 1 to 10 and then terminate. However, when writing the `for` statement that controls the looping logic, I accidentally typed `i--` instead of `i++`. Instead of starting at 1 and going to 10, the script starts at 1 and counts backwards. Because the value of `i` never reaches 11, the script enters into an endless loop and never stops running. Although the script did exactly what it was *told* to do, it did not do what I *intended* it to do.

```
<HTML>

  <HEAD>

    <TITLE>Script 5.5 - Sample logical error</TITLE>

  </HEAD>


  <BODY>


    <SCRIPT LANGUAGE="JavaScript" TYPE="Text/JavaScript">

    <!-- Start hiding JavaScript statements
```

```
document.write(" Let's count from 1 to 10 <BR>")
for (i=1;i<11;i--) {
  document.write(i + "<BR>")
}


// End hiding JavaScript statements -->
</SCRIPT>


</BODY>


</HTML>
```

Another common example of a logic error is one that everybody gets wrong and involves the misuse of the assignment operator in place of the == comparison operator. For example, the following script displays the "We have a match" message even though the values of the apples and oranges variables are not the same. Clearly, this is not the logic I intended. When I rewrote the if statement as if (apples == oranges) and loaded it, the example worked as expected, and the "We do not have a match" message was displayed.

```
<HTML>

  <HEAD>
    <TITLE>Script 5.6 - A second sample logical error</TITLE>
  </HEAD>


  <BODY>


    <SCRIPT LANGUAGE="JavaScript" TYPE="Text/JavaScript">
    <!-- Start hiding JavaScript statements

      apples = 5;
      oranges = 15;
```

```
if (apples = oranges) {

  document.write("We have a match");

}

else {

  document.write("We do not have a match");

}


// End hiding JavaScript statements -->

</SCRIPT>


</BODY>


</HTML>
```

TIP ■
One of the ways I could have debugged the preceding example would have been to add
a checkpoint in the script just before the `if` statement. A *checkpoint* is a statement that
displays the value of a variable so that you know what it has been set to. I will describe
this debugging technique in more detail in a few minutes.
■ ■

Habits of Highly Effective Programmers

Before I delve further into the discussion of debugging your scripts, I thought
I'd provide you with a few tips that you can use to reduce the number of errors
in your scripts and that can make the debugging process a little easier.

✿ **Remember to use plenty of comments.** Comments enable you to
explain why you wrote the script the way you did and to explain particularly difficult sections of code. Comments make it much easier for
others to follow behind you and for you to understand your own code
months or years later.

✪ **Always use indentation to make your code easy to read.** Indenting statements also makes it easier for you to match up beginning and ending tags, curly braces, and other HTML and script elements.

✪ **Write modular code.** Whenever possible, group your statements into functions. Functions let you group related statements, and test and reuse portions of code with minimal effort. Simplify your design by assigning only one task to a function.

✪ **Declare functions and variables at the top of your scripts.** This approach makes those elements easy to find and modify, and is a lot less confusing than embedding them throughout different portions of lengthy scripts. This technique also helps to ensure that the functions and variables are defined before they are referenced.

✪ **Be consistent in the way you name variables and functions.** Try using names that are long enough to be meaningful and that describe the contents of the variable or the purpose of the function.

✪ **Use consistent syntax when naming variables and functions.** In other words, keep them all lowercase or all uppercase; if you prefer Camel-Back notation, use it consistently.

✪ **Do not assume that your script is bug free just because it ran once without an error.** Make sure that you test the script using different browsers and, if possible, with different versions of the same browser.

✪ **Make sure that you test your script using browsers that do not support JavaScript to ensure that your script properly provides alternative content.** Try disabling support in your browsers for things such as frames to make sure that all browsers display your information as you intend it to be displayed.

✪ **Test all possible scenarios.** This includes testing with good and bad data. If your pages have forms, enter invalid data and check to make sure that the validation routines work as you think they will. Test every link and click on every button.

✪ **Test long scripts in a modular fashion.** In other words, do not try to write the entire script before testing any portion of it. Write a piece and get it to work before adding the next portion of code.

- Load your pages using different resolutions to make sure that they look as you expect them to at any size. Also try resizing your browser windows to see how your HTML pages look at different sizes.

- Test every event handler to ensure that it executes as expected.

- Declare variables explicitly using the `var` keyword.

- Use descriptive variable and function names and avoid using single-character names.

- Pay attention when using object names. Core JavaScript objects begin with capitalized letters (for example, `Array`, `Boolean`, `Date`, `Function`, `Math`, `Number`, `Object`, `RegExp`, and `String`).

- Watch your quotation marks. Remember that quotation marks are used in pairs around strings and that both quotation marks must be of the same style (either single or double). If you want to show quotation marks as part of the text message, embed them inside quotation marks of the alternate type (for example, place single quotation marks inside double quotation marks and vice versa).

Using Checkpoints

One very simple debugging technique is to place checkpoints in your script when you are writing and testing it. You can do this by taking advantage of the `document` object's `alert()` method to display the value of variables before and after they are evaluated or changed within the script to make sure that they are being set properly. Another use for checkpoints is to monitor the execution flow of your scripts to make sure that they are executing in the order you anticipate. For example, you can place an `alert()` statement in every function to display a message each time the function is called.

NOTE Alternatively, you can display a message in the current window using the `document.write()` method or open up a new window and write to it. It really does not matter which of these checkpoint techniques you use. Some may work better than others, depending on the circumstances.

Just remember one important thing: Save your visitors some frustration by remembering to remove or comment out all your checkpoints when you are done testing.

Test Before You Write

One of the most difficult things about programming in any language is figuring out the right syntax for a command that you want to execute in your script. One really neat trick you can use in Netscape Communicator or Internet Explorer is to type `javascript:` followed by the statement you want to test in the browser's URL field, as demonstrated in Figure 5.3.

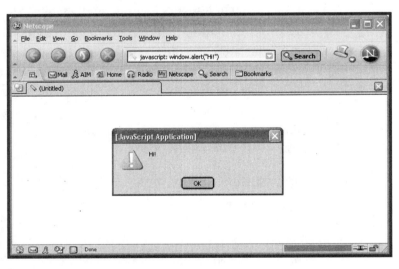

Figure 5.3

You can type JavaScript commands and statements into the browser's URL field to test their results before you use the statements in your scripts.

Trapping Errors with onError

A JavaScript error event is triggered every time a script encounters a problem loading a window, frame, or image. A JavaScript `onerror` event handler routine can be set up to handle these situations. Three arguments are passed to the `onerror` event handler automatically:

- ✪ Error message
- ✪ URL information
- ✪ Line number

The following script demonstrates how to write a function you can place in any of your scripts to display information associated with an occurrence of the error event. A function named `ErrorTrap()` is defined in the head section of the page; the function accepts three arguments. These arguments correspond to the three arguments that are automatically passed to the `onerror` event handler. The `ErrorTrap()` function then formats the error information in an alert pop-up dialog box. The statement `onerror = ErrorTrap` in the script in the head section tells the browser to call the function for any error event.

```html
<HTML>


    <HEAD>

        <TITLE>Script 5.7 - Capturing errors with the onError
event handler</TITLE>


        <SCRIPT LANGUAGE="JavaScript" TYPE="Text/JavaScript">
        <!-- Start hiding JavaScript statements


            function ErrorTrap(msg,url,lineNo) {

                window.alert("Error: " + msg + "\nLine: " + lineNo +
"\nULR: " + url);

            }


            onerror = ErrorTrap;


        // End hiding JavaScript statements -->
        </SCRIPT>


    </HEAD>


    <BODY>
```

```
<SCRIPT LANGUAGE="JavaScript" TYPE="Text/JavaScript">
<!-- Start hiding JavaScript statements
   document.wrrite("");
// End hiding JavaScript statements -->
</SCRIPT>


</BODY>


</HTML>
```

Figure 5.4 shows the pop-up dialog box that is displayed as a result of loading this script. As you can see, all the error information is displayed and, in this example, it points you to the exact location of the problem.

Figure 5.4

The onerror event handler can be used in conjunction with the document object's alert() method to display debugging information.

 TIP You may have noticed that I used the \n character in the alert() statement to format the message output. This special formatting character causes a carriage return and is used to exercise control over how text is laid out in pop-up dialog boxes.

Internet Explorer Error Messages

Internet Explorer can suppress or display JavaScript error messages. This feature is configured on the Advanced property sheet on the Internet Options dialog box (see Figure 5.5) found in the Tools menu. By default, Internet Explorer 6 does not display JavaScript error messages. However, you'll probably find it handy to turn it on when you are creating and testing your JavaScripts. To enable this feature, select the Display a Notification About Every Script Error check box and click on OK.

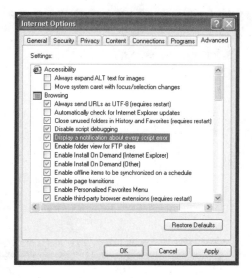

Figure 5.5

Configuring Internet Explorer to display script errors automatically when they occur

The next time you load a Web page that contains a JavaScript error, you will see an Internet Explorer error dialog box similar to the one shown in Figure 5.6. As you can see, you can control the amount of information that is displayed by clicking on the Hide Details button.

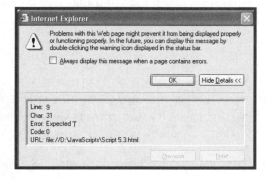

Figure 5.6

Viewing all the details of an Internet Explorer error message

You can safely prevent the display of Internet Explorer error messages by clearing the Display a Notification About Every Script Error option and clicking on OK without losing convenient access to error information.

Instead, when an error is encountered, a small alert icon is displayed in the lower-left corner of the browser, as shown in Figure 5.7. Double-click on the icon to view the error dialog box.

Error message icon

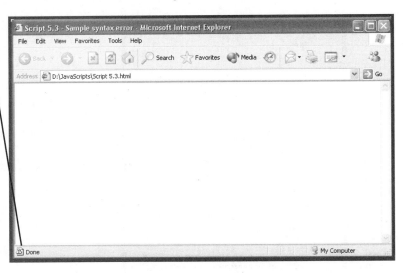

Figure 5.7

When error notification is enabled, you can view Internet Explorer script error messages by double-clicking on the alert icon in the status bar.

Working with the Netscape JavaScript Console

Netscape comes with an integrated JavaScript tool known as the Netscape JavaScript Console. Unfortunately, there is no equivalent tool built into Internet Explorer. As a result, you may find that Netscape Communicator is the better browser to work with when debugging your JavaScripts. Netscape Communicator sends all error messages to the JavaScript Console.

TIP

When I am ready to do some serious debugging, I open the JavaScript Console and leave it displayed at all times. This makes it easier for me to view error messages.

The Netscape JavaScript Console, shown in Figure 5.8, is organized into two sections. The lower section displays a scrollable list of error messages. This section enables you to view current and previous errors. You can open the JavaScript Console at any time by typing `javascript:` in Netscape Communicator's URL field and pressing Enter. I think that you will find the

Console's running history of errors very helpful but, if you prefer, you can click on the Clear button to clear out the messages in the display area.

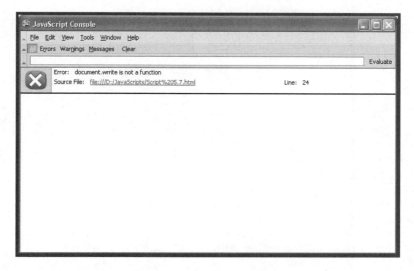

Figure 5.8

Netscape Communicator provides a built-in JavaScript debugger that allows you to view error messages and test command syntax.

Testing JavaScript Statements

The top section of the JavaScript Console contains the Evaluate field, where you can type JavaScript statements and view their results. For example, Figure 5.9 demonstrates how to use the JavaScript Console to test the syntax of two JavaScript statements. The first statement defines a variable, and the second statement displays the value assigned to the variable using the alert() method. Note that in order for this to work the two commands must be separated by a semicolon.

You also can use the Evaluate field to test JavaScript expressions and to perform mathematical calculations to make sure that your formulas will return expected results before you incorporate them into your scripts.

For example, the following text demonstrates how to test the syntax of a function and its statements. As you can see, the statement tests a small function named DisplayMsg() by calling it and passing a single argument. When this statement executes, you'll see an alert dialog box appear.

```
function DisplayMsg(var1) { window.alert(var1) };
DisplayMsg("Hi");
```

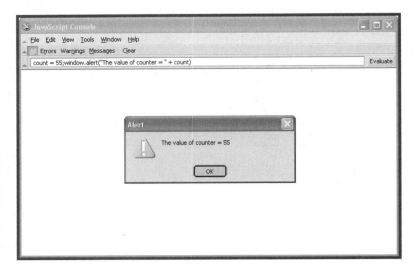

Figure 5.9

You can type
JavaScript
commands into the
Netscape JavaScript
Console to test
their results.

The next example contains three statements. The first statement defines a variable, the second statement changes its value, and the third statement displays an alert dialog box if its conditional test evaluates to true.

```
var oranges = 5; oranges = oranges + 5; if (oranges < 12)
window.alert("Order more oranges");
```

Take a Break

You've just learned how to bake JavaScript cookies as well as how to test and debug your JavaScripts. Now it is time for another break. When you return, I'll guide you through the steps required to build the On-line Bookmall. By the time you are done with this project, you will be ready to spice up your own Web site and tackle even bigger projects. This is the final stretch, and you should be able to see the light at the end of the tunnel. Go ahead and take your break, and I will see you back in a little bit.

Overview of the On-line Bookmall Web Site

The rest of this chapter provides you with the opportunity to put your new JavaScript programming skills to work by creating a Web site called Jerry's

On-line Bookmall. The idea behind this site is that a book vendor (me) has joined several online bookstores' associate programs. These *associate programs* pay a percentage on every sale that is made as a result of somebody entering a bookstore's Web site through Jerry's On-line Bookmall.

This works because each online bookstore provides a specifically formatted link that, when clicked, enables any traffic originating from Jerry's On-line Bookmall to be tracked. Because some people might have an online bookstore at which they like to shop, you might decide against joining just one major online bookstore's associate program.

NOTE You can learn more about each online bookstore's associate program by visiting its Web site, where you can read all about the rules of the program and apply instantly. As you might suppose, bookstores are not the only businesses on the Internet that provide opportunities through associate programs. With just a little surfing, you can find dozens of other opportunities.

Jerry's On-line Bookmall is a relatively small Web site made up of a small collection of HTML pages. The Web site starts off with a typical index page from which other pages in the site are linked. In addition to displaying a welcome message and standard HTML links, the index page contains JavaScript statements that add the following functionality:

- Cookie logic for the collection and display of visitor names
- Code to open a new window and display a featured book selection
- A rotating advertisement banner that promotes other fictitious sites belonging to Jerry
- A browser detection example

The next page in this Web site that uses JavaScript is the navigation frame in the actual bookstore section of the Web site. Here, mouse event handlers are embedded in HTML links that provide rollover effects for five target options, including a welcome page, links to three major online bookstores, and a Jerry's Picks page.

The Jerry's Picks page demonstrates the use of mouse events to post and clear messages on the browser window's status bar. These messages provide additional information about the book over which the visitor moves the mouse pointer.

As you will see, a small collection of carefully placed JavaScripts can make a big impact on any Web site. As you work your way through this sample site, I will point out other ideas for ways to use JavaScript to further enhance the Web site.

NOTE You have already learned a lot about JavaScript in this book. The focus of this final session is on applying much of what you have learned, so I won't waste your time by going over every line of code in excruciating detail and explaining things you have already seen before. Instead, I will lay out the basic structure of the Web site, list its code, and talk at a relatively high level about where and how JavaScript was used. Because of the limited space available in this morning's session, the Web site won't be 100 percent complete, but it will serve as an example and a template from which you can begin your own JavaScript experience.

Crafting the Index Page

The HTML and JavaScript statements that make up the index page of Jerry's On-line Bookmall are listed here.

```
<HTML>


   <HEAD>
     <TITLE>Script 5.8 - Jerry's On-line Bookmall Index
Page</TITLE>


     <SCRIPT LANGUAGE="JavaScript" TYPE="Text/JavaScript">
     <!-- Start hiding JavaScript statements


       //Define an array that will be used to manage banner
advertisements
```

```javascript
MyBannerArray = new Array(3);

MyBannerArray[0]="banner0.jpg";

MyBannerArray[1]="banner1.jpg";

MyBannerArray[2]="banner2.jpg";

currentBanner=0;

noOfBanners=MyBannerArray.length;


function CycleBanner() {

    if (currentBanner==noOfBanners) {

      currentBanner=0;

    }

    document.myBanner.src=MyBannerArray[currentBanner];

    currentBanner++;

    setTimeout("CycleBanner()", 5*1000);

}


    //Declare a variable used to set the cookie expiration
date

ExpirationDate = new Date;

ExpirationDate.setMonth(ExpirationDate.getMonth() + 3);


    //Define a function that stores a cookie on the visitor's
computer

function BakeTheCookie(name) {

  document.cookie = "name=" + name + ";expires=" +

  ExpirationDate.toGMTString();

}


    //Define a function to check for the cookie and use it

    // in the welcome message if found
```

```
function CookieCheck() {
  visitorName = "";
  cookieName = "";
  if (document.cookie != "") {
  visitorName = document.cookie.split("=")[1];
  document.write("<H4>Hello " + visitorName + ",</H4>");
}
  else {
    input = window.prompt("Welcome to the Bookmall. " +
      "What is your name?","");

    //user click on cancel
    if (input != null) {
      //user left blank and clicked on OK
      if (input != "") {
        BakeTheCookie(input);
        document.write("<H4>Welcome " + input + "," +
"</H4>");
      }
      else {
        document.write("<H4>Welcome.</H4>");
      }
    }
    else {
      document.write("<H4>Welcome.</H4>");
    }
  }
}


    //Define a function to load an html page Into a new
window
```

```
function OpenNewWindow() {
     window.open('Script 5.9.html', 'window1',
'width=640,height=420');

     }


     //Define a function that determines the visitor's
browser type
     //and version
     function BrowserCheck() {


          if ((navigator.appName=="Microsoft Internet
Explorer") ||
               (navigator.appName=="Netscape")) {


               if (navigator.appName=="Microsoft Internet
Explorer") {
                    if (navigator.appVersion.indexOf("6.") < 0) {
                         window.alert("Please upgrade to IE version 6
or above.");
                    }
               }


               if (navigator.appName=="Netscape") {
                    if (navigator.appVersion.indexOf("5") < 0) {
                         window.alert("Please upgrade to Netscape
version 7 or above.");
                    }
               }


          } else {
               window.alert("This Web site requires Netscape 7 or
Internet " +
```

```
                                        "Explorer 6 or higher!");
                    }


                }


           // End hiding JavaScript statements -->
           </SCRIPT>


     </HEAD>


     <BODY onLoad="CycleBanner()">


        <TABLE BORDER="0" WIDTH="590">
           <TR>
             <TD>
               <CENTER>
                  <P><IMG NAME="myBanner" SRC="banner0.jpg"></P>
                  <IMG BORDER="0" HEIGHT="78" SRC="bstorelogo.jpg"
WIDTH="636">
               </CENTER>
             </TD>
           </TR>
        </TABLE>
        <TABLE BORDER="0" WIDTH="590" STYLE="HEIGHT: 25px; WIDTH:
643px">
           <TR>
             <TD>
             </TD>
           </TR>
        </TABLE>
```

```
    <TABLE BORDER="0" WIDTH="590" STYLE="HEIGHT: 254px;
WIDTH: 643px">
      <TR>
       <TD>


        <SCRIPT LANGUAGE="JavaScript"
TYPE="Text/JavaScript">
        <!-- Start hiding JavaScript statements


         //Execute the function that determines the
visitor's browser
         //type and version
         BrowserCheck();


         //Execute the function that looks for the Web
site's cookie
         CookieCheck();


         // End hiding JavaScript statements -->
        </SCRIPT>


        <H2 ALIGN="left">
         <FONT COLOR="red">Welcome to Jerry's
Bookmall.</FONT>
         </H2>
        <HR>
        <FONT SIZE="5">F</FONT>or your convenience I have
        assembled a collection of the finest bookstores on
        the World Wide Web. Jerry's On-line Bookmall is
        your one stop shopping place for all your reading
        needs. Whether you are interested in fiction,
        non-fiction, history, literature, or computer books,
```

```
            you will find exactly what you are looking for here.
            Don't forget that you can also purchase your
            favorite toys, videos, and CDs as well. Feel free
            to browse to your heart's content and thanks
            for visiting us!
            <HR>
        </TD>
        <TD>
            <CENTER>
                <H3>Featured Book!</H3>
                <A HREF="javascript:OpenNewWindow()">
<IMG HEIGHT="170"
                SRC="htmlbook.jpg" ALT="Learn HTML In a
Weekend" WIDTH="126">
                </A>
            <BR>
            <B>Learn HTML In a Weekend</B>
            </CENTER>
        </TD>
    </TR>
</TABLE>
<TABLE BORDER="0" STYLE="HEIGHT: 25px; WIDTH: 643px"
WIDTH="590">
    <TR>
        <TD>
            <CENTER>
                <BR>
                [ <A>Main Menu</A> ]
                [ <A HREF="Script 5.10.html">Bookstore</A> ]
                [ <A HREF="script 5.18.html">Email Us</A> ]
            </CENTER>
```

```
        </TD>
      </TR>
    </TABLE>
  </BODY>
</HTML>
```

As you can see, this HTML page and the JavaScripts that it contains are fairly lengthy compared to the other examples you have seen in this book. It begins by defining all the variables and functions used on the page in the head section:

- **ExpirationDate**. A variable used to build the expiration date for the site's cookie.

- **MyBannerArray[]**. An array loaded with three graphic images that will be used to display a rotating banner advertisement.

- **CycleBanner()**. A function that loops continuously through MyBannerArray[] to display the page's banner advertisement.

- **BakeTheCookie()**. A function that, when called, creates and stores a cookie containing the visitor's name on the visitor's computer.

- **CookieCheck()**. A function that, when called, checks to see whether there is a cookie stored on the visitor's computer. If a cookie is not found, the function asks the visitor for his name and then calls the BakeTheCookie() function.

- **OpenNewWindow()**. A function that, when called, opens a new browser window and loads the Web page that presents the Web site's featured book of the month.

- **BrowserCheck()**. A function that, when called, checks to see whether the visitor is using either Netscape Navigator version 4 or higher or Internet Explorer version 4 or higher.

The page's <BODY> tag has been modified so that the first thing that happens is that the CycleBanner() function is executed using onLoad="CycleBanner()". The page itself is arranged using a series of tables that organize and display the information presented. In the middle of the body section, the BrowserCheck() and

`CookieCheck()` functions are called. Next, the link for the featured book has been modified to call the `OpenNewWindow()` function as shown here:

```
<A HREF="javascript:OpenNewWindow()"><IMG HEIGHT="170"
SRC="htmlbook.jpg"

    ALT="Learn HTML In a Weekend" WIDTH="126"></A>
```

The last table on the page provides a simple navigation menu that is used throughout the Web site.

When someone visits Jerry's On-line Bookmall for the first time, or when he visits for the first time in over 90 days (e.g. after the expiration date for the site's cookie has expired as set by `expirationDate.setMonth(expirationDate.getMonth() + 3)`), the `CheckCookie()` function displays the prompt shown in Figure 5.10, asking the visitor to type his name. The `BakeTheCookie()` function then stores the cookie on the visitor's computer.

Figure 5.10

The `document` object's `prompt()` method provides the perfect tool for interactively collecting small pieces of information from visitors.

The Featured Book

When a visitor clicks on the link for the featured book, a new window measuring 640 pixels wide by 420 pixels high opens, and the Web page for the site's featured book is loaded into it. This page contains only HTML, although you might want to add a little JavaScript that uses mouse events to display more detailed information about the book by opening a new window. You might also want to display a message that explains what the rating system is when the visitor moves the pointer over the graphic rating. This could be done using the ALT attribute of the <IMG> tag, by using JavaScript to open a new window, or by enabling the status bar and posting messages to it. The HTML statements that make up this page are listed here:

Figure 5.11

Because of its role as home page, a site's index page is often one of the more lengthy and complex pages, involving heavy use of JavaScript.

```
<HTML>


  <HEAD>

    <TITLE>Script 5.9 - This month's featured book</TITLE>

  </HEAD>


  <BODY>

    <CENTER>

      <H2 ALIGN="left"><IMG BORDER="0" HEIGHT="78"
SRC="bstorelogo.jpg"

        WIDTH="636"></H2>

    </CENTER>
```

```
     <H2 ALIGN="center"><FONT COLOR="#ff0000">This month's
featured book:</FONT></H2>

     <P ALIGN="center"><IMG BORDER="0" HEIGHT="209" SRC="html-
book.jpg"

        ALT="Learn HTML In a Weekend" WIDTH="165"></P>

     <CENTER>

     Learn HTML In a Weekend is your ultimate source for
HTML programming.

     <B>Rating:</B>

       <IMG ALT="" BORDER="0" HEIGHT="15" SRC="star.gif"
WIDTH="14">

       <IMG ALT="" BORDER="0" HEIGHT="15" SRC="star.gif"
WIDTH="14">

       <IMG ALT="" BORDER="0" HEIGHT="15" SRC="star.gif"
WIDTH="14">

       <IMG ALT="" BORDER="0" HEIGHT="15" SRC="star.gif"
WIDTH="14">

       <IMG ALT="" BORDER="0" HEIGHT="15" SRC="star.gif"
WIDTH="14">

     </CENTER>

   </BODY>


</HTML>
```

Figure 5.12 shows what the featured book page looks like when loaded.

Navigating the Bookmall

The actual bookmall opens when the visitor clicks on the Bookmall link at the bottom of the index page. The bookmall is actually a simple HTML page that defines two frames, as shown here. The left frame loads a navigation page from which the visitor selects an option; the right frame holds the contents of the page specified by the selected link.

```
<HTML>
```

Figure 5.12

Opening a new
window is an
effective
presentation tool
for placing extra
emphasis on a
specific page.

```
<HEAD>

    <TITLE>Script 5.10 - Bookmall frame's page</TITLE>

</HEAD>


<FRAMESET COLS="175,*">

    <FRAME SRC="Script 5.11.html" NAME="left" SCROLLING="no"
FRAMEBORDER="1" NORESIZE>

    <FRAME SRC="Script 5.12.html" NAME="right2"
SCROLLING="auto" FRAMEBORDER="1" NORESIZE>

    </FRAMESET>

</FRAMESET>


</HTML>
```

The contents of the navigation page are listed next. JavaScript statements
have been added to the head section to define and preload all the graphic
images used to create the rollover effects for the page. The rest of the page is
contained in the body section and is made up of five HTML links. The first
link reloads a welcome page. The next three links load the URLs for various
online bookstores. I also modified the tags to include the onMouseOver and
onMouseOut events that drive the rollover effects.

NOTE

● ●
This is the point where you would cut and paste the special HTML links that each online bookstore provides you when you join its associates program. Of course, you would have to make a modification to each link to load it in the frame on the right (that is, you have to add the attribute TARGET="right2").
● ●

```html
<HTML>

<HEAD>
  <TITLE>Script 5.11 - Navigation/Rollover page</TITLE>

  <SCRIPT LANGUAGE="JavaScript" TYPE="Text/JavaScript">
  <!-- Start hiding JavaScript statements
      amazon1           =new Image;
      amazon2           =new Image;
      bn1               =new Image;
      bn2               =new Image;
      a1books1          =new Image;
      a1books2          =new Image;
      bookstore1        =new Image;
      bookstore2        =new Image;
      featured1         =new Image;
      featured2         =new Image;
      amazon1.src       ="amazon1.jpg";
      amazon2.src       ="amazon2.jpg";
      bn1.src           ="bn1.jpg";
      bn2.src           ="bn2.jpg";
      a1books1.src      ="a1books1.jpg";
      a1books2.src      ="a1books2.jpg";
      bookstore1.src    ="bookstore1.jpg";
      bookstore2.src    ="bookstore2.jpg";
```

```
      featured1.src        ="featured1.jpg";
      featured2.src        ="featured2.jpg";
   // End hiding JavaScript statements -->
   </SCRIPT>


</HEAD>


<BODY>
   <P><IMG SRC="book.jpg" WIDTH="154" HEIGHT="74" BORDER="0">
</P>
   <A HREF="Script 5.12.html" TARGET="right2"
    onMouseover="document.mybutton1.src=bookstore2.src"
    onMouseout="document.mybutton1.src=bookstore1.src"> <IMG
    SRC="bookstore1.jpg" BORDER="0" NAME="mybutton1"></A><P>
   <A HREF="http://www.amazon.com" TARGET="right2"
    onMouseover="document.mybutton2.src=amazon2.src"
    onMouseout="document.mybutton2.src=amazon1.src">
<IMG SRC="amazon1.jpg"
    BORDER="0" NAME="mybutton2"></A><P>
   <A HREF="http://www.bn.com" TARGET="right2"
    onMouseover="document.mybutton3.src=bn2.src"
    onMouseout="document.mybutton3.src=bn1.src"> <IMG
SRC="bn1.jpg" BORDER="0"
    NAME="mybutton3"></A><P>
  <A HREF="http://www.a1books.com" TARGET="right2"
    onMouseover="document.mybutton5.src=a1books2.src"
    onMouseout="document.mybutton5.src=a1books1.src">
<IMG SRC="a1books1.jpg"
    BORDER="0" NAME="mybutton5"></A><P>
  <A HREF="Script 5.13.html" TARGET="right2"
    onMouseover="document.mybutton6.src=featured2.src"
```

```
    onMouseout="document.mybutton6.src=featured1.src"> <IMG
SRC="featured1.jpg"

    BORDER="0" NAME="mybutton6"></A>

  </BODY>


</HTML>
```

Figure 5.13 shows what the navigation page looks like when it is opened by the browser without the use of frames. The graphic image of the book is not a link; its only purpose is cosmetic. Each of the remaining links represents a different menu selection that will be loaded into the right frame (when the frames are enabled). Each button is green with gold lettering, but when the pointer passes over one of the buttons, it changes to a golden background with green lettering.

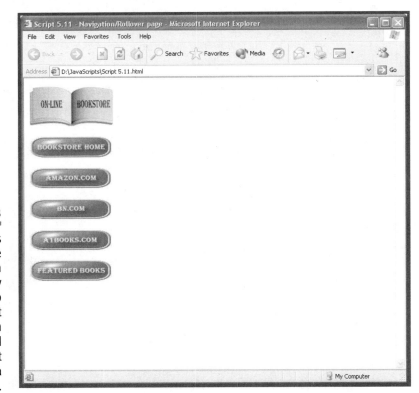

Figure 5.13

When this page is loaded into a frame as a navigation page, it is really just a regular Web page except that its links contain additional attributes that load URLs into a second frame.

The following shows the Web page that is initially loaded into the right frame when the bookmall is loaded. As you can see, it is a simple HTML page that displays basic welcome information. This page provides a lot of opportunities for JavaScript. For example, you could address the visitor by name again, post messages on the status bar, or add some animated effects such as a book that opens and closes.

```
<HTML>

  <HEAD>
    <TITLE>Script 5.12 - Bookstore welcome page</TITLE>
  </HEAD>

  <BODY>
    <TABLE BORDER="0" WIDTH="590">
      <TR>
        <TD>
          <CENTER>
            <IMG SRC="bstorelogo.jpg" BORDER="0" HEIGHT="78"
WIDTH="636">
            <P><H2>Hello and welcome to Jerry's On-line
Bookmall!</H2></P>
            <P>Feel free to shop some of the finest online
bookstores on the Web.</P>
            <P><FONT COLOR="red">Thanks for stopping
by!</FONT></P>
          </CENTER>
        </TD>
      </TR>
    </TABLE>
  </BODY>

</HTML>
```

Figure 5.14 shows what the welcome page looks like when it is opened by the browser outside of any frames.

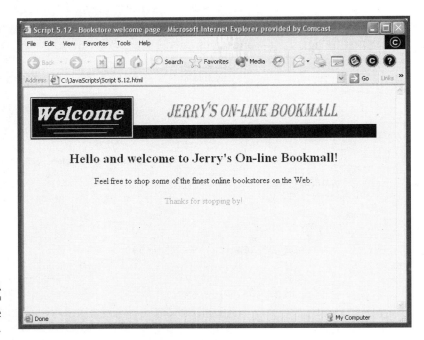

Figure 5.14

Not every page requires JavaScript.

Figure 5.15 shows what the bookmall looks like when visitors come to shop. As you can see, the combination of frames, rollover graphics, and simple HTML present an elegantly simple yet functional interface.

When the visitor is ready to go shopping, he simply clicks on one of the buttons representing an online bookstore. Figure 5.16 shows what happens if the user clicks on the AMAZON.COM button. As you can see, the amazon.com Web site is loaded into the right frame, and the visitor can begin shopping. Because the visitor enters the amazon.com site using the special links on your navigation Web page, you are credited with a portion of every purchase this visitor makes. Best of all, the visitor never really leaves your Web site. This makes it easy for him to jump between other bookstores or to load other pages where you may have added valuable content. This technique makes small Web sites seem much bigger than they actually are. By adding rollover links to other online businesses, you can easily expand the Web site to take advantage of a diverse set of business opportunities.

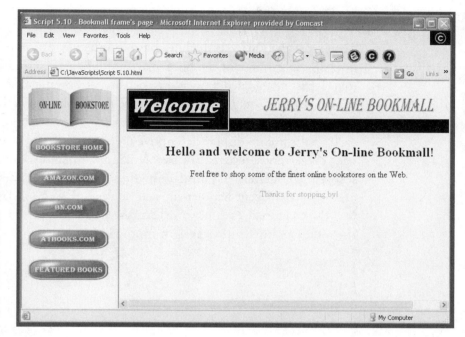

Figure 5.15

When combined, frames, HTML, and JavaScript create one of the most powerful organization and presentation tools available to any Web page designer.

Figure 5.16

Frame technology makes it possible to load URLs from other Web sites into one of your frames so that your visitors can continue to explore the Internet without ever leaving your Web site.

Finishing the Bookmall

The Jerry's Picks page is the last option on the navigation menu. It is loaded into the right frame of the bookmall and presents a selection of four books that Jerry has singled out as his personal recommended picks. A single HTML `<TABLE>` tag is used to organize the display of the book images. An `onMouseOver` and an `onMouseOut` event handler have been embedded into each book's link to display descriptive messages in the browser window status bar. These mouse events call two JavaScript functions located in the head section. The `PostMsg()` function writes the message passed to it from the `onMouseOver` event handler in each book's link as a message on the status bar; the `ClearMsg()` function clears the message from the status bar when the mouse pointer moves away from the link.

```
<HTML>


  <HEAD>
    <TITLE>Script 5.13 - Jerry's picks page</TITLE>


      <SCRIPT LANGUAGE="JavaScript" TYPE="Text/JavaScript">
      <!-- Start hiding JavaScript statements


        //Define a function that writes the message onto the
browser's statusbar
        function PostMsg(msg) {

          window.status = msg;
        }         //Define a function that clears the message
off of the browser's status bar
        function ClearMsg() {

          window.status="";

        }


        // End hiding JavaScript statements -->
      </SCRIPT>
```

```
    </HEAD>


    <BODY>


        <TABLE BORDER="0" WIDTH="590">
          <TR>
            <TD>
              <CENTER>
                  <H2 ALIGN="left"><IMG BORDER="0" HEIGHT="78"
SRC="bstorelogo.jpg"

                        WIDTH="636"></H2>
                  <BR>
                  <H1> Jerry's picks of the month!</H1>
          <A HREF="Script 5.14.html"
onMouseOver="PostMsg('Electrify Your Web Site In

        a Weekend'); return true;"
onMouseOut="ClearMsg();"><IMG

        SRC="electrify.jpg" BORDER="0" ALT="Electrify Your Web
Site In a

        Weekend"></A>
          <A HREF="Script 5.15.html" onMouseOver="PostMsg('Learn
Microsoft Windows Me

        Millenium Edition In a Weekend'); return true;"

        onMouseOut="ClearMsg();"><IMG SRC="me.jpg" BORDER="0"
ALT="Learn

        Microsoft Windows Me Millenium Edition In a Weekend"></A>
          <A HREF="Script 5.16.html" onMouseOver="PostMsg('Learn
Windows 98 In a

        Weekend'); return true;" onMouseOut="ClearMsg();">
<IMG SRC="w98.jpg"

        BORDER="0" ALT="Learn Windows 98 In a Weekend"></A>
          <A HREF="Script 5.17.html" onMouseOver="PostMsg('Learn
HTML on the MAC In a
```

```
              weekend'); return true;" onMouseOut="ClearMsg();"><IMG
SRC="mac.jpg"
              BORDER="0" ALT="Learn HTML on the MAC In a week-
end"></A>

          </CENTER>

        </TD>

      </TR>

      </TABLE>


    </BODY>


</HTML>
```

Figure 5.17 shows how the Jerry's Picks page appears in the bookmall. Notice that the status bar is displaying a message for the *Electrify Your Web Site In a Weekend* book because the mouse pointer is currently positioned over that book's graphic. Each book's image is actually a link that opens a new page in the right frame. Optionally, you might prefer to borrow some of the JavaScript logic in the index page to display each book's linked page in a new window outside the frame rather than inside it.

The next four pages show the contents of the Web page associated with each of the four books. These pages contain only HTML and are organized using a single table. The code for the first of these pages is shown here. This page represents the *Electrify Your Web Site In a Weekend* book.

```
<HTML>


  <HEAD>
    <TITLE>Script 5.14 - Book pick number 1</TITLE>
  </HEAD>


  <BODY>
```

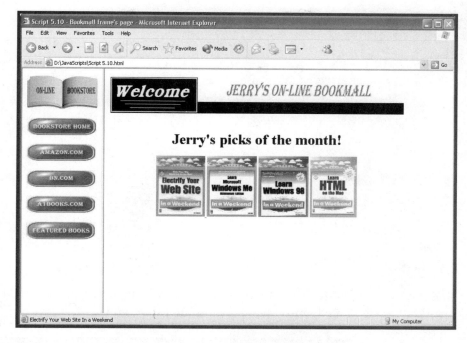

The Jerry's Picks
page provides
descriptive
information about
each book, using
the browser's
status bar.

```
        <H2 ALIGN="left"><IMG BORDER="0" HEIGHT="78"
SRC="bstorelogo.jpg"

            WIDTH="636"></H2></CENTER>

        <BR>

        <TABLE BORDER="3" WIDTH="590" STYLE="HEIGHT: 254px;
WIDTH: 633px">

            <TR>

                <TD>

                    <H2 ALIGN="left">

                        <FONT COLOR="red">Electrify Your Web Site In a
Weekend</FONT>

                    </H2>

                    <P ALIGN="left">Learn everything that you need to
know to start

                        building your own super-charged Web site!</P>

                </TD>
```

```
<TD>

    <H3 ALIGN="center">Featured Book!</H3>

    <P ALIGN="center"><IMG ALT="" BORDER="0"
HEIGHT="133"

        SRC="electrify.jpg" WIDTH="108"></P>

   </TD>

  </TR>

 </TABLE>


</BODY>


</HTML>
```

Figure 5.18 show what the preceding example looks like when loaded directly into the bookstore site using frames.

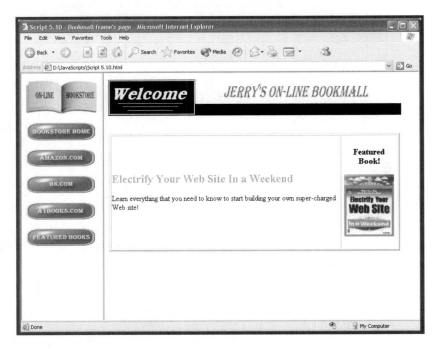

The visitor can select individual books to view more detailed information.

This next page represents the *Learn Microsoft Windows ME In a Weekend* book. Its structure is the same as the previous example in that it relies only on the use of HTML. After all, just because JavaScript is powerful and can do many things doesn't means it has to be used on every page. Like any other tool, it is better used in some places and not in others.

```
<HTML>


  <HEAD>

    <TITLE>Script 5.15 - Book pick number 2</TITLE>

  </HEAD>


  <BODY>

    <H2 ALIGN="left">

     <IMG BORDER="0" HEIGHT="78" SRC="bstorelogo.jpg"
WIDTH="636">

    </H2>

    <BR>

    <TABLE BORDER="3" WIDTH="590" STYLE="HEIGHT: 254px;
WIDTH: 633px">

      <TR>

        <TD>

          <H2 ALIGN="left"><FONT COLOR="red">Learn Microsoft
Windows ME

          Millenium Edition In a Weekend</FONT></H2>

          <P ALIGN="left">Learn everything that you need to
know about this

          exciting Microsoft operating system.</P>

        </TD>

        <TD>

          <H3 ALIGN="center">Featured Book!</H3>

          <P ALIGN="center"><IMG ALT="" BORDER="0"
HEIGHT="133" SRC="me.jpg"
```

```
            WIDTH="108"></P>

        </TD>

      </TR>

    </TABLE>

  </BODY>


</HTML>
```

Figure 5.19 shows how the preceding page looks when selected by visitors to Jerry's On-line Bookmall.

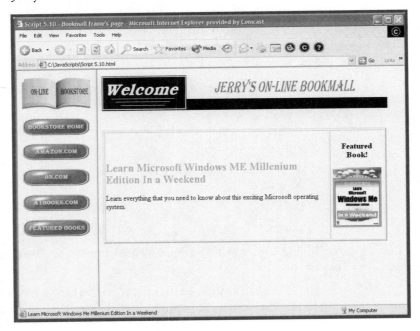

Figure 5.19

Looking at one of Jerry's picks as it is seen by visitors to the bookmall

The next two scripts show the HTML contents for the pages that represent the last two of Jerry's picks. These pages are structured similarly to the previous two examples and are provided here for consistency. The first script is for the *Learn Windows 98 In a Weekend* book:

```
<HTML>
```

```
<HEAD>

  <TITLE>Script 5.16 - Book pick number 3</TITLE>

  </HEAD>


  <BODY>

    <H2 ALIGN="left"><IMG BORDER="0" HEIGHT="78"
SRC="bstorelogo.jpg"

        WIDTH="636"></H2>

    <BR>

    <TABLE BORDER="3" WIDTH="590" STYLE="HEIGHT: 254px;
WIDTH: 633px">

      <TR>

       <TD>

         <H2 ALIGN="left">

           <FONT COLOR="red">Learn Windows 98 In a
Weekend</FONT>

         </H2>

         <P ALIGN="left">Learn everything that you need to
know about this

           exciting Microsoft operating system.</P>

       </TD>

       <TD>

         <H3 ALIGN="center">Featured Book!</H3>

         <P ALIGN="center"><IMG ALT="" BORDER="0"
HEIGHT="133" SRC="w98.jpg"

           WIDTH="108"></P>

       </TD>

      </TR>

    </TABLE>

  </BODY>


</HTML>
```

The next Web page shows the HTML statements that display the description for the *Learn HTML on the Mac In a Weekend* book:

```
<HTML>


  <HEAD>
    <TITLE>Script 5.17 - Book pick number 4</TITLE>
  </HEAD>


  <BODY>
    <H2 ALIGN="left"><IMG BORDER="0" HEIGHT="78"
SRC="bstorelogo.jpg"
        WIDTH="636"></H2></CENTER>
    <BR>
    <TABLE BORDER="3" WIDTH="590" STYLE="HEIGHT: 254px;
WIDTH: 633px">
      <TR>
        <TD>
          <H2 ALIGN="left">
            <FONT COLOR="red">Learn HTML on the MAC In a
Weekend</FONT>
          </H2>
          <P ALIGN="left">Learn everything that you need to
know to begin
            creating exciting Web sites using your Mac.</P>
        </TD>
        <TD>
          <H3 ALIGN="center">Featured Book!</H3>
          <P ALIGN="center"><IMG ALT="" BORDER="0"
HEIGHT="133" SRC="mac.jpg"
            WIDTH="108"></P>
        </TD>
      </TR>
```

```
      </TABLE>

    </BODY>


  </HTML>
```

Receiving Customer E-Mail

The final Web page in Jerry's On-line Bookmall is a simple HTML page with a link that, when clicked, opens the visitor's e-mail client and places the specified e-mail address in the address field. Although this page contains no JavaScript, I am listing it here to give you a complete view of all the pages in this Web site.

```
<HTML>


  <HEAD>

    <TITLE>Script 5.18 - email page</TITLE>

  </HEAD>


  <BODY>

    <TABLE BORDER="0" WIDTH="590">

      <TR>

        <TD>

          <IMG BORDER="0" HEIGHT="78" SRC="bstorelogo.jpg"
WIDTH="636">

            <CENTER>

              <BR>

              <BR>

              <BR>

              <BR>

              <H3>If you have any suggestions or comments we
would appreciate hearing from you.</H3>
```

```
          <P><B>Please email us at:</B><A
HREF="mailto:jlf04@yahoo.com">jlf04@yahoo.com</P>
          <BR>
          <BR>
          <BR>
          <BR>
          <BR>
          <BR>
          <BR>
          [ <A HREF="script 5.8.html">Main Menu</A> ]
          [ <A HREF="script 5.10.html">Bookstore</A> ]
          [ <A>Email Us</A> ]
        </CENTER>
      </TD>
    </TR>
  </TABLE>


  </BODY>
</HTML>
```

Figure 5.20 shows what the e-mail page looks like when loaded.

What's Next?

Congratulations! You are ready to begin creating your own exciting adventure on the Internet where, with a little imagination, hard work, and JavaScript, you can begin building world-class Web pages. From this point on, this book will focus on teaching you the ins and outs of JScript development. So go get yourself some lunch; when you return this afternoon, we'll get started on making you more efficient by showing you how to develop scripts that automate all sorts of tasks on your computer.

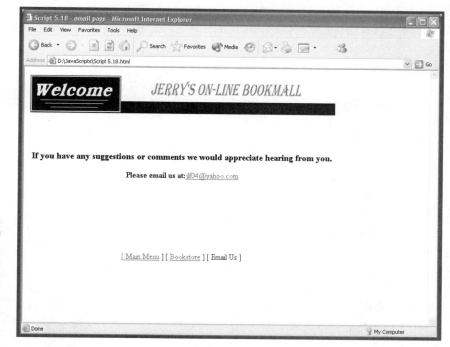

Figure 5.20

Every good Web site provides a way for visitors to communicate with the site's owner; e-mail provides the easiest solution.

Learning How to Use JScript and the WSH

➤ The objects that make up the WSH core object model

➤ JScript's runtime objects

➤ How to access the Windows file system and examine disk and file properties

➤ How to create report and log files

➤ How to create JScripts that perform file and folder administration tasks

Okay, it's time to switch directions a bit. Starting this afternoon and going through the rest of the evening, this book will focus exclusively on how to use what you have already learned in order to teach you how to work with JScript and the WSH. As you will see this afternoon, you already know how to program using JScript; all that you need to do is learn how to work with the WSH object model.

By accessing and manipulating WSH objects, your JScripts will be able to automate all sorts of Windows tasks. Your JScripts will be able to access and manipulate the contents of files and folders. You'll be able to develop JScripts that can create report and log files. You will also be able to create JScripts that can read and process text files. In addition, you will learn how to copy, move, rename, and delete text files and folders.

On top of all this, this evening you'll learn how to write JScripts that can access local and network printers and drives. You'll also see how to work directly with the Windows desktop, Start menu, and registry. You'll learn how to use the WSH to write messages to the Windows event log and execute Windows commands and command-line utilities.

An Overview of the WSH Object Model

The WSH object model provides JScript with access to Windows resources. Simply put, the WSH object model does for JScripts what the browser DOM does for JavaScripts. Instead of exposing browser objects, the WSH provides access to an assortment of Windows objects, which in turn provides access to dozens of object properties and methods that provide direct access and control over an assortment of Windows resources.

The WSH object model consists of 14 different objects. Figure 6.1 lists each of these objects and shows how they relate to one another.

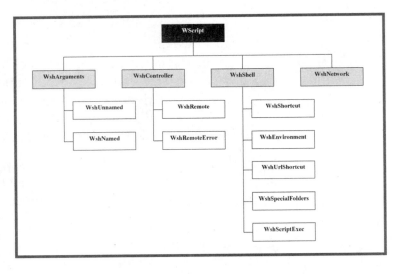

Figure 6.1

Methods and properties belonging to the WSH objects provide direct access to an assortment of Windows resources.

The `WScript` object sits at the top of the WSH object model. By default, an instance of the `WScript` object is created automatically at script execution. Therefore, you can access all of the `WScript` object's properties and methods without having to first set up a reference to it. However, all of the other objects in the WSH object model must first be defined, or *instantiated*, before you can start working with their properties and methods.

The `WScript` object is sometimes referred to as a *public* object. In addition to the `WScript` object, the WSH supports three other public objects. These objects are the `WshController`, `WshShell`, and `WshNetwork` objects. To instantiate these other three objects, you have to use the `WScript` object's `CreateObject()` method. All the other objects that make up the WSH object model are instantiated using one of the properties or methods provided by one of the four WSH public objects. Table 6.1 lists the other 10 WSH objects and identifies the properties or methods used to instantiate them.

TABLE 6.1 NON-PUBLIC WSH OBJECTS	
Object	**Method of Instantiation**
WshArguments	WScript.Arguments
WshNamed	WScript.Arguments.Named
WshUnnamed	WScript.Arguments.Unnamed
WshRemote	WshController.CreateScript()
WshRemoteError	WshRemote.Error
WshShortcut	WshShell.CreateShortcut()
WshUrlShortcut	WshShell.CreateShortcut()
WshEnvironment	WshShell.Environment
WshSpecialFolders	WshShell.SpecialFolders
WshScriptExec	WshShell.Exec()

Each WSH object provides access to its own collection of properties and methods. Table 6.2 provides a complete list of WSH objects and their associated properties.

TABLE 6.2   WSH OBJECTS AND THEIR PROPERTIES AND METHODS

Object	Description
`WScript`	This object provides access to numerous properties and methods and to the other objects that make up the WSH object model. Properties: `Arguments`, `BuildVersion`, `FullName`, `Interactive`, `Name`, `Path`, `ScriptFullName`, `ScriptName`, `StdErr`, `StdIn`, `StdOut`, and `Version` Methods: `ConnectObject()`, `CreateObject()`, `DisconnectObject()`, `Echo()`, `GetObject()`, `Quit()`, and `Sleep()`
`WshArguments`	This object provides access to any command-line arguments passed to the script at the beginning of its execution. Properties: `Item`, and `Length`; `Named` and `Unnamed` Methods: `Count()` and `ShowUsage()`
`WshNamed`	This object provides access to a collection of named command-line arguments. Properties: `Item` and `Length` Methods: `Count()` and `Exists()`
`WshUnnamed`	This object provides access to a collection of unnamed command-line arguments. Properties: `Item` and `Length` Methods: `Count()`
`WshController`	This object is used to set up remote script execution. Properties: This object does not support any properties. Methods: `CreateScript`

TABLE 6.2 WSH OBJECTS AND THEIR PROPERTIES AND METHODS *(CONTINUED)*

Object	Description
WshRemote	This object provides control over the execution of remote scripts. Properties: Status and Error Methods: Execute() and Terminate()
WshRemoteError	This object provides the capability to retrieve error information for remote scripts. Properties: Description, Line, Character, SourceText, Source, and Number Methods: This object does not support any methods.
WshNetwork	This object provides the capability to access and manipulate network printers and drives. Properties: ComputerName, UserDomain, and UserName Methods: AddWindowsPrinterConnection(), AddPrinterConnection(), EnumNetworkDrives(), EnumPrinterConnection(), MapNetworkDrive(), RemoveNetworkDrive(), RemovePrinterConnection(), and SetDefaultPrinter()
WshShell	This object provides the capability to access and manipulate environment variables, Windows applications, the Windows registry, and the Windows event log. Properties: CurrentDirectory, Environment, and SpecialFolders Methods: AppActivate(), CreateShortcut(), ExpandEnvironmentStrings(), LogEvent(), Popup(), RegDelete(), RegRead(), RegWrite(), Run(), SendKeys(), and Exec()

TABLE 6.2	**WSH OBJECTS AND THEIR PROPERTIES AND METHODS** *(CONTINUED)*

Object	Description
WshShortcut	This object provides access to properties and methods that can be used to create Windows shortcuts. Properties: Arguments, Description, FullName, Hotkey, IconLocation, RelativePath, TargetPath, WindowStyle, and WorkingDirectory Method: Save()
WshUrlShortcut	This object provides access to properties and methods that can be used to create URL shortcuts. Properties: FullName and TargetPath Methods: Save()
WshEnvironment	This object provides the capability to retrieve data stored in environment variables. Properties: Item and Length Methods: Remove() and Count()
WshSpecialFolders	This object provides the capability to configure the Windows desktop, Start menu, and Quick Launch toolbar. Properties: Item, Length Methods: Count()
WshScriptExec	This object provides access to error information generated by scripts started with the Exec() method. Properties: ExitCode, ProcessID, Status, StdOut, StdIn, and StdErr Methods: Terminate()

WSH Object Properties

Properties belonging to WSH objects provide access to information about the resources they represent. By modifying object properties, JScripts can manipulate their execution environment. Table 6.3 lists all of the properties supported by WSH objects and provides a brief description of their purposes.

TABLE 6.3 SUMMARY OF WSH OBJECT PROPERTIES	
Property	**Description**
Arguments	Returns the WshArguments object's arguments or sets and retrieves shortcut arguments
AtEndOfLine	Returns either True or False, depending on whether the stream's end-of-line marker has been reached
AtEndOfStream	Returns either True or False, depending on whether or not the end of the input stream has been reached
BuildVersion	Retrieves the build version number for the WSH
Character	Returns the character in a line of code where an error occurred
Column	Returns the current column position within the input stream
ComputerName	Returns the computer's assigned name
CurrentDirectory	Retrieves or modifies a script's working directory
Description	Returns a shortcut's description
Environment	Establishes a reference to the WshEnvironment object
Error	Exposes the WshRemoteError object in order to provide access error information
ExitCode	Returns the exit code of a script run using Exec()

TABLE 6.3 SUMMARY OF WSH OBJECT PROPERTIES *(CONTINUED)*	
Property	**Description**
FullName	Returns the path for the specified shortcut or executable program
HotKey	Sets or retrieves the keystroke sequence associated with a shortcut
IconLocation	Sets or retrieves a shortcut's icon location
Interactive	Sets or retrieves a script execution mode
Item	Retrieves the specified item from a collection, provides access to items stored in the WshNamed object, or retrieves an item stored in the WshUnnamed object
Length	Returns a count of enumerated items
Line	Returns the current line in the input stream or retrieves line number where an error occurred
Name	Returns a text string specifying the name of the WScript object
Number	Returns the error number associated with an error
Path	Returns the path of the folder containing CScript and WScript execution hosts
ProcessID	Retrieves the process ID assigned to a process started with the WshScriptExec object
Relativepath	Sets or retrieves a relative shortcut path
ScriptFullName	Returns the script's full path and name
ScriptName	Returns the script's name
Source	Identifies the object that generated a script error
SourceText	Returns the source code responsible for creating an error

TABLE 6.3	SUMMARY OF WSH OBJECT PROPERTIES *(CONTINUED)*
Property	**Description**
SpecialFolders	Provides access to the Windows Start menu folder, the Windows desktop folder, and other special folders
Status	Returns information about the execution status of a remote script
StdErr	Provides the capability to write text to the error output stream
StdIn	Provides the capability to read from the input stream
StdOut	Provides the capability to write text to the output stream
TargetPath	Returns the path for the specified shortcut
UserDomain	Returns the name of the Windows domain of which the computer running the script is a member
UserName	Returns the user account name of the user who is currently logged on to the computer
Version	Returns the current version number of the WSH
WindowStyle	Returns the specified shortcut's window style
WorkingDirectory	Returns the specified shortcut's working directory

NOTE You've probably already noticed back in Table 6.2 that many objects provide access to the same properties, providing you with different ways of accessing some information.

Accessing WSH Object Properties

You work with WSH object properties in pretty much the same manner that you learned how to work with object properties when writing JavaScripts. For example, the following JScript demonstrates how to access and display values assigned to properties belonging to both the WScript and WshNetwork objects.

```
//*****************************************************************
//************
//Script Name: Script 6.1.js

//Author: Jerry Ford

//Created: 09/12/03

//Description: This JScript shows how to access properties
belonging to the

//WScript and WshNetwork objects
//*****************************************************************
//************

//Initialization Section

  //Instantiate the WshShell object
  var wshObject = WScript.CreateObject("WScript.Shell");

  //Instantiate the WshNetwork object
  var wshNetwork = WScript.CreateObject("WScript.Network")

//Main Processing Section

  //Call the function that displays script information

  DisplayScriptInfo()

  //Call the function that displays network information

  DisplayNetworkInfo()
```

```
   //Terminate script execution

   WScript.Quit()

//Procedure Section

   //This subroutine displays script information


   function DisplayScriptInfo() {

     wshObject.Popup("Execution Environment: \t" +
WScript.Name + "\r\r" +

       "Version: \t\t\t" + WScript.Version + "\r\r" +

       "Location of Execution Host: \t" +WScript.Path + "\r\r" +

       "Script name and path: \t" + WScript.ScriptFullname +
"\r\r);


   }


   //This subroutine displays network information

   function DisplayNetworkInfo() {

     wshObject.Popup("Domain Name: \t" + wshNetwork.UserDomain
+ "\t\t\r\r" +

       "User Name: \t" + wshNetwork.UserName   + "\r\r" +

       "Computer Name: \t" + wshNetwork.ComputerName + "\r\r);


   }
```

This script begins by first instantiating the WshShell and WshNetwork objects. Instances of both objects are established by executing the WScript object's CreateObject() method and specifying the appropriate WSH object as shown here.

```
var wshObject = WScript.CreateObject("WScript.Shell");
var wshNetwork = WScript.CreateObject("WScript.Network")
```

Once instantiated, the properties and methods associated with the `WshShell` object can be accessed by referencing `wshObject`. Likewise, the properties and methods associated with the `WshNetwork` object can be accessed by referring to `wshNetwork`.

Next, two function calls are made. The first call is made to the `Display ScriptInfo()` function. It uses the `WshShell` object's `Popup()` method to display a text string in a graphical pop-up dialog as shown here.

```
wshObject.Popup("Execution Environment: \t" + WScript.Name +
"\r\r" +
   "Version: \t\t\t" + WScript.Version + "\r\r" +
   "Location of Execution Host: \t" +WScript.Path + "\r\r" +
   "Script name and path: \t" + WScript.ScriptFullname +
"\r\r");
```

As you can see, the text string that is displayed consists of a number of elements, all of which are concatenated together. The information displayed by the `DisplayScriptInfo()` function includes the name of the scripting environment, its version number, the location of the execution host used to run the script, and the full path and name of the script itself.

NOTE You probably noticed in the previous example the use of the \r and \t switches. These two switches provide the capability to control the formatting of text within the pop-up dialog. The \t switch equates to a tab operation, thus allowing you to pad extra spaces anywhere within the dialog. The \r switch provides the capability to perform a carriage return, allowing you to control when line breaks occur.

The second function call made by the script is to `DisplayNetwork-Info()`. This function uses the `WScript` object's `Popup()` method to display information stored in `WshNetwork` object properties. The information displayed here includes the name of the Windows domain of which the computer is a member, the name of the user who started the script, and the name of the computer running the script.

The last statement executed by the script is `WScript.Quit()`. This statement executes the `WScript` object's `Quit()` method. This method terminates the script's execution. Figures 6.2 and 6.3 demonstrate the output that was displayed when I ran this script.

Figure 6.2

Displaying information about the script and its execution environment

Figure 6.3

Displaying information about the computer and network on which the script is executing

WSH Object Methods

By executing WSH object methods, your JScripts can directly affect their execution environment and manipulate the resources located within it. This includes performing such tasks as the creation and deletion of files and folders, adding and removing data to and from the Windows registry, and manipulating the Windows desktop and Start menu. Table 6.4 is a complete list of methods supported by WSH objects.

Working with WSH Object Methods

The following example demonstrates how a JScript can use WSH object methods to control Windows resources. In this case, the script uses methods belonging to the `WshShell` object to interact with and control the Windows Notepad application.

TABLE 6.4 SUMMARY OF WSH OBJECT METHODS

Method	Description
AddPrinterConnection()	Sets up a new printer connection to a locally installed printer using an MS-DOS printer port
AddWindowsPrinterConnection()	Sets up a new printer connection to either a local or network printer
AppActivate()	Activates the specified application window
Close()	Terminates an open text stream
ConnectObject()	Sets up a connection to a specified object
Count	Returns the number of switches found in the WshNamed and WshUnnamed objects
CreateObject()	Instantiates a new object reference
CreateScript()	Instantiates a WshRemote object representing a remote script
CreateShortcut()	Provides the capability to create new Windows shortcuts
DisconnectObject()	Terminates a connection to the specified object
Echo()	Displays a text string in either a pop-up dialog or the Windows command console
EnumNetworkDrives()	Returns information about currently mapped network drives
EnumPrinterConnections()	Returns information about current network printer connections
Exec()	Runs an application in a child command shell and provides access to its StdIn, StdOut, and StdErr streams
Execute()	Starts the execution of a remote script object

TABLE 6.4 SUMMARY OF WSH OBJECT METHODS *(CONTINUED)*

Method	Description
`Exists()`	Determines whether a key exists within the `WshNamed` object
`ExpandEnvironmentStrings()`	Retrieves an environmental variable's expanded value
`GetObject()`	Returns an `Automation` object
`GetResource()`	Returns the value of a resource as specified by the `<resource>` tag
`LogEvent()`	Records a text string in the Windows application event log
`MapNetworkDrive()`	Establishes a mapped network drive connection
`Popup()`	Displays a text string in a graphical pop-up dialog
`Quit()`	Terminates a script's execution
`Read()`	Retrieves a string of a specified length from the input stream
`ReadAll()`	Retrieves all the data currently in the input stream
`ReadLine()`	Retrieves an entire line of data from the input stream
`RegDelete()`	Deletes the specified registry key or value
`RegRead()`	Retrieves the specified registry key or value
`RegWrite()`	Creates the specified registry key or value
`Remove()`	Deletes the specified environment variable
`RemoveNetworkDrive()`	Removes a connection to a network drive

TABLE 6.4 SUMMARY OF WSH OBJECT METHODS *(CONTINUED)*

Method	Description
RemovePrinterConnection()	Removes a connection to a network printer
Run()	Starts a new process
Save()	Saves the specified shortcut
SendKeys()	Sends keystrokes to the specified window or application
SetDefaultPrinter()	Defines the default Windows printer
ShowUsage()	Retrieves instruction, if available, on the manner in which a script is supposed to be run
Sign()	Adds a signature to a script that has been stored in a string.
SignFile()	Signs or adds a digital signature to a script
Skip()	Skips a specified number of characters when reading data from the input stream
SkipLine()	Skips one line of data when reading from the input stream
Sleep()	Pauses a script's execution for a specified number of seconds
Terminate()	Stops the execution of a process started by Exec()
Verify()	Validates the digital signature returned as a string
VerifyFile()	Validates a digitial signature that was signed or added to a script
Write()	Places the specified text string in the output stream
WriteBlankLines()	Places a blank line of data in the output stream
WriteLine()	Places the specified text string in the output stream, followed by a carriage return

```
//*************************************************************
*************
//Script Name: Script 6.2.js

//Author: Jerry Ford

//Created: 09/12/03

//Description: This JScript shows how to use methods belonging
to the

//WScript object in order to open Notepad and type a text string
//*************************************************************
*************


//Initialization Section

  //Instantiate the WScript Shell
  var wshObject = WScript.CreateObject("WScript.Shell");


//Main Processing Section

  //Call the function that starts the Notepad application
  OpenNotepad();


  //Pause for 1 second before continuing
  PauseExecution(1000);


  //Call the function that writes text
  WriteSampleText();


  //Terminate the script's execution
  WScript.Quit();


//Procedure Section
```

```
//This subroutine Display network information

function OpenNotepad() {

  wshObject.Run("Notepad");

}

//Pause for script execution for a specified number of seconds

function PauseExecution(timeLimit) {

  WScript.Sleep(timeLimit);

}


//Type a text string into the currently active application

function WriteSampleText() {

  wshObject.SendKeys(Date() + "       Daily Journal Entry");
  wshObject.SendKeys("~");
  wshObject.SendKeys("~");


}
```

This script begins by instantiating the WshShell object using the WScript object's CreateObject() method as shown here.

```
var wshObject = WScript.CreateObject("WScript.Shell");
```

Next, the script's `Main Processing Section` executes three function calls. The first function that is called is `OpenNotepad()`. It starts the Notepad application by executing the `WshShell` object's `Run()` method. The next function called is `PauseExecution()`, which is passed an argument of `1000`. The function takes this argument and uses it when executing the `WScript` object's `Sleep()` method. This method pauses the script's execution for a specified number of milliseconds. This allows the Notepad application time to start up before the script calls the `Write-SampleText()` function.

The `WriteSampleText()` function uses the `WshShell` object's `Send-keys()` method to type a series of keystrokes into the Notepad application as shown here.

```
wshObject.SendKeys(Date() + "     Daily Journal Entry");
wshObject.SendKeys("~");
wshObject.SendKeys("~");
```

The first of these three statements sends a text string to the Notepad application. This string consists of the current date and a small text string that have been concatenated together. The next two statements in the function emulate the Enter keystroke and result in the execution of two carriage returns. Figure 6.4 shows how the Notepad application appears on the screen after the script has run and entered its data.

JScript Runtime Objects

In addition to the objects that make up the WSH object model, your JScripts also have access to a series of runtime objects that are made available to it at execution time. These runtime objects provide your JScripts with access to properties and methods that you can use to work with the Windows file system.

Using the properties and methods provided by JScript's runtime objects, you'll be able to automate an assortment of tasks, including the creation, deletion, renaming, copying, and moving of Windows files and folders.

In addition, you'll be able to develop JScripts that can create report and log files. You'll also be able to open and read text files programmatically. Table 6.5 provides a list of JScript runtime objects and lists their properties and methods.

Figure 6.4

Using `WshShell` methods to interact with and control Windows applications

TABLE 6.5 JSCRIPT RUNTIME OBJECTS	
Object	**Description**
Dictionary	Stores data key, item pairs
	Properties: `CompareMode`, `Count`, `Item`, `Key`
	Methods: `Add`, `Exists`, `Items`, `Keys`, `Remove`, `RemoveAll`
Drive	Provides the capability to access disk drive properties
	Properties: `AvailableSpace`, `DriveLetter`, `DriveType`, `FileSystem`, `FreeSpace`, `IsReady`, `Path`, `RootFolder`, `SerialNumber`, `ShareName`, `TotalSize`, `VolumeName`
	Methods: This object does not support any methods.

TABLE 6.5   JSCRIPT RUNTIME OBJECTS   *(CONTINUED)*

Object	Description
Drives Collection	Provides the capability to access information about disk drives
	Properties: Count, Item
	Methods: This object does not support any methods.
File	Provides the capability to access file properties
	Properties: Attributes, DateCreated, DateLastAccessed, DateLastModified, Drive, Name, ParentFolder, Path, ShortName, ShortPath, Size, Type
	Methods: Copy, Delete, Move, OpenAsTextStream
Files Collection	Provides the capability to process all the files in the specified folder
	Properties: Count, Item
	Methods: This object does not support any methods.
FileSystemObject	Provides the capability to access the Windows file system and to work with other runtime objects
	Properties: Drives
	Methods: BuildPath, CopyFile, CopyFolder, CreateFolder, CreateTextFile, DeleteFile, DeleteFolder, DriveExists, FileExists, FolderExists, GetAbsolutePathName, GetBaseName, GetDrive, GetDriveName, GetExtensionName, GetFile, GetFileName, GetFolder, GetParentFolderName, GetSpecialFolder, GetTempName, MoveFile, MoveFolder, OpenTextFile

	TABLE 6.5 JSCRIPT RUNTIME OBJECTS *(CONTINUED)*	

Object	Description
Folder	Provides the capability to access folder properties
	Properties: `Attributes, DateCreated, DateLastAccessed, DateLastModified, Drive, Files, IsRootFolder, Name, ParentFolder, Path, ShortName, ShortPath, Size, SubFolders, Type`
	Methods: `Copy, Delete, Move, OpenAsTextStream`
Folders Collection	Provides the capability to process all the subfolders stored in a specified folder
	Properties: `Count, Item`
	Method: `Add`
TextStream	Provides for sequential file access
	Properties: `AtEndOfLine, AtEndOfStream, Column, Line`
	Methods: `Close, Read, ReadAll, ReadLine, Skip, SkipLine, Write, WriteBlankLines, WriteLine`

Runtime Object Properties

JScript runtime objects provide access to a large collection of properties. By accessing or modifying these properties, you can interact with the Windows file system in a variety of ways. Table 6.6 provides a complete listing of JScript runtime properties.

TABLE 6.6 JScript Runtime Object Properties	
Property	**Description**
AtEndOfLine	Returns a value of true or false based on whether the location of the file pointer precedes the end-of-line marker.
AtEndOfStream	Returns a value of true or false based on whether the end of the file has been reached
Attributes	Sets or returns file and folder attributes
AvailableSpace	Returns the amount of free space on the specified drive
Column	Returns the current column position within a file
CompareMode	Sets or returns the comparison mode used when comparing a Dictionary object's string keys
Count	Returns a value representing the number of items in a collection or Dictionary object
DateCreated	Returns the creation date and time for a specified file or folder
DateLastAccessed	Returns the date and time that the specified file or folder was last accessed
DateLastModified	Returns the date and time that the specified file or folder was last modified
Drive	Returns a string representing the drive letter where the specified file or folder resides
DriveLetter	Returns a string representing a specified drive's drive letter
Drives	Returns a Drives collection that represents all the Drive objects found on the computer
DriveType	Returns a string representing a specified drive's type

TABLE 6.6	JSCRIPT RUNTIME OBJECT PROPERTIES *(CONTINUED)*
Property	**Description**
Files	Returns a Files collection that represents all the File objects located inside a specified folder
FileSystem	Returns a string representing the file system type implemented on a specified drive
FreeSpace	Returns a value representing the amount of free space available to the user on a specified drive
IsReady	Returns a value of true or false, depending on whether a drive is currently available
IsRootFolder	Returns a value of true or false, depending on whether a folder is the root folder
Item	Sets or returns an item based on the specified Dictionary object key
Key	Specifies a Dictionary object key
Line	Returns the current line number where the pointer is located in the TextStream file
Name	Sets or returns a file or folder's name
ParentFolder	Returns an object reference to a file or folder's parent folder
Path	Returns the path for a specified file, folder, or drive
RootFolder	Returns a Folder object representing the root folder on the specified drive
SerialNumber	Returns the serial number for a specified disk volume
ShareName	Returns the share name for a specified network drive
ShortName	Returns a file or folder's 8.3 character name

TABLE 6.6	JSCRIPT RUNTIME OBJECT PROPERTIES *(CONTINUED)*
Property	**Description**
ShortPath	Returns the short path for a file or folder's 8.3 character name
Size	Returns a value representing file or folder's size (in bytes)
SubFolders	Returns a Folders collection made up of all the folders located inside a specified folder
TotalSize	Returns a value representing the amount of free space (in bytes) remaining on a drive
Type	Returns a specified file or folder's type
VolumeName	Sets or returns the volume name for a specified drive

Runtime Object Methods

JScript's runtime objects also provide access to dozens of methods. Using these methods, listed in Table 6.7, you can create JScripts that can take full control of the Windows file system.

TABLE 6.7	JSCRIPT RUNTIME OBJECT METHODS
Method	**Description**
Add() (Dictionary)	Adds key and item pairs to a Dictionary object
Add() (Folders)	Adds a Folder to a collection
BuildPath()	Appends a name to the end of a path
Close()	Closes an open TextStream file
Copy()	Copies the specified file or folder

TABLE 6.7 JSCRIPT RUNTIME OBJECT METHODS *(CONTINUED)*

Method	Description
CopyFile()	Copies one or more specified files
CopyFolder()	Recursively copies a folder and its contents
CreateFolder()	Creates the specified folder
CreateTextFile()	Creates the specified text file
Delete()	Deletes the specified file or folder
DeleteFile()	Deletes the specified file
DeleteFolder()	Deletes the specified folder and its contents
DriveExists()	Returns a value of true or false based on the existence of the specified drive
Exists()	Returns a value of true or false based on the existence of a key in a Dictionary object
FileExists()	Returns a value of true or false based on whether a specified file is found
FolderExists()	Returns a value of true or false based on whether a specified folder is found
GetAbsolutePathName()	Returns a full pathname
GetBaseName()	Returns a file name for the specified file without its file extension
GetDrive()	Returns a Drive object reference based on the specified path
GetDriveName()	Returns the name of a specified drive
GetExtensionName()	Returns a specified file's file extension
GetFile()	Returns a File object reference

TABLE 6.7	JSCRIPT RUNTIME OBJECT METHODS *(CONTINUED)*
Method	**Description**
`GetFileName()`	Returns the last file name or folder in a specified path
`GetFileVersion()`	Returns a specified file's version number
`GetFolder()`	Returns a `Folder` object reference for the specified path
`GetParentFolderName()`	Returns the name of the parent folder
`GetSpecialFolder()`	Returns the name of the specified special folder
`GetTempName()`	Returns the name of a specified temporary file or folder
`Items()`	Returns an array made up of the items stored in a `Dictionary` object
`Keys()`	Returns an array made up of the keys stored in a `Dictionary` object
`Move()`	Moves a specified file or folder
`MoveFile()`	Moves one or more specified files
`MoveFolder()`	Moves one or more specified folders
`OpenAsTextStream()`	Opens the specified file and returns a `TextStream` object reference to the file
`OpenTextFile()`	Opens the specified file and returns an object reference to that file
`Read()`	Returns a string containing a specified number of characters from a file
`ReadAll()`	Reads all the contents of a file
`ReadLine()`	Reads an entire line from the specified file

TABLE 6.7	**JSCRIPT RUNTIME OBJECT METHODS** *(CONTINUED)*
Method	**Description**
Remove()	Deletes a Dictionary object's key-item pair
Skip()	Skips x number of character positions when reading a file
SkipLine()	Provides the capability to skip a line when reading a file
Write()	Writes a string to the specified file
WriteBlankLines()	Writes x number of newline characters to the specified file
WriteLine()	Writes an entire line of text to the specified file

Take a Break

Okay, you have just completed your introduction to the WSH object model and the JScript runtime object model. As you have seen, these objects and their associated properties and methods provide JScript with extensive automation capabilities on computers running Windows. Now it is time for a quick break. When you return, you will learn how to develop JScripts that create and process text files. In addition, you will learn how to write JScripts that can automate the administration of Windows files and folders.

Working with the Windows File System

The primary JScript runtime objects are the FileSystemObject and Dictionary objects. The Dictionary object provides the capability to set up an array whose contents can be accessed using keys instead of by index position. All other JScript runtime objects are derived from FileSystemObject.

The `Dictionary` object provides all the benefits provided by arrays with better flexibility when it comes to retrieving data that is stored with an associated key (which can be used later to retrieve the item's value). Use of the `Dictionary` object is an advanced programming topic that is beyond the scope of this book. To learn more about the `Dictionary` object, check out *Microsoft JScript Professional Projects*, published by Premier Press.

To use `FileSystemObject`, you must first instantiate it. This is done as demonstrated here.

```
var fsoObject = new ActiveXObject
("Scripting.FileSystemObject");
```

In this example, `fsoObject` is the name I assigned to the object reference for the `FileSystemObject`. Using this reference, you can access any of the `FileSystemObject` object's properties and methods, as well as instantiate other runtime objects. For example, the following JScript demonstrates how to instantiate the `FileSystemObject` and then use its `GetDrive()` method to instantiate the `Drive` object in order to use that object's `FreeSpace` property. The end result is a script that reports the total amount of free space available on the computer's C drive.

```
//************************************************************
//*************
//Script Name: Script 6.3.js
//Author: Jerry Ford
//Created: 09/12/03
//Description: This JScript shows how to use JScript runtime
//objects to access information about the computer C: drive
//************************************************************
//*************
```

```javascript
//Initialization Section

  //Instantiate the FileSystemObject object
  var fsoObject = new
ActiveXObject("Scripting.FileSystemObject");


  //Instantiate the Drive object
  var diskDrive =
fsoObject.GetDrive(fsoObject.GetDriveName("c:"));



//Main Processing Section

  //Call the function that displays drive information
  GetDriveInfo();

  //Terminate the script's execution
  WScript.Quit();



//Procedure Section

  //This subroutine displays the amount of drive free space

  function GetDriveInfo() {

    WScript.Echo("The amount of free space currently
available on C: is " +
      ((diskDrive.FreeSpace / 1024) / 1024) + " MB");

  }
```

The script begins by instantiating the `FileSystemObject` followed by the `Drive` objects as shown here.

```
var fsoObject = new
ActiveXObject("Scripting.FileSystemObject");

var diskDrive =
fsoObject.GetDrive(fsoObject.GetDriveName("c:"));
```

Once the `FileSystemObject` object has been established, its `Get-Drive()` method is used to create the `Drive` object reference. Notice that the reference returned is for the computer's C drive.

Next the script calls the `GetDriveInfo()` function, which is shown here.

```
function GetDriveInfo() {


    WScript.Echo("The amount of free space currently available
on C: is " +

      ((diskDrive.FreeSpace / 1024) / 1024) + " MB");


}
```

This function uses the `WScript` object's `Echo()` method to display a string. This string consists of text that includes an embedded reference to the `Drive` object's `FreeSpace` property. The value returned by this property is the amount of unused disk space (in bytes) on the specified disk drive. This value is then divided by 1,024 twice in order to convert it to MB. Finally, the script terminates its own execution with the `WScript.Quit()` statement.

This script uses the `WScript` object's `Echo()` method to display its output. This method displays text output differently, depending on whether it is executed in a script run from the Windows command line or the Windows desktop. Figures 6.5 and 6.6 demonstrate effects of running this script from both of these locations.

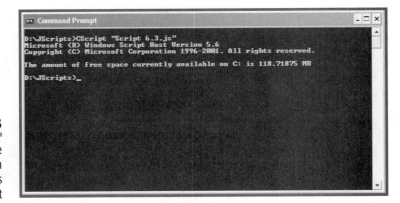

Figure 6.5

The result of the script when run from the Windows command prompt

Figure 6.6

The result of the script when run from the Windows desktop

Opening and Closing Files

Having looked at the previous example, you should have a pretty good idea of how the FileSystemObject works and how to use it to instantiate other runtime objects, as well as how to use other runtime objects to access the Windows files system. Let's dig a little deeper in and learn how to use JScript's runtime object to create custom report and log files.

As demonstrated in the previous example, the first thing to do is to instantiate the FileSystemObject as shown here.

```
var fsoObject = new
ActiveXObject("Scripting.FileSystemObject");
```

Once this is done, you should next check to find out whether the report or log file you plan on working with already exists, as demonstrated here.

```
if (fsoObject.FileExists("c:\\MyDocs\\Summary.txt"))
```

Take note of the use of the double backslashes in the previous statements. I had to use two slashes instead of one because in JScript, the \ character is a special character, so to use it I had to escape it, which means that I had to precede it with another slash character.

In this example, the `FileSystemObject` object's `FileExists()` method is used to determine whether a file named `Summary.txt` already exists in a folder called `MyDocs` on the computer's C drive. By first checking for the existence of a file, you provide the opportunity to decide which of the following should happen:

- The script should open it and append new data to the end of it.
- The script should create it if it does not exist.
- The script should overwrite it with a new empty file.

To work with files, you first must open them. This is accomplished using the `FileSystemObject` object's `OpenTextFile()` method. This method requires that you pass it the following information:

- The file's name and its path
- The mode in which the file should be opened
- Instruction on whether or not to create the file if it does not already exist

Table 6.8 lists the constants that define the mode in which the `OpenTextFile()` method opens text files.

Unfortunately, you can open a file only using one of the modes listed in Table 6.8. Therefore, if your script needs to both read and write to an output file, you will have to make sure that you close the file and reopen it using the appropriate mode each time you need to perform a different type of file processing operation.

TABLE 6.8	OPENTEXTFILE() CONSTANTS	
Constant	**Function**	**Value**
ForReading	Opens the specified file in read mode	1
ForWriting	Opens the specified file in write mode	2
ForAppending	Opens the specified file in append mode	8

Table 6.9 lists the two available choices that determine whether or not a new file will be created if one does not already exist.

TABLE 6.9	OPENTEXTFILE() OPTIONS
Value	**Description**
True	Opens an existing file or creates and then opens a new file
False	Opens an existing file but will not create a new file if the specified file does not exist

Make sure that you take special care to specify the correct operation when opening a file. Otherwise, you'll run into problems. For example, if you open a file in ForWriting mode and a file of the same name already exists, that file will be overridden with a new file, resulting in the loss of all data previously stored in the file. By the same token, if you want to create a fresh new report each time your script runs, make sure that you open the output file in ForWriting mode and not in ForAppending mode. Otherwise, you'll end up with a report that keeps growing and growing, which is fine if you are creating a log file and not a fresh copy of a report.

NOTE

Now seems like an opportune moment for me to mention that when you run a JScript using the WSH on a computer running Windows NT, XP, 2000, or 2003, that script runs using the same security access rights and permissions assigned to your user account. Therefore, if you do not have the capability to access or modify a given file manually, your scripts will not be able to work with it, either.

NOTE

The trick to processing text files effectively using JScripts is to understand the purpose and location of the file pointer. The file pointer marks the location within a file where the next character typed will be placed. When a new file is first opened, the file pointer will be at row 0 and column 0. The first character entered into the file results in the pointer moving to column 1 in row 0. If a carriage return operation occurs, the file pointer moves to column 0 in the next row. Knowing the location of the file pointer is especially important if you need to read data from or write data to a file with a fixed record format, in which data is organized in fixed column positions.

When you open an existing file in `ForReading` mode, all existing data is overridden because the file pointer is automatically repositioned back to row 0 and column 0. On the other hand, if you open an existing file in `ForAppending` mode the file point is automatically placed at the end of the file.

To see how all this works, let's look at the following example. In this script, a file named `Sample.txt` is to be opened and a small text string written to it. The script begins by checking to see if the file already exists. If it does, then the file is opened in `ForAppending` mode. Otherwise, it is opened in `ForWriting` mode.

```
//****************************************************************
*************

//Script Name: Script 6.4.js
//Author: Jerry Ford
//Created: 09/14/03
```

```
//Description: This JScript demonstrates how to open a file
//and then write data to it
//*************************************************************
*************


//Initialization Section


  var fsoObject = new
ActiveXObject("Scripting.FileSystemObject");


//Main Processing Section


  //Determine what mode the output file should be opened in
  if (fsoObject.FileExists("c:\\MyDocs\\Sample.txt")) {
    var outputFile = fsoObject.OpenTextFile("c:\\MyDocs\\
Sample.txt", 8, "True")

    AppendToFile()
  } else {
    var outputFile =
fsoObject.OpenTextFile("c:\\MyDocs\\Sample.txt", 2, "True");

    WriteToFile()
  }


  //Close the output file when done working with it
  CloseFile()


  //Terminate the script's execution
  WScript.Quit();


//Procedure Section
```

```
function WriteToFile() {


  outputFile.WriteLine(Date() + "   -   File opened in
ForWriting Mode.");


}


function AppendToFile() {


  outputFile.WriteLine(Date() + "   -   File opened in
ForAppending mode.");


}


function CloseFile() {

  outputFile.Close();


}
```

The script begins by instantiating the `FileSystemObject`. Next, it uses the `FileSystemObject` object's `FileExists` property to determine whether or not a file named `Sample.txt` already exists in `c:\MyDocs`, as shown below. If it does exist, the `AppendToFile()` function is executed. Otherwise, the `WriteToFile()` function is called.

```
//Determine what mode the output file should be opened in
if (fsoObject.FileExists("c:\\MyDocs\\Sample.txt")) {
  AppendToFile()
} else {
  WScript.Echo("The file does not exist")
}
```

NOTE

This script assumes that the folder C:\MyDocs already exists. If it doesn't, an error will occur. Therefore, you might want to modify the script to verify that this folder exists as well.

The AppendToFile() function, shown below, uses the FileSystemObject object's OpenTextFile() method to set up a reference to C:\MyDocs\Sample.txt. Note that the second parameter passed to OpenTextFile() is 8, which tells the method to open the file in ForAppending mode. The FileSystemObject object's WriteLine() method is then executed. This method writes a text string to the file and performs a carriage return. I'll go over the use of this method in greater detail a little later in this chapter.

```
function AppendToFile() {


  outputFile.WriteLine(Date() + "  -  File opened in
ForAppending mode.");


}
```

The WriteToFile() function, shown here, is very similar to the AppendToFile() function except that it opens the file in ForWriting mode, and an additional parameter with a value of True is passed to the OpenTextFile() that instructs the parameter to create the file if it does not already exist.

```
function WriteToFile() {


  outputFile.WriteLine(Date() + "  -  File opened in
ForWriting Mode.");


}
```

Finally, the `CloseFile()` function is called, and the script terminates its own execution. This function uses the `FileSystemObject` object's `CloseFile()` method to close the file and write the end-of-file marker.

```
function CloseFile() {

  outputFile.Close();

}
```

NOTE

Always make sure that your JScripts close any open file before they stop executing. Failure to do so may result in an error the next time you try to access the file, because the end-of-file marker will be missing.

When you run this script for the first time, you should see a line of text similar to this:

```
Sat Sep 20 06:08:58 2003   -   File opened in ForWriting Mode.
```

Figure 6.7 shows how `Sample.txt` will look after running the script a few more times.

Figure 6.7

Creating a text file and appending new data to the end of it

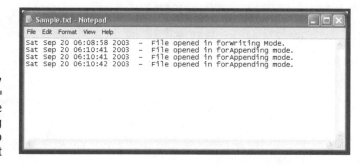

Creating Report and Log Files

Once you have opened a file in either `ForWriting` or `ForAppending` mode, you can begin to write output to it. There are several ways you can do this. First of all, you can write output a few characters at a time. This often is a good technique to use when creating formatted reports that present data in rows and columns.

You also can write output a line at a time. This facilitates the creation of free-form reports and log files. For example, you might want to create a script log file to which you record all error messages generated by your scripts. Another way to write output to text files is to write blank lines. You may want to add blank lines to text files in order to improve readability and to offset specific sections of reports.

Writing Output a Few Characters at a Time

If you want, you can write a specific number of characters to an output file. This is done using the `FileSystemObject` object's `Write()` method. The `Write()` method writes whatever text you pass to the line in the output file where the file pointer is currently positioned. After writing the new text, the file pointer is advanced to the right, but a carriage return is not performed. Therefore, the next write operation will occur on the same line as the previous write operation, and its output will be appended to the end of the previous output.

To see how this works, take at look at the following example:

```
var fsoObject = new ActiveXObject("Scripting.
FileSystemObject");

var outputFile = fsoObject.OpenTextFile("c:\\MyDocs\\
Sample.txt", 2, "True");

outputFile.Write("Once upon a time there were ");

outputFile.Write("three little bears.");

outputFile.Close();
```

First the `FileSystemObject` object is instantiated. Then an object reference is set up for a file named `Sample.txt`. The file opens in `ForWriting` mode. The `Write()` method is then executed twice, and each time a different text string is written, after which the file is closed.

NOTE Note that the previous example assumed that the folder `c:\MyDocs` already existed. If it did not exist when the script was run, an error would occur. Therefore, it is always a good idea to check and make sure that a folder exists before you attempt to access its contents. You can accomplish this using the `FileSystemObject` object's `CreateFolder()` method, which I will cover a little later.

Figure 6.8 shows how the text will look when written to the output file.

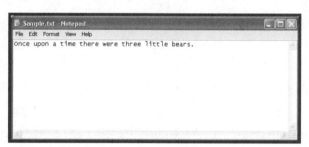

Figure 6.8

Creating a small text file using the `FileSystem Object` object's `Write()` method

Writing Output a Line at a Time

Usually, you'll want to write output to text files a line at a time. You can do this using the `FileSystemObject` object's `WriteLine()` method. For example, the following script uses the `WriteLine()` method in place of the `Write()` method used in the previous example:

```
var fsoObject = new ActiveXObject("Scripting.FileSystemObject");

var outputFile = fsoObject.OpenTextFile("c:\\MyDocs\\
Sample.txt", 2, "True");

outputFile.WriteLine("Once upon a time there were ");

outputFile.WriteLine("three little bears.");

outputFile.Close();
```

When this script runs, the output from the two `WriteLine()` methods is written to the output file on two different lines, as demonstrated in Figure 6.9.

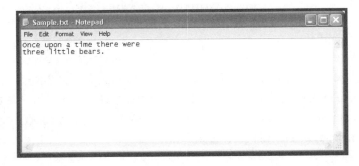

Figure 6.9

Writing output to files a line at a time

Formatting Output Files with Blank Lines

You can add blank lines to your output files when generating reports in order to make them more attractive and easier to read. To do so, you will need to use the `FileSystemObject` object's `WriteBlankLines()` method. This method appends a blank line to the end of the output file and then performs a carriage return.

As a demonstration of how to use the `WriteBlankLines()` method, take a look at the following JScript:

```
//*****************************************************
*************

//Script Name: Script 6.5.js

//Author: Jerry Ford

//Created: 09/14/03

//Description: This JScript demonstrates how to create and

//format a typical reports file.

//*****************************************************
*************


//Initialization Section
```

```
//Instantiate the FileSystemObject

var fsoObject = new
ActiveXObject("Scripting.FileSystemObject");


//Set up an object reference for the output file

var outputFile = fsoObject.OpenTextFile("c:\\MyDocs\\
Sample.txt", 2, "True");


//Set up an object reference for the computer's hard drive

var hardDrive = fsoObject.GetDrive("c:")


//Main Processing Section


WriteToFile()


CloseTheFile()


//Terminate the script's execution

WScript.Quit();


//Procedure Section


function WriteToFile() {

  outputFile.WriteBlankLines(1);

  outputFile.WriteLine("=======================================
===========");

  outputFile.WriteBlankLines(1);

  outputFile.WriteLine(Date() + "     C: Drive Analysis:");

  outputFile.WriteBlankLines(1);

  outputFile.WriteLine("=======================================
==============");
```

```
   outputFile.WriteBlankLines(1);

   outputFile.WriteBlankLines(1);


   outputFile.WriteLine("Serial No. \t\t" +
hardDrive.SerialNumber);

   outputFile.WriteBlankLines(1);


   outputFile.WriteLine("Volume Name \t\t" +
hardDrive.VolumeName);

   outputFile.WriteBlankLines(1);


   outputFile.WriteLine("Drive Type \t\t" +
hardDrive.DriveType);

   outputFile.WriteBlankLines(1);


   outputFile.WriteLine("File System \t\t" +
hardDrive.FileSystem);

   outputFile.WriteBlankLines(1);


   outputFile.WriteLine("Total Size  \t\t" +
hardDrive.TotalSize);

   outputFile.WriteBlankLines(1);


   outputFile.WriteLine("Free Space \t\t" +
hardDrive.FreeSpace);

   outputFile.WriteBlankLines(1);


   outputFile.WriteLine("=====================================
==============");

}


function CloseTheFile() {

  outputFile.Close();

}
```

This script begins by instantiating the `FileSystemObject` object. It then sets up object references to the script's output file using `ForWriting` mode and to the computer's C drive using the `FileSystemObject` object's `GetDrive()` method. Next the `WriteToFile()` function is called, which is responsible for writing the formatted report to the output file. The `CloseTheFile()` function is then called to close the output file, and the script then terminates its own execution.

NOTE

The `WriteBlankLines()` method also enables you to pass a number representing the number of blank lines you want to write.

Figure 6.10 shows the output that this script generated when it was run on my computer.

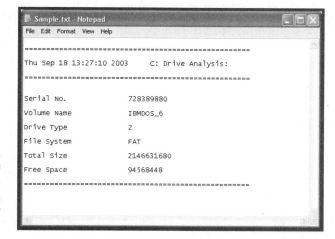

Figure 6.10

Adding blank lines to reports makes them easier to read.

Processing File Contents

It's not much harder to read and process a text file using JScript than it is to create and write to it. The first thing that you have to do is use the `FileSystemObject` object's `FileExists()` method to perform a check to determine whether or not the file you want to read exists. If it does exist, your script can open and begin to read it. The next thing that your script will need to do is to make sure that the file contains some data to process. You can do this using the `TextStream` object's `AtEndOfStream` property. In addition, the `AtEndOfStream` property will need to be checked just before each additional read operation to make sure that the end of the file has not been reached.

The following example demonstrates how to use JScript to read and process the output file created by the previous script:

```
//***********************************************************
*************
//Script Name: Script 6.6.js
//Author: Jerry Ford
//Created: 09/14/03
//Description: This JScript demonstrates how to read and
//process data stored in text files.
//***********************************************************
*************


//Initialization Section


//Instantiate the FileSystemObject
var fsoObject = new ActiveXObject("Scripting.FileSystemObject");


//Define variable that will be use to set up an object
//reference to the input file
var inputLine


//Main Processing Section


if (fsoObject.FileExists("c:\\MyDocs\\Sample.txt")) {
```

```
    var inputFile = fsoObject.OpenTextFile("c:\\MyDocs\\
Sample.txt", 1, "True");


    ProcessTheFile()


}


CloseTheFile()


//Terminate the script's execution
WScript.Quit();


//Procedure Section


//Verify that the input file exists and process it
function ProcessTheFile() {

  while (!inputFile.AtEndOfStream) {
    inputLine = inputFile.ReadLine();
    WScript.Echo(inputLine);
  }


}


function CloseTheFile() {

  inputFile.Close();


}
```

This script begins by instantiating the `FileSystemObject`. Next it defines a variable that will be used later to set up an object reference to the `c:\MyDocs\Sample.txt` file. The script then checks to see if the `Sample.txt` file exists. If it does exist, the file object reference is established and the `ProcessTheFile()` function is called. This function uses a `while` loop to read data a line at a time from the input file. It iterates until the end of file is reached. Once the entire file has been read, the `CloseTheFile()` function executes, and the script terminates is own execution.

Figure 6.11 shows the output that is displayed when this script is run from the Windows command prompt.

Figure 6.11

Creating a JScript that reads and displays the contents of an entire file

Skipping Lines when Processing Files

In the preceding example, the script read a report stored in an input file from top to bottom, including the report's header section. You can set up your script so that it skips portions of input files when processing them. For example, in the preceding example, you might want to modify the script to skip the first five lines, which consists of a header and blanks lines.

The `FileSystemObject` provides two methods for skipping portions of input files:

○ `Skip()`. Skips the processing of a specified number of characters

○ `SkipLine()`. Skips the processing of a single line

Using the Skip() method, you can skip a given number of characters when processing data stored in formatted reports that have known column positions. Typically, you'd use this method in conjunction with the FileSystemObject object's Read() methods, which I'll go over in just a bit. The following JScript statement demonstrates how to use this method to skip the processing of the next 10 characters in an input file with an object reference of inputFile:

```
inputFile.skip(10);
```

Unlike the Skip() method, the SkipLine() method does not accept an argument that enables you to specify the number of lines to be skipped. Instead, you can use it only to skip one line at a time, as demonstrated here:

```
inputFile.skipLine();
```

However, you can always wrap this statement inside a loop to skip multiple lines. For example, the following JScript statements set up a loop that will skip the next 10 lines in the input file:

```
for (i=0; i<10; i++) {
  inputFile.skipLine()
}
```

Processing Formatted Data

For files that contain known starting and ending column positions, you may want to read the data stored in the input file using the FileSystemObject object's Read() method. For example, suppose that you had an input file called employee.txt that contained the following data:

```
_____

Company Employee File

_____
```

Last Name	First name	User ID	Phone Number	Address
Masterson	Mollissa	mm987601	804-444-0000	8446 Somewhere Dr.
Peterson	William	pw987701	804-555-0000	6755 Park Ave.
Dickens	Alexander	da435401	804-666-0000	4565 Nowhere Park
Williamson	Marrideth	wm937401	703-777-0000	4654 Overthere Dr.
Thompson	Gerald	tg994401	804-888-0000	6221 Lonely Street
Patterson	Martha	pm747401	703-999-0000	3345 Party Lane

This file consists of 13 lines, each of which is 80 characters long. It stores information about company employees. All employee user IDs begin at column position 28 and end at column position 35. The following JScript code reads this file and extracts a list of user IDs.

```
var fsoObject = new ActiveXObject("Scripting.FileSystemObject");

var inputFile = fsoObject.OpenTextFile("c:\\myDocs\\
Employee.txt", 1, "True");


for (i=0; i<7; i++) {

  inputFile.skipLine()

}


while (!inputFile.AtEndOfStream) {

  inputFile.skip(27)

  userID = inputFile.Read(8);

  WScript.Echo(userID);

  inputFile.skip(46)

}


inputFile.Close();
```

The first thing that happens in this script is that the `FileSystemObject` is instantiated. Then an object reference is set up for the input file. Next, a `for` loop is set up that uses the `SkipLine()` method to skip the processing of the first 7 lines in the input file. A while loop is set up that extracts the user ID of each employee using the Skip() method to skip the first 27 characters on each line, the Read() method to extract the next 8 characters, and the Skip() method to skip the rest of the characters on that line of the file, thus moving the file pointer down to the first column of the next row in the file. The while loop runs until inputFile.AtEndOfStream is true, which occurs when the last line in the file has been processed.

If you were to save and run this example using the CScript execution host, you would see the outline shown in Figure 6.12.

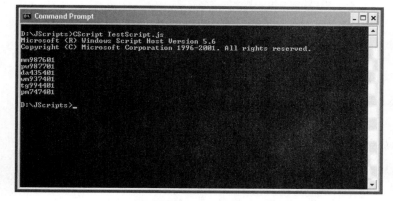

Figure 6.12

Using the Read() method to process data stored in a formatted file

Processing the Contents of an Entire File

In addition to reading an input file a line at a time or a few characters at a time, you also have the option of reading the entire input file in a single read operation using the FileSystemObject object's ReadAll() method. For example, the following JScript code displays the entire contents of c:\MyDocs\Sample.txt, using the WScript object's Echo() method.

```
var fsoObject = new
ActiveXObject("Scripting.FileSystemObject");

var inputFile = fsoObject.OpenTextFile("c:\\MyDocs\\Sample.txt",
1, "True");
```

```
reportFile = inputFile.ReadAll();

inputFile.Close();

WScript.Echo(reportFile);
```

When run, this example uses the ReadAll() method to store all the data in the input file in a variable called reportFile. The input file is then closed, and the file's contents are displayed, as shown in Figure 6.13.

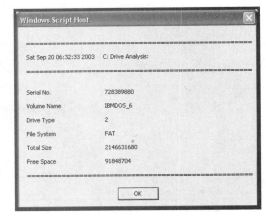

Figure 6.13

Using the
ReadAll()
method to process
all the content
of a file in
one operation

Administering Files and Folders

In addition to using JScript's runtime objects to create and process files, you can use them to automate a number of file and folder administration tasks, including copying, moving, and deleting files and folders. For example, you might want to delete files after they have reached a certain age.

Using methods that belong to the FileSystemObject, you can copy, move, or delete one or more file or folders. Optionally, you can use methods belonging to the File object to administer files and methods belonging to the Folder object to automate the handling of folders.

Working with the FileSystemObject Object

The FileSystemObject provides a large collection of methods that you can use to automate any number of file administration tasks. These methods include:

- **CopyFile()**. Copies one or more files to a specified folder.
- **MoveFile()**. Moves one or more files to a specified folder.
- **DeleteFile()**. Deletes one or more files from a specified folder.
- **FileExists()**. Determines whether a file contains any data.

In addition to methods that work with files, the FileSystemObject has methods for administering folders, as shown here:

- **CopyFolder()**. Copies one or more folders to a specified folder.
- **MoveFolder()**. Moves one or more folders to a specified folder.
- **DeleteFolder()**. Deletes one or more folders from a specified folder.
- **FolderExists()**. Determines whether a folder already exists.
- **CreateFolder()**. Creates a new empty folder.

TIP

Always remember to use the FileExists() and FolderExists() methods to determine whether or not a file or folder already exists before attempting to perform a file or folder operation. That way you can avoid any unnecessary errors by either creating the file or folder if it does not exist or by terminating the execution of your script.

Copying, Moving, and Deleting Files

The FileSystemObject object's CopyFile() method provides the capability to copy one or more files to a specified folder. To use this method, you must first instantiate the FileSystemObject, as demonstrated here:

```
var fsoObject = new ActiveXObject("Scripting.FileSystemObject");
```

```
fsoObject.CopyFile("c:\\MyDocs\\Employee.txt", "c:\\Temp\\
Employee.txt");
```

In this example, a file named `Employee.txt` is copied from the computer's `c:\MyDocs` folder to its `c:\Temp` folder. You can modify this example as shown here to copy more than one file at a time.

```
var fsoObject = new
ActiveXObject("Scripting.FileSystemObject");
fsoObject.CopyFile("c:\\MyDocs\\*.*", "c:\\Temp");
```

In this example, all the files located in the `c:\MyDocs` folder are copied to the `c:\Temp` folder.

NOTE You can use either the * or the ? wildcard characters when using any of the `File SystemObject` methods. Wildcard characters enable you to select one or more files based on matching character patterns in file names. The ? character is used to match a single character, whereas the * character is used to match any number of characters. For instance, if you specify `Jan3?.doc`, a match will occur with any 5-character file name that begins with `Jan3` and has a `.doc` file extension. Similarly, if you specify `Jan.*`, any file with a file name of `Jan` will match, regardless of its file extension.

If you want to move a file to a different folder instead of copying it, you can use the `FileSystemObject` object's `MoveFile()` method, as demonstrated here:

```
var fsoObject = new
ActiveXObject("Scripting.FileSystemObject");
fsoObject.MoveFile("c:\\MyDocs\\Sample.txt",
"c:\\Temp\\Sample.txt");
```

In this example, a file named `Sample.txt` located in the `c:\MyDocs` folder is moved to the `c:\Temp` folder.

You also can delete one or more files using the `FileSystemObject` object's `DeleteFile()` method, as demonstrated here:

```
var fsoObject = new
ActiveXObject("Scripting.FileSystemObject");

fsoObject.DeleteFile("c:\\Temp\\*.txt");
```

In this example, all files with a .txt file extension that reside in the
c:\Temp folder are deleted.

Creating, Copying, Moving, and Deleting Folders

There is not too much of a difference in working with folders and
working with files. Instead of using the FileExists() method, you use
the FolderExists() method. Similarly, there are like-named methods
for copying, moving, and deleting folders. For example, the following
JScript statements demonstrate how to use the FolderExists() method
to determine whether or not the c:\Scripts folder already exists.

```
var fsoObject = new
ActiveXObject("Scripting.FileSystemObject");

if (!fsoObject.FolderExists("c:\\JScripts")) {
  var newFolder = fsoObject.CreateFolder("c:\\JScripts");
  WScript.Echo("JScripts folder created on C:")
} else {
  WScript.Echo("Folder already exists!");
}
```

In this example, the JScripts folder is created if it does not exist.
Otherwise a message is displayed stating that the folder already exists.

To copy a folder, you can use the FileSystemObject object's CopyFolder()
method. This method copies a folder and all of its contents, as demonstrated by the following example:

```
var fsoObject = new
ActiveXObject("Scripting.FileSystemObject");

fsoObject.CopyFolder("c:\\JScripts", "d:\\JScripts");
```

In this example, the `c:\JScripts` folder and all its contents are copied to `d:\JScripts`. If you change the name of the destination folder, you can copy and rename a folder in one operation, as demonstrated here:

```
var fsoObject = new
ActiveXObject("Scripting.FileSystemObject");
fsoObject.CopyFolder("c:\\JScripts", "d:\\Scripts");
```

Here the `c:\JScripts` folder is copied to the computer's D drive as `Scripts`.

You can use the `MoveFolder()` method to move a folder to a different location, as demonstrated here:

```
var fsoObject = new ActiveXObject("Scripting.
FileSystemObject");
fsoObject. MoveFolder("c:\\JScripts", "c:\\Temp\\JScripts");
```

Like the `CopyFolder()` method, the `MoveFolder()` method moves the specified folder and all its contents to its new location.

You can delete folders using the `FileSystemObject` object's `Delete-Folder()` method, as demonstrated here:

```
var fsoObject = new
ActiveXObject("Scripting.FileSystemObject");
fsoObject.DeleteFolder("c:\\Temp\\JScripts");
```

In this example, the `JScript` subfolder and all its contents are deleted from the `c:\Temp` folder.

NOTE Delete folders with great care. Remember that the folder and all its contents will be deleted. Also, be extra careful when using wildcard characters with the `DeleteFolder()` method to make sure that you don't accidentally delete folders that you did not intend to delete.

Working with the File Object

While the `FileSystemObject` object provides the capability to work with one or more files at a time, the `File` object is limited to just working with a single file at a time. In order to work with the `File` object, you must first instantiate the `FileSystemObject` and then use its `GetFile()` method to instantiate the `File` object. Once you have done this, you will be able to use any of the following `File` object methods:

- ⚙ `Copy()`. Copies a single file to a specified folder.
- ⚙ `Delete()`. Removes a single file from a specified folder.
- ⚙ `Move()`. Moves a single file to a specified folder.

The following example demonstrates how to use the `File` object's `Copy()` method to copy a file from one location to another:

```
var fsoObject = new
ActiveXObject("Scripting.FileSystemObject");

var sourceFile =
fsoObject.GetFile("c:\\JScripts\\TestScript.js");

sourceFile.Copy("c:\\Temp\\TestScript.js");
```

In this example, a file called `TestScript.js` is copied from the `c:\JScripts` folder to the `c:\Temp` folder.

NOTE   The `Copy()` method works with one file at a time. Therefore, it does not support the use of wildcard characters.

The `File` object's `Move()` method works very similarly to the `Copy()` method, as demonstrated here:

```
var fsoObject = new
ActiveXObject("Scripting.FileSystemObject");

var sourceFile =
fsoObject.GetFile("c:\\JScripts\\TestScript.js");
```

```
sourceFile.Move("c:\\Temp\\TestScript.js");
```

In this example, a file named `TestScript.js` is moved from the `c:\JScripts` folder to the `c:\Temp` folder.

The `File` object's `Delete()` method provides the capability to delete a single file, as demonstrated here:

```
var fsoObject = new
ActiveXObject("Scripting.FileSystemObject");

var sourceFile = fsoObject.GetFile("c:\\Temp\\TestScript.js");

sourceFile.Delete();
```

In this example, a file named `TestScript.js` is deleted from the `c:\Temp` folder.

Working with the Folder Object

The `Folder` object is very similar to the `File` object except that it works with folders instead of files. The `Folder` object provides access to several methods, which are listed here:

- ✪ `Copy()`. Copies a single folder to a specified folder.
- ✪ `Delete()`. Removes a single folder from a specified folder.
- ✪ `Move()`. Moves a single folder to a specified folder.

NOTE Because its methods only allow you to work with one folder at a time, you cannot use wildcard characters with any of the `Folder` object's methods.

The `Folder` object is limited to working with a single folder at a time. To use it, you must first instantiate the `FileSystemObject` object and then use the `FileSystemObject` object's `GetFolder()` method to set up a `Folder` object reference.

NOTE

Because the `File` and `Folder` objects support the same set of methods, it is easy to get mixed up when working with them. Take great care not to do this; otherwise, you might end up copying, moving, or deleting entire folders when you only meant to administer like-named files.

The `Folder` object's `Copy()` method copies a folder and all its contents to a new location. The following example demonstrates how to use this method:

```
var fsoObject = new
ActiveXObject("Scripting.FileSystemObject");

var sourceFolder = fsoObject.GetFolder("c:\\JScripts");

sourceFolder.Copy("D:\\JScripts");
```

In this example, the `c:\JScripts` folder is copied to the computer's D drive. As you probably expect, the `Folder` object's `Move()` method moves a folder and all its contents from one location to another, as demonstrated in the following example:

```
var fsoObject = new
ActiveXObject("Scripting.FileSystemObject");

var sourceFolder = fsoObject.GetFolder("c:\\JScripts");

sourceFolder.Move("c:\\Temp\\JScripts");
```

Here the `c:\JScripts` folder is copied and made a subfolder of the `c:\Temp` folder. Finally, you can use the `Folder` object's `Delete()` method to delete a single folder, as demonstrated here:

```
var fsoObject = new
ActiveXObject("Scripting.FileSystemObject");

var sourceFolder = fsoObject.GetFolder("c:\\Temp\\JScripts");

sourceFolder.Delete();
```

In this example, the `JScript` subfolder and all its contents are deleted from the `c:\Tempo` folder.

What's Next?

By this point you should have a pretty good understanding of how to write JScripts that can create, process, and administer Windows files and folders. It's time to break for dinner. When you return for this evening's final session, you will learn how to create JScripts that perform an assortment of useful tasks, including the configuration of the Windows desktop and Start menu. You also will learn how to work with the Windows registry and write messages to the Windows application event log programmatically. On top of all this, you will find out how to create new user accounts, control Windows services, and even work with network resources. Have a good break, and I'll see you in a bit.

Using JScript to Automate Windows Tasks

➤ How to create, configure, and delete shortcuts

➤ How to use shortcuts to configure the Windows desktop, Start menu, and Quick Launch toolbar

➤ How to execute any Windows command or command-line utility from within your JScripts

➤ How to write a message to the Windows application event log

➤ How to start and retrieve data from the Windows registry

➤ How to connect to network resources

I n tonight's final lesson you are going to learn how to create JScripts that automate a host of different Windows tasks. Therefore, the chapter will be switching from topic to topic pretty quickly. I think that you'll find the variation of topics and pace a lot of fun. For starters, you will learn how to create JScripts that can interact with and configure the Windows desktop, Start menu, and Quick Launch toolbar.

Next you will find out how to control Windows services and create new user accounts. Then you will learn how to connect to and work with network resources. After that you will learn how to store and retrieve data and script configuration settings in the Windows registry. You'll then learn about the Windows application event log and find out how to write messages to it, which you'll find particularly useful in saving error information for later review.

You will also learn how to execute any Windows command or command-line utility from within a JScript. I'll then wrap up everything by showing you how to set up the scheduled execution of your JScripts so that you can run them even when you are away form your computer. If you are ready, let's get started.

Automating Windows Desktop Tasks

Tonight's final chapter will begin by showing you how to create JScripts that can configure Windows programmatically in a number of different ways using shortcuts. Shortcuts provide easy access to Windows resources and help make you more productive by reducing the number of steps required to locate and open a file, folder, application, or other Windows resource. For example, by placing a shortcut on your desktop, you provide quick access to a resource. By placing shortcuts on the Windows Start menu, you reduce desktop clutter. You can also reduce desktop clutter by placing shortcuts on the Windows Quick Launch toolbar. This toolbar provides single-click access to resources represented by shortcuts. When enabled, the Quick Launch toolbar resides on top of the Windows Taskbar.

You may be surprised at the number of resources you can administer using shortcuts. These Windows resources include

- The Windows desktop
- The Windows Start menu
- The Quick Launch toolbar
- Windows folders

Working with Shortcuts

Shortcuts represent links to other Windows resources. When you open a shortcut, Windows automatically locates and opens the resource associated with it just as if you had opened the actual resource. You work with shortcuts every day. You probably have some on the Windows desktop. The Windows Start menu is made up of them.

You can create shortcuts manually by clicking on an object, dragging the pointer to a new location, and then selecting Create Shortcut Here when prompted by Windows. You also can create new shortcuts using the Windows Create Shortcut Wizard, which you can start by right-clicking on an open area of the Windows desktop and selecting New followed by Shortcut.

Creating a single shortcut manually is relatively easy. Creating a bunch of them takes more time. If you work on a number of different computers (you may have more than one computer at home as well as a computer at work and school that you use), and you like to keep things consistent, creating a shortcut on one computer means re-creating that shortcut over and over again. In addition, if you replace one of your computers, you have to re-create your collection of shortcuts all over again. Alternatively, you could create a JScript that creates all your shortcuts for you. Then all you have to do to configure any computer is to run your script, which you might keep with you on a floppy disk.

A shortcut is identified by the presence of a small black arrow in the lower left corner of its icon, as shown in Figure 7.1.

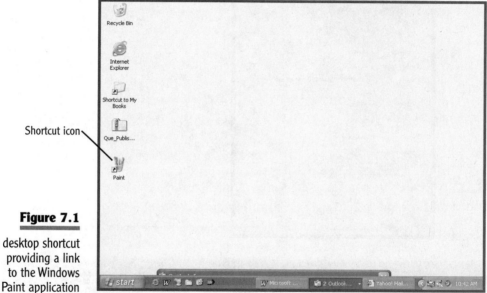

Shortcut icon

Figure 7.1

A desktop shortcut providing a link to the Windows Paint application

You can examine the properties for any Windows shortcut by right-clicking on it and selecting Properties, as demonstrated in Figure 7.2.

As you can see, this shortcut is to the Windows Paint program. A shortcut contains a lot of information about the Windows resource it represents. Table 7.1 defines each of the pieces of information stored in the shortcut.

Windows uses folders as the primary organizational structure for managing its file system. In addition, folders are used to configure the Windows desktop, Start menu, and Quick Launch toolbar. By adding or removing a shortcut to the appropriate folder, you can configure the appearance and functionality of any of those resources. For example, you can add a shortcut to the Windows desktop for a user by copying it to `C:\Documents and Settings\UserName\Desktop`.

`UserName` represents the account name used by the user to log in to the computer. Figure 7.3 shows the folder where all the icons that reside on my desktop are stored.

Figure 7.2

Examining shortcut properties for the Paint shortcut

TABLE 7.1 WINDOWS SHORTCUT PROPERTIES

Property	Description
`Target`	Specifies the path and file name of the Windows resource
`Start in`	Specifies the default working directory
`Shortcut key`	Specifies a keystroke sequence that will open the shortcut
`Run`	Specifies the type of window to be used to open the application (normal window, minimized, or maximized)
`Comment`	An optional description of the shortcut

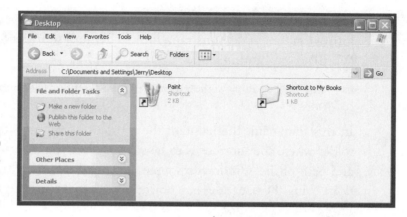

Figure 7.3

The shortcuts associated with an individual user's desktop

All I have to do is create a new shortcut and move or copy it into `C:\Documents` and `Settings\`*Jerry*`\Desktop` to make it appear on my Windows desktop.

NOTE

> If you share your computer with others and want to share a shortcut with them by placing it on their Windows desktops, you can do so by moving or copying it to C:\Documents and Settings\All Users\Desktop.

Scripting Shortcut Creation

The first step in creating a shortcut is to instantiate the `WshShell` object, as shown here:

```
var wshObject = WScript.CreateObject("WScript.Shell");
```

Next you are going to need someplace to save the shortcut. For example, to save a new shortcut on the Windows desktop, you will need to set up a reference to a special folder called `Desktop`. To accomplish this, you will need to use the `WshShell` object's `SpecialFolders()` property as shown here:

```
desktopFolder = wshObject.SpecialFolders("Desktop");
```

Now that you have a place to put the shortcut, it is time to instantiate the `WshShortcut` object and define the shortcut. This is accomplished using the `WScript` object's `CreateShortcut()` method. For example, the following statement demonstrates how to define a shortcut for the Windows WordPad application:

```
var newShortcut = wshObject.CreateShortcut(desktopFolder +
"\\WordPad.lnk");
```

In this statement, the name of the shortcut is concatenated to the special folder where the shortcut is to be stored. Next you must specify the name and path of the Windows resource that the shortcut will represent. This is done using the `WshShortcut` object's `TargetPath` property, as shown here:

```
newShortcut.TargetPath = "c:\\Program Files\\Windows NT\\
Accessories\\WordPad.exe";
```

NOTE Depending on which version of Windows your computer is running, the WordPad application may have a different path than the one shown in this example.

Finally, it's time to save the shortcut using the `WshShortcut` object's `Save()` method, as shown here:

```
newShortcut.Save();
```

The following script shows how these statements look when added together as a complete JScript.

```
//************************************************************
//************
//Script Name: Script 7.1.js
//Author: Jerry Ford
//Created: 09/12/03
//Description: This JScript creates a desktop shortcut for
//the Windows WordPad application
//************************************************************
//************
```

```
//Initialization Section


  //Instantiate the WshShell object
  var wshObject = WScript.CreateObject("WScript.Shell");


  //Set up a reference to the Desktop special folder
  desktopFolder = wshObject.SpecialFolders("Desktop");


  //Instantiate the WshShortcut object
  var newShortcut = wshObject.CreateShortcut(desktopFolder +
"\\WordPad.lnk");


//Main Processing Section


  //Call the function that creates the shortcut


  CreateShortcut()


  //Terminate script execution


  WScript.Quit()


//Procedure Section


  //set the location of the WordPad application and save the
shortcut


  function CreateShortcut() {


    newShortcut.TargetPath = "c:\\Program Files\\Windows
NT\\Accessories\\WordPad.exe";
```

```
newShortcut.Save();


}
```

 NOTE The `Desktop` special folder is just one of a number of special folders maintained by Windows. Others include these:

- **StartMenu.** Represents the Windows Start menu.
- **Programs.** Represents the All Programs or Programs menu.

In addition to these, there are a number of special folders that are applicable to all uses of a computer. These folders include

- **AllUsersDesktop.** Stores content that is displayed on every user's desktop.
- **AllUsersStartMenu.** Stores content that is displayed on every user's Start menu.
- **AllUsersPrograms.** Stores content that is displayed on every user's All Programs or Programs menu.

Setting up Shortcuts for Windows Folders

Most of the time you will probably find yourself creating shortcuts and saving them in Windows special folders. However, there may be times when you will want to add one or more shortcuts to regular Windows folders. For example, if you find that having too many shortcuts on your Windows desktop makes things look cluttered, you might want to consider creating a folder on your desktop and storing your shortcuts in that folder. That way they are only a couple of clicks away.

When working with regular folders instead of a special folder, you need to instantiate the `FileSystemObject` and use it to set up a folder reference, as demonstrated here:

```
var fsoObject = new ActiveXObject("Scripting.FileSystemObject");

var destinationFolder = fsoObject.GetFolder("c:\\MyDocs");

var wshObject = WScript.CreateObject("WScript.Shell");

var newShortcut = wshObject.CreateShortcut(destinationFolder +
"\\Notepad.lnk");

newShortcut.TargetPath = "%windir%\\notepad.exe";

newShortcut.Save();
```

In this example, a shortcut is created for the Windows Notepad application, which is saved in a folder called MyDocs located on the computer's C drive.

NOTE

You may have noticed the use of variable %windir% in the previous example. %windir% is an example of an environment variable created and maintained by Windows. %windir% specifies the location of the folder where the Windows system files are stored. This also is the folder where the Windows Notepad application is installed. You can reference environment variables from within your scripts just as easily as you can define and reference your own variables.

Different versions of windows place the system files in different locations. By referencing %windir% within your scripts, you can find the system files without having to worry about where they actually reside.

Deleting Unused Shortcuts

If you no longer need a shortcut, you can delete it. You can write a script that removes your shortcuts. For example, if you like to stay up to date with the latest technologies, you may find yourself purchasing a new computer every year or two and selling your old computer. Since you'll probably want to clean up your old computer before you sell it, you might want to write a JScript to perform this task, as demonstrated here:

```
var wshObject = WScript.CreateObject("WScript.Shell");
```

```
desktopFolder = wshObject.SpecialFolders("Desktop");

var fsoObject = new ActiveXObject("Scripting.FileSystemObject");

var newShortcut = fsoObject.GetFile(desktopFolder +
"\\WordPad.lnk");

newShortcut.Delete();
```

As you can see, this script deletes the WordPad shortcut that was created earlier on the Windows desktop using the `WshShortcut` object's `Delete()` method. In similar fashion, you can delete the shortcut that was added to the `C:\MyDocs` folder, as demonstrated here:

```
var fsoObject = new
ActiveXObject("Scripting.FileSystemObject");

fsoObject.DeleteFile("c:\\MyDocs\\Notepad.lnk");
```

This time, instead of the `WshShortcut` object's `Delete()` method, the `FileSystemObject` object's `DeleteFile()` method is used.

Configuring Shortcut Properties

As you saw earlier in this chapter, shortcuts contain a number of properties which affect their behavior. You can use the `WshShortcut` object to configure shortcut properties. Table 7.2 provides a list of `WshShortcut` properties that you can work with.

NOTE Of all of the `WshShortcut` properties, only the `TargetPath` property must be specified in order to create and save a new shortcut.

As an example of how to work with `WshShortcut` properties, take a look at the following script:

```
//*************************************************************
************
//Script Name: Script 7.2.js
//Author: Jerry Ford
```

TABLE 7.2 PROPERTIES BELONGING TO THE WSHSHORTCUT OBJECT

Property	Description
Arguments	Specifies arguments to be passed at startup to the application
Description	Adds a comment to the shortcut
Hotkey	Defines a combination of keystrokes that can be used to open the shortcut
IconLocation	Identifies the shortcut's icon
RelativePath	Sets the relative path for the object represented by the shortcut
TargetPath	Specifies the name and path to the object represented by the shortcut
WindowStyle	Sets the window style to use when opening the application
WorkingDirectory	Sets a default folder to be used by the application when saving files

```
//Created: 09/12/03

//Description: This JScript creates a desktop shortcut for
//the Windows WordPad application
//*************************************************************
*************



//Initialization Section

   //Instantiate the WshShell object
   var wshObject = WScript.CreateObject("WScript.Shell");


   //Set up a reference to the Desktop special folder
```

```
    desktopFolder = wshObject.SpecialFolders("Desktop");


  //Instantiate the WshShortcut object
  var newShortcut = wshObject.CreateShortcut(desktopFolder +
"\\Personal Journal.lnk");


//Main Processing Section


  //Call the function that creates the shortcut


  CreateShortcut()


  //Terminate script execution


  WScript.Quit()


//Procedure Section


  //set the location of the WordPad application and save the
shortcut


  function CreateShortcut() {


    newShortcut.TargetPath = "c:\\Program Files\\Windows NT\\
Accessories\\WordPad.exe";
    newShortcut.Arguments = "c:\\MyDocs\\Journal.rtf";
    newShortcut.Hotkey = "CTRL+Alt+P";
    newShortcut.IconLocation = "c:\\Program Files\\Windows NT\\
Accessories\\WordPad.exe, 2";
    newShortcut.WindowStyle = 1;
    newShortcut.Description = "Personal diary file";
```

```
newShortcut.WorkingDirectory = "C:\\Temp";

newShortcut.Save();


}
```

As you can see, what makes this script different from all previous examples is the manipulation of `WshShortcut` properties other than the `TargetPath` property. The shortcut created by this script opens the WordPad application and loads a file called `C:\Mydocs\Journal.rtf`. The WordPad application can be opened by double-clicking on it or by pressing the Ctrl, Alt, and P keys simultaneously. In addition, the script specifies that the second indexed icon associated with the `WordPad.exe` file should be used to represent the shortcut. WordPad will be opened in normal windows and will use the `C:\Temp` folder as its working directory.

If you right-click on the shortcut and select Properties, as shown in Figure 7.4, you will see how all these properties have been set, including the `Description` property.

Figure 7.4

The properties configured by the JScript for the WordPad shortcut

NOTE

Specific icons represent many Windows resources. However, some contain a built-in indexed list of optional icons. You can view these icons and determine which ones are which by right-clicking on the application's icon, selecting Properties, and then clicking on the Change Icon button. For example, if you do this for the WordPad application, you will see the list of icons shown in Figure 7.5.

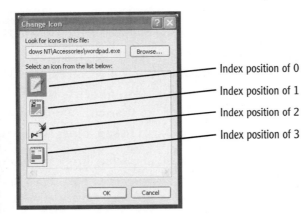

Index position of 0
Index position of 1
Index position of 2
Index position of 3

Figure 7.5

Selecting the icon to be used to represent a shortcut

Using Shortcuts to Configure the Windows Start Menu

At this point you know how to create a shortcut on the Windows desktop and in regular Windows folders. Now let's take a look at how to use short-cuts to configure the Windows Start menu. The Windows Start menu is organized as a collection of special folders. Therefore, all you have to do to create a new menu item is add a shortcut to the appropriate special folder.

The following JScript statements demonstrate how to add a shortcut to the Notepad application to the All Programs submenu under the Windows Start menu.

```
var wshObject = WScript.CreateObject("WScript.Shell");
destionationFolder = wshObject.SpecialFolders("Programs");
```

```
var newShortcut = wshObject.CreateShortcut(destionationFolder
+ "\\notepad.lnk");

newShortcut.TargetPath = "%windir%\\notepad.exe";

newShortcut.Save();
```

Figure 7.6 shows how the Windows Start menu looks after the previous example has been run.

The Windows Notepad shortcut

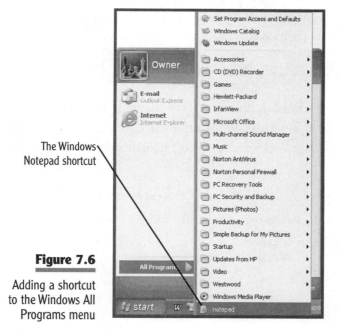

Figure 7.6

Adding a shortcut to the Windows All Programs menu

Using Shortcuts to Configure the Quick Launch Toolbar

The Windows Quick Launch toolbar resides on the Windows Taskbar, as demonstrated in Figure 7.7. It displays a list of shortcuts and provides single-click access to Windows resources that they represent. By default, the Quick Launch toolbar displays shortcuts for Internet Explorer, Outlook Express, and the Windows desktop.

Figure 7.7

The Quick Launch
toolbar provides
quick access to
Windows resources

NOTE The Quick Launch toolbar actually is just one of a collection of optional toolbars that you can tell Windows to display on the Taskbar. If you do not see it, you can enable it by right-clicking on an open area on the Windows Taskbar, clicking on Toolbars, and then selecting Quick Launch.

The special folder associated with the Quick Launch toolbar is called AppData. To reference it you must set up a reference to it as well as specify its location within the AppData special folder, as demonstrated in the following example:

```
var wshObject = WScript.CreateObject("WScript.Shell");

quickLaunchToolbar = wshObject.SpecialFolders("AppData");

destinationFolder = quickLaunchToolbar +
"\\Microsoft\\Internet Explorer\\Quick Launch";

var newShortcut = wshObject.CreateShortcut(destinationFolder +
"\\notepad.lnk");

newShortcut.TargetPath = "%windir%\\notepad.exe ";

newShortcut.Save();
```

Executing Windows Commands

Okay, enough for shortcuts. Let's look at how to execute Windows commands from within your JScripts. To do this, you will have to use the WshShell object's Run() method. As you will see, using this method, you can create scripts that automate the execution of any Windows command or command-line utility.

Controlling Windows Services

Windows NT, XP, 2000, and 2003 provide much of their functionality in the form of services. A *service* is simply a software program that provides the operating system with a specific set of capabilities. For example, the Printer Spooler service handles all the work involved in printing print jobs. Likewise, the Plug and Play service is responsible for detecting and helping to install new hardware.

Windows automatically starts a large number of services, whether you use them or not. Each active service consumes a small portion of Windows CPU and memory resources. By stopping services that you do not need to use, you may be able to improve the performance of your computer just a bit.

 NOTE To see a list of services running on your computer, right-click on My Computer and select Manage. Then expand the Services and Applications node on the console tree that will be displayed and select Services. A list of installed services will be displayed on the right side of the console, along with their status and a brief explanation of their purposes.

You can control the execution of Windows services from the Windows command prompt using any of the following commands.

- **NET START.** Starts a Windows service.
- **NET PAUSE.** Pauses the execution of a Windows service.
- **NET CONTINUE.** Resumes the execution of a paused Windows service.
- **NET STOP.** Stops a Windows service.

The following JScript statements demonstrate how to use the WshShell object's Run() method to stop the Windows Alerter service:

```
var wshObject = WScript.CreateObject("WScript.Shell");
wshObject.Run("net stop Alerter", 0, "True");
```

Once the service is stopped, the following statements can be used to start it again:

```
var wshObject = WScript.CreateObject("WScript.Shell");

wshObject.Run("net start Alerter", 0, "True")
```

Creating New User Accounts

Windows NT, XP, 2000, and 2003 operating systems also provide command-line support for the creation and configuration of user accounts via the following commands:

- **net user**. Provides the capability to create and delete user accounts from the Window command line.
- **net group**. Provides the capability to add user accounts to global group accounts.
- **net localgroup**. Provides the capability to add user accounts to local groups.

The following JScript statements demonstrate how to create a new user account:

```
var wshObject = WScript.CreateObject("WScript.Shell");

cmdResult = wshObject.Run("net user WilliamF qwerty /add", 0);
```

In this example, an account named WilliamF is created with a temporary password of qwerty. The user account is established on the computer where the script runs. If the computer is part of a Windows-based local area network and you have administrative privileges over the Windows domain, you can modify the previous example by adding the /Domain switch, as demonstrated below, to create the user account as a domain-level account.

```
var wshObject = WScript.CreateObject("WScript.Shell");

cmdResult = wshObject.Run("net user WilliamF qwerty /add
/domain", 0);
```

Working with Networks and Network Resources

If your computer is connected to a home or corporate network, you can also create JScripts that interact with and control network resources (assuming that you have security privileges over those resources). To make this happen, you need to work with the WshNetwork object. This object provides access to several properties that provide information about the network to which a computer is attached. These properties include:

- **UserName**. Returns the account name of the user currently logged on.

- **ComputerName**. Returns the name of the computer as it will appear to other network users.

- **UserDomain**. Returns the name of the domain to which the computer is currently logged in.

In addition to these properties, the WshNetwork object also provides access to a number of methods. Using these methods, your JScripts can connect to and access network drives and printers. These methods include:

- **EnumNetworkDrives**. Returns information about current network drive connections.

- **MapNetworkDrive**. Establishes a connection to a network drive or folder.

- **RemoveNetworkDrive**. Deletes a connection to a network drive or folder.

- **EnumPrinterConnection**. Returns information about current network printer connections.

- **AddPrinterConnection**. Establishes a connection to a network printer.

- **RemovePrinterConnection**. Deletes a connection to a network printer.

- **SetDefaultPrinter**. Establishes a printer as the printer to which all print jobs are automatically submitted.

NOTE

A *network drive* is a disk drive that network users can access in order to store or retrieve files. A *network folder* is a single folder whose contents have been shared over a network. A *network printer* is a printer device that accepts and prints print jobs from users connected to a network. By establishing connections to network drives, folders, and printers, you make them look and act as if they are connected to your computer locally.

The following JScript statements demonstrate how to set up a connection to a network drive or folder:

```
var WshNetwork = WScript.CreateObject("WScript.Network");
WshNetwork.MapNetworkDrive("x:", "\\\\FileSvr\\d");
```

In this example, a network connection is established to the D drive on a computer named `FileSvr`. The connection is represented by the drive letter assignment of `x:`, which will be displayed in the My Computer dialog along with all locally connected network drives, as demonstrated in Figure 7.8.

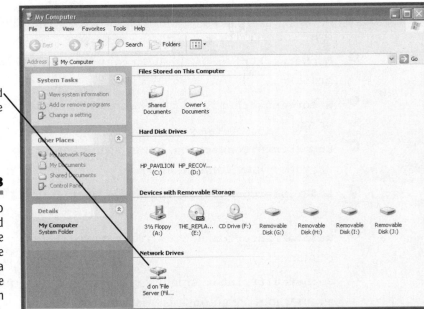

Mapped
Network Drive

Figure 7.8

Connections to network drives and folders are identified by the depiction of a network cable connection beneath the icon.

Remember that to connect to a network resource you must use the Universal Naming Convention (UNC). Also remember that the \ character represents a special character in JScript and that you must escape it by preceding it with another \ when you want to use it. Therefore, in order to specify a UNC address of \\FileSvr\d in a JScript, you must write it out as \\\\FileSvr\\d.

If you no longer need access to a network drive, you may want to delete its connection. You can do this using the WshNetwork object's RemoveNetworkDrive() method, as demonstrated here:

```
var WshNetwork = WScript.CreateObject("WScript.Network");

WshNetwork.RemoveNetworkDrive("x:");
```

In this example, the WshNetwork object is instantiated, and then the previously established network drive connection is deleted.

Taking a Break

Time for one last break before we begin the sprint to this evening's finish line. You've already learned a lot this evening, including how to create and configure shortcuts, how to control Windows services, how to create new user accounts, and how to connect to network resources. There is still plenty left to do, including learning how to work with the Windows registry and application event log. Take a 15 to 30 minute break, and when you return we'll start back up.

Interacting with the Windows Registry and Application Event Log

In addition to the Windows desktop, Start menu, Quick Launch toolbar, printers, disk drives, files, and folders, you can create JScripts that interact with and control other Windows resources. These other resources include the Windows registry and the Windows application event log.

The Windows application event log is one of a collection of log files maintained by Windows operating systems. As Windows applications run, they record event messages in the log that provide a record of their activities. In addition, applications usually record error messages in the Windows application event log. You can modify your JScripts to write information to this log as well, especially error messages.

The Windows registry is a specialized database built into Windows operating systems in which information about all computer hardware and software is stored. In addition, the registry contains information about users and Windows configuration settings. You can create JScripts that take advantage of the Windows registry by using it to store script configuration settings that you might otherwise hard code within your scripts.

Recording Messages in the Windows Application Event Log

Windows computers automatically maintain a collection of log files where messages are recorded. These log files include

- **Application log.** Stores event messages recorded by Windows applications.
- **Security log.** Stores security and audit event messages.
- **System log.** Stores event messages generated by the Windows operating system.

 NOTE The Windows application event log is supported only on Windows NT, XP, 2000, and 2003. If you want to record log information on other Windows operating systems, you will need to create and maintain your own custom log file.

Messages generated by Windows applications are written to the application event log. You can open the Windows application event log and view its contents by right-clicking on the My Computer icon and selecting Manage. This opens the Computer Management console. To view a list of events currently stored in the application event log, expand the Event Viewer node until you see the Application node and then select it, as demonstrated in Figure 7.9.

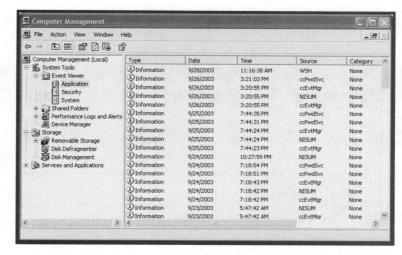

Figure 7.9

Viewing a list of messages currently stored in the Windows application event log

As you can see, a number of different pieces of information are displayed about the event message, including its type and the time and date it was recorded. To view detailed information about an event, double-click on it.

Using the WshShell object's LogEvent() method, you can modify your JScripts so that they can record messages to the Windows application event log, thus creating a central repository for all your script message reporting. For example, the following JScript statements demonstrate how to record a message in the application log:

```
var WshShell = WScript.CreateObject("WScript.Shell");

WshShell.LogEvent(0, "Script 7.X has finished executing
without any errors.");
```

As you can see, this example begins by instantiating the WshShell object. It then uses the LogEvent() method to record a message to the application log. The information passed to the LogEvent() method consists of two arguments. The first argument is a numeric value that indicates the type of error being recorded to the application event log. There are six different event types that you can specify when coding this argument, as outlined in Table 7.3. The second argument passed to the LogEvent() method is the text string to be recorded in the log.

Figure 7.10 shows how the message this example records to the Windows application event log appears when viewed on a computer running Windows XP.

TABLE 7.3 SUPPORTED EVENT TYPES	
Value	**Event Type**
0	A successful event
1	An error event
2	A warning event
4	An informational event
8	A successful audit event
16	A failed audit event

Figure 7.10

The message posted to the application event log by the JScript

As you can see from this example, it does not take a lot of work to modify your JScripts to begin recorded messages to the Windows application event log.

TIP

At a minimum, you may want to start setting up your JScripts so that they record messages to the Windows application event log indicating when they start, finish, or experience an error.

Interacting with the Windows Registry

The Windows registry provides you with a central repository where you can store and retrieve script configuration settings. All data is stored within the registry in a tree-like hierarchy. The registry is made up of five high-level root keys, as outlined in Table 7.4.

TABLE 7.4 ROOT LEVEL REGISTRY KEYS		
Key	**Abbreviation**	**Contents**
HKEY_LOCAL_MACHINE	HKLM	Contains configuration data for settings that globally affect the computer
HKEY_CLASSES_ROOT	HKCR	Stores information regarding Windows file extension associations
HKEY_CURRENT_USER	HKCU	Stores information related to the user who is currently logged on to the computer
HKEY_USERS	—	Stores information about all users of the computer
HKEY_CURRENT_CONFIG	—	Stores information about current configuration settings

NOTE Depending on which Windows operating system you are working on, other root keys may be present.

NOTE The Windows registry stores information that is essential to the proper operation of your computer and its software and hardware. It is therefore critical that you take extra care anytime you work with it. Even a small mistake can result in disastrous effects, potentially preventing your computer from restarting.

Within the registry, data is stored in keys and values. A *key* is a container that stores other keys or values. The actual data stored in the registry is stored within *values*. It may help you to think of registry keys as being like Windows folders and values as being like Windows files.

The registry stores all data using the following format:

```
Key : KeyType : Value
```

Key specifies the name of a registry key or subkey. KeyType identifies the type of data that is stored in the key. Value represents the data that is stored. The Windows registry supports the storage of many different types of data, including the following.

- **REG_SZ**. Represents a text string.
- **REG_MULTI_SZ**. Represents multiple strings.
- **REG_EXPAND_SZ**. Represents a string that can be expanded such as %windir%.
- **REG_BINARY**. Represents a binary value.
- **REG_DWORD**. Represents a hexadecimal DWORD value.

Windows provides a registry editor called Regedit, shown in Figure 7.11, that you can use to view and modify the Windows registry. To start this utility, click on Start, Run and then type Regedit and click on OK.

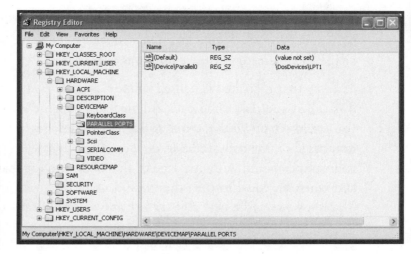

Figure 7.11

Viewing the
structure of the
Windows registry
using the
Regedit utility

Using methods provided by the WshShell object, you can programmatically read, write, and delete data stored in the Windows registry. The registry-related methods provided by the WshShell object include:

- **RegWrite()**. Provides the capability to create registry keys and values and to modify existing ones.
- **RegRead()**. Provides the capability to read registry keys and values.
- **RegDelete()**. Provides the capability to delete registry keys and values.

Storing Data in the Windows Registry

Using the WshShell object's RegWrite(), method you can create new registry subkeys and values. All you have to do is to pass it the complete path within the registry where you want a new key or value to be created. For example, the follow JScript statements create a new key and value under the HKEY_Current_User root key:

```
var WshShell = WScript.CreateObject("WScript.Shell");

WshShell.RegWrite("HKCU\\MyJScripts\\Logging", "On");
```

When run, this example creates a new key and value in the Windows registry under the HKEY_CURRENT_USER root key. However, if either the key or the value already exists, it simply is overwritten.

The key that is created is named MyJScripts. The value that is stored in it is called Logging. The data assigned to the value is On. For example, you could set up your JScripts to log error messages and other information based on the data stored in the Logging value. When set equal to On, your scripts would write message to the Windows applications event log, and when set equal to Off, they would not write event messages. Figure 7.12 shows how the new registry key and value appear once created.

TIP

■ ■

To help work safely within the registry, create one key within which you add other subkeys and values. That way, you will always have a consistent place within the registry where you store your data, thus reducing the possibility of accidentally overwriting data stored in another part of the registry.

■ ■

Reading Date Stored in the Windows Registry

Reading data from the registry is just as easy as writing it there. For starters, you need to instantiate the WshShell object. You can then use the WshShell object's RegRead() method to read the data stored in any value, as demonstrated here:

```
var WshShell = WScript.CreateObject("WScript.Shell");
logMode = WshShell.RegRead("HKCU\\MyJScripts\\Logging");
if (logMode == "On") {
  WshShell.LogEvent(0, "Script 7.X is now executing.");
}
```

In this example, the value stored in HKCU\JScripts\Logging is read and, if the data stored in it is equal to On, a message is written to the Windows application event log.

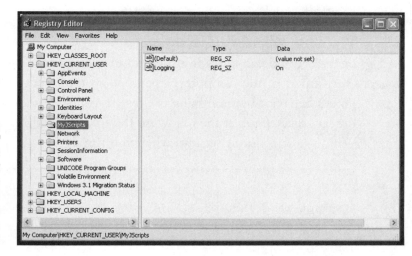

Figure 7.12

Verifying that the new registry subkey and value have been added under the HKEY_Current _User root key

Deleting Data Stored in the Windows Registry

If you no longer need to use data that you have stored in the Windows registry, it is a good idea to remove it. This can be done using the WshShell object's RegDelete() method. For example, the following JScript statements show how to delete the HKCU\MyJScripts\Logging value:

```
var WshShell = WScript.CreateObject("WScript.Shell");

WshShell.RegDelete("HKCU\\MyJScripts\\Logging");
```

This example removes the Logging value while leaving the MyJScripts subkey still in place. This is useful in situations where you have stored other subkeys or values under the MyJScripts subkey. However, if you are completely done with the key, you can remove it and all the subkeys and values stored beneath it using the following example:

```
var WshShell = WScript.CreateObject("WScript.Shell");

WshShell.RegDelete("HKCU\\MyJScripts\\");
```

NOTE

To delete a registry subkey using JScript, you must append the \\ character to the end of the subkey name.

Performing System Configuration Via the Windows Registry

Because Windows stores information in the registry that affects virtually every aspect of the computer's operation, you often can change the computer's behavior by modifying the registry values. As an example of what I mean, take a look at the following JScript. This script reconfigures your Windows screensaver settings when you run it.

```
//***********************************************************
*************
//Script Name: Script 7.3.js
//Author: Jerry Ford
//Created: 09/21/03
//Description: This JScript configures the Windows screensaver
//***********************************************************
*************


//Initialization Section

  var getConfirmation;


  //Instantiate the WshShell object
  var wshObject = WScript.CreateObject("WScript.Shell");


//Main Processing Section

  //Get confirmation before continuing


  getConfirmation = wshObject.Popup("This script configure
the Windows " +

    "screen saver. \r\r Do you want to continue?", 10,
"Please " +

    "confirm", 36)
```

```
if (getConfirmation == 6) {

  ChangeScreenSaver()

  NotifyUser()

}


//Terminate script execution

WScript.Quit()

//Procedure Section

//This subroutine changes desktop settings

function ChangeScreenSaver() {

  //Turn on the Windows screen saver
  wshObject.RegWrite("HKCU\\Control
Panel\\Desktop\\ScreenSaveActive", 1);


  //Turn on password protection
  wshObject.RegWrite("HKCU\\Control
Panel\\Desktop\\ScreenSaverIsSecure", 1);


  //Set up a 20 minute delay
  wshObject.RegWrite("HKCU\\Control
Panel\\Desktop\\ScreenSaveTimeOut", 1200);


  //Enable the Mystify screen saver
  wshObject.RegWrite("HKCU\\Control Panel\\Desktop\\
SCRNSAVE.EXE", "C:\\" +

    "\\Windows\\System32\\ssmyst.scr");
```

```
}


function NotifyUser() {


    WScript.Echo("The next time you log in the changes will
take effect.")


}
```

This script begins by defining the getConfirmation variable and instantiating the WshShell object in the script's Initialization section. Next the WshShell object's Popup() method is used to display a pop-up dialog that prompts the user for permission to modify screensaver settings, as shown in Figure 7.13.

Figure 7.13

Prompting the user for confirmation before allowing the JScript to finish executing

If the user elects to allow the script to run, the value assigned to getConfirmation will be set to 6, in which case the ChangeScreenSaver() and NotifyUser() functions are executed. The ChangeScreenSaver() function performs four RegWrite() operations. The first one modifies the value assigned to HKCU\Control Panel\Desktop\ScreenSaveActive by changing it to 1. This has the effect of enabling the screensaver in the event that it is currently turned off. Next, the value of HKCU\Control Panel\Desktop\ScreenSaverIsSecure is set to 1. This enables password protection, which will force the user to reenter his password (if he has one) in order to reauthenticate with the operating system.

Next, the value of HKCU\Control Panel\Desktop\ScreenSaveTimeOut is set equal to 1200, which is the number of seconds the operating system should wait for no user activity to occur before starting the execution of the screensaver. Finally, the value of `HKCU\Control Panel\Desktop\SCRNSAVE.EXE` is set equal to `C:\Windows\System32\ssmyst.scr`. `ssmyst.scr` is the name of the Mystify screensaver.

Once the `ChangeScreenSaver()` function has finished, the `NotifyUser()` function executes. This function displays a text message in a pop-up dialog notifying the user that the changes made by the script will take effect the next time the user logs into Windows, as shown in Figure 7.14.

Figure 7.14

The script notifies the user after the screensaver settings have been reconfigured.

NOTE By default, Windows stores its screensavers in `C:\Windows\System32`. They can be identified by their `.scr` file extension. To see which ones are which, just double-click on them to see them run.

You can verify the changes made by the JScript by looking at the Screen Saver property sheet on the Display Properties dialog. To open this dialog, right-click on an open area of the Windows desktop and select Properties. Figure 7.15 shows how the screensaver setting will look after the script has finished executing.

Automating Script Execution

Depending on what you design your JScripts to do, you might want to run them at times when you are not working on your computer. For example, you might want to write a JScript that runs the Windows `defrag.exe` command-line utility. This command-line utility provides the capability to run the Windows Disk Defragmenter utility, which defrags files that are stored on hard disk drives.

Figure 7.15

Reconfiguring
Windows
screensaver settings
via modifications to
the Windows
registry

The unfortunate thing about working the `defrag.exe` is that it is very resource intensive and makes working on your computer almost impossible while it is running. Therefore, most people generally start the defrag process at times when they know that they will not be using their computers. Another way to tackle this situation is to create a JScript that runs `defrag.exe` and then to schedule the execution of this script so that it runs during the middle of the night. For example, the following two-line JScript demonstrates how this script might look:

```
Set WshShl = WScript.CreateObject("WScript.Shell")
WshShl.Run "c:\Windows\System32\defrag C: /f"
```

Windows provides two different ways to schedule the execution of your JScripts. Both of these options use the built-in Windows Scheduler service. The first option is to use the AT command. This command provides the capability to create, display, and delete scheduled tasks from the Windows command prompt. The second option available to you is to use the Windows Scheduled Task Wizard, which guides you through a series of steps that collect information from you that is required to set up a task that manages the scheduled execution of your script. Both of these scheduling options are discussed further in the sections that follow.

Scheduling Script Execution from the Windows Command Line

You can execute the Windows AT command from the Windows command prompt or from within a script. When it is executed from the Windows command prompt, you can view and administer scheduled tasks interactively. When it is executed from within a script, you can create a JScript that automates the creation and administration of scheduled tasks.

To view a list of currently scheduled tasks on your computer, open the Windows command prompt, type AT, and press the Enter key, as demonstrated here:

```
C:\>at

Status ID    Day            Time          Command Line
_____

         1   Each M W F     11:30 PM      cmd /c TestScript.js
         2   Each M W F     10:30 PM      cmd /c Cleanup.js
         3   Each F         10:00 PM      cmd /c Archive.js
C:\>
```

As you can see, the output produced in this example shows three scheduled tasks, each of which is associated with a different JScript. The first script is called TextScript.js and has been set up to run as a scheduled task that executes at 11:30 P.M. every Monday, Wednesday, and Friday. The second script is called Cleanup.js and has been set up to run at 10:30 P.M. every Monday, Wednesday, and Friday. The third JScript is Archive.js and has been scheduled to execute at 10:00 P.M. every Friday. Also, take note that each scheduled task is assigned a unique status ID.

The following example demonstrates how to create a new scheduled tasks for a script called CopyTempFiles.js:

```
AT 23:59 /EVERY:Su CMD /C CopyTempFiles.js
```

The scheduled tasks set up by this statement will execute the script just before midnight every Sunday night. If this were the fourth scheduled task set up on the computer, it would be assigned a status ID of 4. By passing the number 4 to the AT command as an argument along with the /DELETE switch, as demonstrated below, you can delete the scheduled task.

```
AT 4 /DELETE
```

Alternatively, if you want to delete all currently configured scheduled tasks, you can run the AT command with the /DELETE switch without specifying any status ID, as shown here:

```
AT /DELETE
```

One benefit to using the AT command instead of the Windows Scheduled Task Wizard is that the AT command supports the capability to set up the scheduled tasks remotely on other network computers, as demonstrated here:

```
AT \\NtkFileServer 22:00 /EVERY:M,T,W,Th,F,S,Su CMD /C
CopyTempFiles.js
```

In this example, a scheduled task is set up to run a script called Copy-TempFiles.js on a computer named NtkFileServer at 10:00 P.M., seven days a week.

NOTE Note the use of the \\ characters in front of the network computer's name in the previous example. This is an example of using the Universal Naming Convention or UNC notation in which network resources are referenced in the format of ***ComputerName**\ ***Path**SharedResource*.

NOTE To learn more about the AT command, open the Windows command prompt and type AT HELP.

To wrap up our discussion of the AT command, let's use the command to schedule the execution of the two-line Defrag.js script shown earlier in this section so that it will run automatically every Friday night, as shown here:

```
at 23:30 /every:F cmd /c Defrag.js
```

NOTE When you run a JScript from the Windows command prompt or from the Windows desktop, the script executes under the context of your security privileges. In addition, it has access to your currently configured execution environment. In other words, if you have connections set up for network resources that the script needs in order to execute, its uses them. However, if you set up a JScript to run after hours, when you are not using your computer, it will not have access to your network drive connections. Therefore, you will have provide the script with the capability to establish its own connection, as demonstrated previously in this chapter.

Running the Windows Scheduled Task Wizard

If you prefer to work with wizards, you can use the Windows Scheduled Task Wizard to configure the automated execution of your JScripts. The wizard guides you through the setup process and will help you to set up any of the following automated execution schedules:

- Daily
- Weekly
- Monthly
- One Time Only
- When My Computer Starts
- When I Log On

By default, scheduled tasks run using the authority provided by a special built-in account known as LocalSystem. The problem with this account is that it has very limited security permissions. As a result, some of your scripts may fail to run. Fortunately, using the Windows Scheduled Task Wizard, you can configure scheduled tasks to run using a different user account, one with sufficient security privileges to get the job done.

TIP To keep things simple, you may want to create a special user account with sufficient security privileges to handle the automated execution of your JScripts. Also, you may want to set up this special user account so that its password never expires. Otherwise, your JScripts will stop executing the next time you change the account's password.

Setting Up a Scheduled Task

The following procedure outlines the steps involved in creating a new scheduled task using the Windows Scheduled Task Wizard.

1. Click on Start and Control Panel. The Windows Control Panel appears.

2. Click on Performance and Maintenance. The Performance and Maintenance dialog appears.

3. Click on Scheduled Tasks. The Scheduled Tasks folder appears.

4. Double-click on the Add Scheduled Task icon. The Scheduled Task Wizard begins to run. Click on Next to begin.

5. A list of applications is displayed, as shown in Figure 7.16. Click on Browse to locate your JScript and then click on Open.

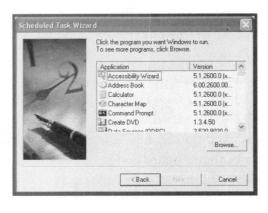

Figure 7.16

Locate the JScript you want to set up to run as a scheduled task

6. Enter a descriptive name for the task and select a task schedule, as shown in Figure 7.17. Click on Next.

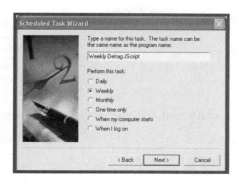

Figure 7.17

Always give your scheduled tasks descriptive names.

7. If you selected the Daily option, you'll next see a dialog prompting you to select from the following list of options:

   ○ **Start time.** Sets the time the task is to be run.

   ○ **Perform this task.** Configures the task to run daily, on weekdays, or every __ days.

   ○ **Start date.** Sets the date on which the task should start running.

   Make your selections and click on Next, and then skip to step 13.

8. If you selected the Weekly option, you'll next see a dialog prompting you to select from a list of options, as shown in Figure 7.18.

   ○ **Start time.** Sets the task's start time.

   ○ **Every __ weeks.** Configures the task to run every *X* number of weeks.

   ○ **Select the day(s) of the week below.** Sets one or more days of the week on which the task should run.

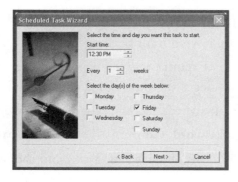

Figure 7.18

Configuring your JScript to run on a weekly basis

Make your selections and then click on Next and then skip to step 13.

9. If you selected the Monthly option, you'll next see a dialog prompting you to select from the following list of options:

   ✿ **Start time.** Sets the time the task is to be run.

   ✿ **Day.** Sets the date of the month on which the task is to run.

   ✿ **The __.** Specifies the day of the month on which the task is to run.

   ✿ **Of the month(s).** Sets the months in which the task is to run.

   Make your selections and click on Next, and then skip to step 13.

10. If you selected the One Time Only option, you will be prompted to select from the following list of options:

    ✿ **Start time.** Sets the task's start time.

    ✿ **Start date.** Sets the task's start date.

    Make your selections and click on Next, and then skip to step 13.

11. If you selected the When My Computer Starts option, you will be prompted to provide the following information, as shown in Figure 7.19.

    ✿ **Enter the user name.** Sets the name of a user account whose security privileges should be used when running the task.

    ✿ **Enter the password.** Sets the account's password.

    ✿ **Confirm password.** Confirms the account's password.

    Make your selections and click on Next, and then skip to step 14.

12. If you selected the When I Log On option, you will be prompted to provide the following information:

    ✿ **Enter the user name.** Sets the name of a user account whose security privileges should be used when running the task.

    ✿ **Enter the password.** Sets the account's password.

    ✿ **Confirm password.** Confirms the account's password.

    Make your selections and click on Next, and then skip to step 14.

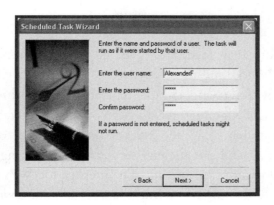

Figure 7.19

Setting up a
scheduled task to
run using a user
account with
sufficient security
privileges

13. The wizard then prompts you to provide the following information:

   ○ **Enter the user name.** Sets the name of a user account whose security privileges should be used when running the task.

   ○ **Enter the password.** Sets the account's password.

   ○ **Confirm password.** Confirms the account's password.

14. Click on Finish.

Once created, the new scheduled task is stored in the Scheduled Tasks folder, as shown in Figure 7.20.

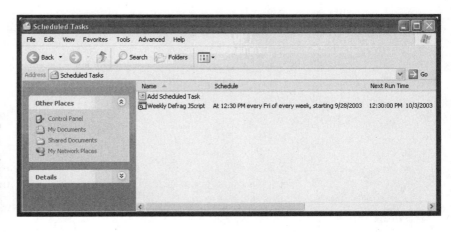

Figure 7.20

Viewing the
scheduled task
created by the
Windows
Scheduled
Task Wizard

What's Next?

Congratulations, you made it to the end of this book, and in doing so have learned everything that you need to know to begin programming using both JavaScript and JScript. In accomplishing this goal, you have gained the knowledge required to begin creating interactive Web pages and to start automating Windows tasks. But don't stop now. Think of this as the beginning and not the end of your programming education. You can learn a lot more by surfing the Internet for Web sites that cover JavaScript and JScript. Most important of all, start writing your own scripts. There is no better way to learn than by doing. Good luck!

What's on the
Web Site?

To save you the time and effort required to re-key all of the examples that you have seen in this book, copies of each script are available for download from http://www.courseptr.com as shown in Figure D.1.

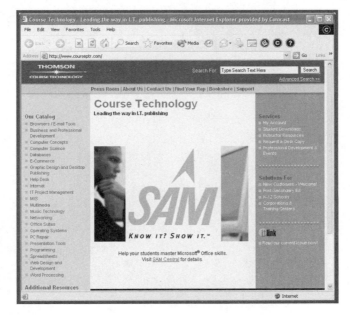

Integrating JavaScript with HTML

I have organized the book's scripts into Zip files by chapter. This way you'll be able to download only the scripts that you need. However, if you prefer, you can download them all at once in a single Zip file as well. In addition to the sample scripts for both JavaScript and JScript, you'll also find that any graphic images used by sample scripts in a given chapter have been included in that chapter's download file.

GLOSSARY

abort. An event that occurs when the user aborts the loading of a page and triggers the `onAbort` event handler.

ActiveX. A proprietary Microsoft technology for embedding Windows components into Web pages.

alert() method. A document object method that can be called to display an alert dialog box for the user. This dialog box displays a text message and waits for the user to click on the OK button before returning control to the calling statement.

anchor object. Represents a location in a Web page that is the target of a link.

applet. A small program written in Java that executes on the client computer.

applet object. An object created by the HTML `<APPLET>` tag that provides access to that applet.

area object. A type of link object that provides access to an area in an imagemap.

argument. A piece of data passed to a function as input.

array. A logical collection of related data that is indexed and can be manipulated programmatically.

array object. An object that enables you to work with arrays in JavaScript.

blur. An event detected by the browser when an object loses focus because a different object has received the focus. The `blur` event triggers the `onBlur` event handler.

Boolean. A variable that can store either a `true` or `false` value.

Boolean object. An object that treats a Boolean value as an object.

break. A JavaScript statement you can use to terminate the processing of a loop.

browser. A software application that displays Web pages and may provide a JavaScript environment.

button object. A representation of a button on a form that has its own methods and properties and is subject to various events.

camelback. A type of programming notation that uses a combination of uppercase and lowercase letters to create descriptive names.

case. A JavaScript statement that is used in conjunction with the `switch` statement to test for a particular condition.

change. An event detected by the browser when the user changes an object (such as the contents of a form's text field) that triggers the `onChange` event handler.

CGI (Common Gateway Interface). An interface or communications specification used in creating Web server-based applications using languages such as PERL.

checkbox object. A representation of a check box on a form. The object has its own methods and properties and is subject to various events.

check points. A debugging technique that displays the value of variables during the processing of a script so that the variables can be checked when the script is tested. Check points also can be used to verify the logical flow of your scripts.

click. An event detected by the browser when the user clicks the mouse button while the pointer is placed over an object. This event triggers the `onClick` event handler.

collection. An array that provides a reference to a group of objects.

cookie. A small piece of information stored on client computers that contains information collected when users visit Web sites.

comments. Statements added to Web pages and scripts that are ignored by the browser but that provide valuable information to anyone editing or reading the page or script.

compiling. The process of converting a program to machine code before it is executed.

concatenation. The process of combining two or more strings into a single string.

confirm() method. A document object method that can be called to display a confirmation dialog box for the user. This dialog box displays a text message and waits for the user to click on the OK or Cancel button before returning control to the calling statement.

continue. A JavaScript statement that allows you to skip the remaining statements in a loop and to continue on with the loop's next iteration.

CScript. A WSH script execution host that supports text-based scripts that run in the background from the Windows command prompt.

date object. An object that allows your script to access and manipulate time and date information.

dblClick. An event detected by the browser when the user double-clicks the mouse button while the pointer is placed over an object. This event triggers the `onDblClick` event handler.

debug. The process of testing and fixing errors in programs and scripts.

dense array. An array that is populated with data at the time of its creation.

`Dictionary`. A VBScript runtime object that stores data using key and item pairs.

`document` object. An object that provides access to the document that is currently loaded into a browser window and whose properties and methods provide access to viewing and changing the page content.

DOM (Document Object Model). A browser object model that provides JavaScript with access to all the elements on an HTML page.

`do...while`. A type of loop that executes as long as a given condition remains `true`.

`drive`. A JScript runtime object that provides access to a disk drive.

`drives`. A JScript runtime collection that provides access to all the drives on the computer.

element. An individual entry in an array that may be referenced by a name or an index number.

`else`. The counterpart to the `if` statement that provides an alternative action when the `if` condition proves `false`.

`error`. An event detected by the browser when there is an error with a window, frame, or image. This event triggers the `onError` event handler.

event. The occurrence of a predefined action such as a mouse click on an object in a Web page.

event object. An object that provides access to properties that describe an event.

event handler. A JavaScript construct that executes automatically when a given event occurs. For example, the `onClick` event handler executes when the `Click` event occurs for an object.

execution host. An application such as the WSH or a Web browser that interprets and executes scripts.

expression. A statement that evaluates the value of variables and constants.

file. A JScript runtime object that provides direct access to a file.

`fileUpload` object. An object that represents the file upload HTML element.

`Files Collection`. A JScript runtime collection that provides access to files stored within a given folder.

`FileSystemObject`. One of two primary runtime objects that provides access to the Windows file system and to other runtime objects.

`focus`. An event detected by the browser when the user selects an object (such as a form text field). This event triggers the `onFocus` event handler.

`folder`. A JScript runtime object that provides access to a folder.

`Folders Collection`. A JScript runtime collection that provides access to subfolders stored within a given folder.

`for`. A JavaScript statement that repeats a series of statements until a condition proves `false`.

for...in. A loop that iterates repeatedly through a specified object's list of properties.

form object. An object created by the HTML <FORM> tag that provides access to all the elements on a form.

frame object. An object created by the HTML <FRAME> tag that allows JavaScript to reference frames.

function. A collection of JavaScript statements that performs a specific action and can be referenced and called repeatedly from different locations in the Web page.

function object. A JavaScript statement that is compiled as a function.

GIF. A format for saving graphic images. GIF files typically are larger than JPEG files and provide slightly lower image quality, but take less time to load.

global variable. A variable whose scope is such that its value is available throughout the Web page.

hidden object. A text-based object that is not displayed on a form but that can be accessed programmatically.

history object. An array containing information about all the URLs that have been loaded into the browser window.

HomeSite. A program editor that supports both HTML and JavaScript languages. HomeSite includes such advanced features as color coding, integrated browser support, visual layout, code templates, and wizards.

HREF. A hypertext reference used to specify a URL.

Hypertext Markup Language (HTML). A programming language used to deliver text and graphic information over the Internet.

IDE (integrated development environment). A software application that facilitates the development of scripts or programs and provides tools for testing and debugging scripts and programs.

if. A conditional statement that tests whether a condition is true of false.

image object. An object created by the HTML <IMG> tag that provides access to image attributes.

Internet Explorer. A popular Internet browser developed by Microsoft that supports JScript, VBScript, ActiveX, and other advanced features.

interpreted language. A language used to develop programs or scripts that are not compiled in advance before execution. Instead, each statement in an interpreted language script is processed as it is read.

Java. An object-oriented language descended from C and C++. A variation of Java allows small programs known as applets to be added to Web pages.

JavaScript. A programming language developed by Netscape that supports the development of client-side scripts that execute inside of Internet browsers.

JavaScript Console. A Netscape Navigator debugging utility that receives JavaScript error messages and allows you to test JavaScript commands and expressions.

JPEG. A format for saving high-quality graphic images. JPEG files typically are smaller than GIF files and provide superior image quality, but take slightly longer to load.

JScript. Microsoft's version of JavaScript. The only Internet browser that currently supports JScript is Internet Explorer.

keyDown. An event detected by the browser when the user presses a keyboard key. This event triggers the onKeyDown event handler.

keyPress. An event detected by the browser when the user presses and releases a keyboard key. This event triggers the onKeyPress event handler.

keyUp. An event detected by the browser when the user releases a keyboard key. This event triggers the onKeyUp event handler.

label. A JavaScript statement that allows you to associate a label with a JavaScript statement so that it can be referenced from other parts of a script.

layer object. An object that represents an HTML layer.

link object. An object that represents an HTML hypertext link.

LiveScript. A scripting language introduced in Netscape Navigator version 2.0 and later renamed JavaScript.

load. An event that occurs when the browser finishes loading a Web page. This event triggers the onLoad event handler.

load-time error. An error that occurs when loading Web pages in a browser and typically involves basic syntax issues.

local variable. A variable whose scope is such that its value is limited to the function in which it is declared.

location object. An object that provides access to the window object's location property.

logic errors. Errors that occur as a result of human error and produce unexpected results.

loop. The process of repeating a set of instructions indefinitely.

Lynx. A text-based, non-graphical Internet browser noted for its speed and exceptional performance.

Netscape JavaScript Debugger. A debugging tool that runs in the form of a Java applet inside the Netscape browser. It works with Netscape browser versions 4.02 and above.

Math object. An object that provides access to various mathematical functions and constants.

method. A function associated with an object.

Microsoft Script Debugger. A debugging tool compatible with Internet Explorer that can be used to debug ActiveX, VBScript, and JavaScript.

mimeType object. A predefined JavaScript object that provides access to a specific browser-supported MIME type.

mouseDown. An event detected by the browser when the user presses a mouse button over an object. This event triggers the object's onMouseDown event handler.

mouseMove. An event detected by the browser when the user moves the mouse. This event triggers the object's onMouseMove event handler.

mouseOut. An event detected by the browser when the user moves the mouse off an object. This event triggers the object's onMouseOut event handler.

mouseOver. An event detected by the browser when the user moves the mouse over an object. This event triggers the object's onMouseOver event handler.

mouseUp. An event detected by the browser when the user releases a mouse button over an object. This event triggers the object's onMouseUp event handler.

Netscape Navigator. A popular Internet browser that supports JavaScript, plug-ins, and other advanced features.

navigator object. An object that provides access to the information about the version of Netscape Navigator supported by the browser.

new. A JavaScript keyword that supports the declaration of new JavaScript objects.

number object. A predefined object that allows numbers to be represented as objects.

null. An empty value.

object. A programming construct that contains its own properties and methods.

object. A root object from which all objects are derived.

object-based language. A programming language providing some but not all of the features of an object-oriented programming language.

onAbort. An event handler that is triggered when the browser detects the abort event, indicating that the user has aborted the loading of the Web page.

onBlur. An event handler that is triggered when the browser detects the blur event, indicating that an object has lost focus.

onChange. An event handler that is triggered when the browser detects the change event, indicating that an object (such as form text field) has been changed.

onClick. An event handler that is triggered when the browser detects the click event, indicating that a user has clicked the mouse while the pointer is over an object.

onDblClick. An event handler that is triggered when the browser detects the dblClick event, indicating that a user has double-clicked the mouse while the pointer is over an object.

onerror. An event handler that is triggered when the browser detects the error event, indicating that an error has occurred with a window, frame, or image.

onFocus. An event handler that is triggered when the browser detects the focus event, indicating that an object has been selected or has received focus.

onKeyDown. An event handler that is triggered when the browser detects the keyDown event, indicating that the user has pressed a keyboard key.

onKeyPress. An event handler that is triggered when the browser detects the `keyPress` event, indicating that a user has pressed a keyboard key.

onKeyUp. An event handler that is triggered when the browser detects the `keyUp` event, indicating that a user has released a pressed keyboard key.

onLoad. An event handler that is triggered when the browser detects the `load` event, indicating that a Web page has been completely loaded by the browser.

onMouseDown. An event handler that is triggered by the `mouseDown` event, indicating that the user has pressed a mouse button over an object.

onMouseMove. An event handler that is triggered by the `mouseMove` event, indicating that the user has moved the mouse.

onMouseOut. An event handler that is triggered by the `mouseOut` event, indicating that the user has moved the pointer off an object.

onMouseOver. An event handler that is triggered by the `mouseOver` event, indicating that the user has moved the pointer over an object.

onMouseUp. An event handler that is triggered by the `mouseUp` event, indicating that the user has released a mouse button over an object.

onReset. An event handler that is triggered when the browser detects the `reset` event, indicating that the user has clicked on a form's Reset button.

onResize. An event handler that is triggered when the browser detects the `resize` event, indicating that the user has changed the dimensions of a browser window.

onSelect. An event handler that is triggered when the browser detects the `select` event, indicating that the user has selected an object such as a form's text field.

onSubmit. An event handler that is triggered when the browser detects the `submit` event, indicating that the user has clicked on a form's Submit button.

onUnload. An event handler that is triggered when the browser detects the `unLoad` event, indicating that a Web page has been closed by the browser.

Opera. A new Internet browser that supports JavaScript, plug-ins, and other advanced features.

option object. An object created by the HTML `<OPTION>` tag that provides access to the list of options in a select list.

parameter. An argument passed to a script at runtime as input.

password object. An object created by the HTML `<INPUT>` tag's `TYPE="password"` option that represents a form's password field.

PERL. A programming language often used in conjunction with CGI to deliver server-based Web content.

plug-ins. Add-on modules that can be installed to add or extend the capabilities of the Netscape browser.

plug-in object. An object whose properties represent all the browser's plug-ins.

program. A collection of stored programming statements that constitute a script or application.

prompt() method. A document object method that can be called to display a prompt dialog box for the user. This dialog box displays a text message and enables the user to type a response before clicking on either the OK or Cancel button and returning control to the calling statement.

property. A variable associated with an object that controls or describes a particular object feature.

RAD (rapid application development). A specialized programming tool or suite of tools designed to support the rapid creation of programs and applications.

radio object. A representation of a radio button on a form. This object has its own methods and properties and is subject to various events. Radio buttons are created in groups; only one option in a group can be selected at a time.

registry. A specialized Windows database that stores configuration information about software, hardware, system, user, and application settings.

reserved words. A collection of language-specific words that cannot be used as variable and function names within a script.

reset. An event detected by the browser when the user clicks on a form's Reset button. This event triggers the onReset event handler.

reset object. A specialized type of button object that has its own methods and properties and is subject to various events. The reset object is used to clear the contents of a form and to restore the form's default values.

resize. An event detected by the browser when the user changes the dimensions of a browser window. This event triggers the onResize event handler.

rollover. A graphical effect that swaps between two images as the pointer selects or passes over a graphic image. A rollover is used to simulate a selection or identify the focus of a selected graphic image.

runtime error. An error that occurs when a script attempts to do something that is against the rules, such as referencing an undefined function or variable.

scope. The portion of a Web page in which a variable can be accessed, either locally or globally.

screen object. An object that contains information about the current screen display.

script. A group of program statements that is interpreted by a Web browser or the WSH as an executable file.

scripting engine. A language-specific interpreter that processes script statements and converts them into a format that can be executed by the computer.

select. An event detected by the browser when the user selects an object, such as a form text field. This event triggers the `onSelect` event handler.

select object. An object created by the HTML `<SELECT>` tag that provides access to a form's select list.

statement. A line of code in a Web page or JavaScript.

status bar. The area located at the bottom of Internet browsers that is used to display text-based messages.

string. A group of text characters such as `"Hello world!"`

string object. An object that references the value of a string and provides methods for working with the string.

style object. An object that describes the style used by HTML elements and whose properties provide access to specific style attributes.

submit. An event detected by the browser when the user clicks on a form's Submit button, causing the form's contents to be sent to a Web server or e-mailed to a designated e-mail address. This event triggers the `onSubmit` event handler.

submit object. A specialized type of `button` object on a form that has its own methods and properties and is subject to various events. The `submit` object is used to submit form data to a Web server for processing or to e-mail form contents.

switch. A JavaScript statement that enables you to test for multiple conditions using a series of `case` statements.

table. An HTML construct that enables page content to be organized and presented within predefined tables.

text object. A representation of a single-line text field on a form that has its own methods and properties and is subject to various events.

textarea object. A representation of a multiline text box on a form that has its own methods and properties and is subject to various events.

unLoad. An event that occurs when the browser closes a Web page. This event triggers the `onUnload` event handler.

URL (Universal Resource Locator). An address used to identify a site on the World Wide Web.

validation. The process of verifying that the data typed into a form conforms to required specifications.

var. A keyword used to declare a variable explicitly.

variable. A programming construct that provides for the storage and retrieval of data in memory that can be accessed by its name.

VBScript. A scripting language developed by Microsoft as an alternative to JavaScript. VBScript is derived from the Visual Basic programming language. The only Internet browser that currently supports VBScript is Internet Explorer.

Visual JavaScript. A professional developer's tool for building large cross-platform applications. It includes a WYSIWYG HTML editor and supports visual JavaScript development. In addition, you can use this tool to cut and paste prebuilt HTML, Java, and JavaScript components into JavaScript applications.

while. A loop that iterates until a condition proves `false`.

window object. An object that represents a browser window or frame and whose methods can be used to control the window or frame.

WScript. The root or parent object in the WSH object model or a WSH script execution host that supports the presentation of data in graphical pop-up dialogs.

WSH (Windows Script Host). A Windows scripting environment that supports the execution of different scripting languages and provides object-based access to Windows resources.

WSH Core Object Model. A core component of the Windows Script Host that provides object-based access to Windows resources.

WshArguments. A WSH object that provides access to command-line arguments.

WshController. A WSH object that provides the capability to create remote scripts.

WshEnvironment. A WSH object that provides access to environment variables.

WshNamed. A WSH object that provides access to named command-line arguments.

WshNetwork. A WSH object that provides access to network resources.

WshRemote. A WSH object that provides the capability to run remote scripts.

WshRemoteError. A WSH object that provides access to errors generated by remote scripts.

WshScriptExec. A WSH object that provides access to error information from remote scripts run using `Exec()`.

WshShell. A WSH object that provides access to environment variables and the Windows registry.

WshShortcut. A WSH object that provides the capability to create shortcuts.

WshSpecialFolders. A WSH object that provides access to Windows folders.

WshUnnamed. A WSH object that provides access to unnamed command-line arguments.

WshUrlShortcut. A WSH object that provides the capability to create URL shortcuts.

WWW. The World Wide Web.

WYSIWYG. What you see is what you get.

INDEX